John Mill, Gilbert Goudie

The diary of the Reverend John Mill

minister of the parishes of Dunrossness, Sandwick and Cunningsburgh in Shetland,

1740-1803

John Mill, Gilbert Goudie

The diary of the Reverend John Mill
minister of the parishes of Dunrossness, Sandwick and Cunningsburgh in Shetland, 1740-1803

ISBN/EAN: 9783337017750

Printed in Europe, USA, Canada, Australia, Japan

Cover: Foto ©Thomas Meinert / pixelio.de

More available books at **www.hansebooks.com**

PUBLICATIONS

OF THE

SCOTTISH HISTORY SOCIETY

VOLUME V

———◆———

MILL'S DIARY

JUNE 1889

THE DIARY OF THE
REVEREND JOHN MILL

MINISTER OF THE PARISHES OF DUNROSSNESS
SANDWICK AND CUNNINGSBURGH IN

SHETLAND

1740-1803

WITH SELECTIONS FROM LOCAL RECORDS
AND ORIGINAL DOCUMENTS RELATING
TO THE DISTRICT

Edited with Introduction and Notes by

GILBERT GOUDIE, F.S.A. Scot.

EDINBURGH

Printed at the University Press by T. and A. Constable
for the Scottish History Society

1889

PREFACE.

THE MS. Diary of the Rev. John Mill was brought under my notice in the year 1879 by the late Mr. Bruce of Sumburgh, in the possession of whose family it appears to have been since the decease of the author in 1805. Mr. Bruce gave me permission to make use of the MS. in any way that might be deemed suitable; and its publication in the present form, as an issue of the Scottish History Society, has the cordial concurrence of his son and successor.

The transcript made by myself has, by the aid of my wife, been carefully collated with the original, which, in arrangement and orthography, has been closely adhered to.

The Diary is, primarily and essentially, of local interest, and the aim in view in editing it has been, by the addition of notes and original illustrative matter, to make it of some value as a contribution to the topographical literature of the part of the country to which it refers.

At the same time, it is believed that the Diary possesses features which should claim for it an interest beyond the merely local or personal, inasmuch as it sets before us a vivid representation of domestic manners and Church life and feeling at a time comparatively near to us, and yet in many respects widely divergent from what now usually prevails.

It abounds throughout in living human interest, and shows not only a vigorous actor in the little world—a remote and unique one—which lay around him, but also a keen observer in the larger sphere of contemporary life and history of which, as an educated and capable man, he was a warmly interested spectator.

The extracts from records and original documents given in the Appendix are of various dates, but are all of strictly local character, and it is conceived will add materially to the historical and topographical interest of the volume.

The transcriptions and preparation for the press have been the work of spare hours amid many pressing activities; and this may to some extent explain, if it cannot excuse, imperfections in the editing of which I am very sensible.

Acknowledgments are due to the Council of the Society of Antiquaries of Scotland for woodcuts courteously put by them at my disposal; and to Mr. Thomas Graves Law for invaluable hints in the arrangement and preparation of the work.

G. G.

39 NORTHUMBERLAND STREET,
EDINBURGH, *March* 1, 1889.

CONTENTS

1747-1749.

1750-1752.

1753.

1754-1757.

CONTENTS

1765.

1766-1767.

1768-1769.

1770-1771.

CONTENTS

1780.

1781.

1782.

1783.

1784.

1785-1786.

1787.

1788.

CONTENTS

1796.

1797.

1798.

CONTENTS

APPENDIX.

INTRODUCTION.

THE Rev. John Mill, author of the Diary, was an active and zealous parish minister, and at the same time a man of parts, and an industrious writer. In addition to the Diary, and a Collection of ' Speeches,' or Addresses for Communion Seasons, the Kirk-Session Minutes of his parish, for the long period of nearly sixty years, were penned by him. These manuscript productions have remained practically unknown. Equally so a printed volume on *The Holy Catholic Church delineated in her Faith and Practice*, etc., issued by him in 1773 under the veil of anonymity, died in the course of time to public memory, and the knowledge of it was only recovered by an accident. His Account of the Parish of Dunrossness, in the old *Statistical Account of Scotland* (1793), is almost as completely out of view, buried in one of the numerous volumes of that great work.

Mill's writings possess an interest and value both from the force of his own individuality, and from the nature of his life and surroundings in the far-off northern isles where he lived and laboured. It is the picture of life, manners, religion, in the second half of last century, which he presents to the student of history, that constitutes the claim of his Diary to appear in this series of the Scottish History Society.

All that was hitherto known of Mill was gleaned by Dr. Hew Scott, and recorded in the *Fasti Ecclesiæ Scoticanæ*, Part v. p. 426, as follows :—

1743. JOHN MILL. Licensed by the Presbytery of Fordyce
14th November 1739; called to Dunrossness 19th October 1742, and ordained 27th April succeeding. In July
1799, when in his 88th year, he allowed the pious itinerant, Captain Haldane, to preach in the church, and
after hearing sermon, warned his hearers to take heed
to the words they had heard, especially as this visit was
a new and unprecedented occurrence in their history.
Mr. Mill died 13th February 1805, in his 94th year,
and 62d of his ministry, the last survivor of the original
contributors to the Ministers' Widows' Fund at its commencement, 25th March 1744. He married, 2d October
1754, Anne, daughter of Mr. Young of Sandsting,
Aberdeenshire; she died at Prestonpans 29th June
1816. Publication—Account of the Parish (Sinclair's
Stat. Acc. vii.) [*Presby. Reg.*; Haldane's *Memoir*, etc.]
This account is defective, and to some extent erroneous, but
the means of amplification and rectification are now available
in the pages of the Diary, which was unknown to Dr. Scott.
Mill's parentage appears not to have been ascertained; and,
the earlier portion of the Diary having been lost, the facts can
only be gathered from casual references. He was born in
Shetland ('Lerwick, the place of my nativity'—Diary, 1753—
where his father left some property, more than once referred
to). The last entry in the Diary, January 1, 1803, records
that he was born on February 23, 1712. His mother, as stated
in the entry for January 1788, was born 100 years earlier,
namely, in the Revolution year, 1688. The family consisted
of nine children, five sons and four daughters, whose histories
are briefly related in the entry of July 12, 1782.

Though it is nowhere so stated, there is now no doubt that
his father was the Rev. James Milne, first minister of Lerwick
after its disjunction from the parish of Tingwall in 1701. In
the *Fasti* the narrative regarding the father is as follows:—

LERWICK.

1704. JAMES MILNE. Called in 1703, and ordained 6th
April 1704; died in February 1718, in the fourteenth
year of his ministry. He married, 2d January 1707,
Mrs. Isabel Bruce, who died 12th November 1771.

No particulars appear to have been gathered as to the ances-
try of this clergyman, but Mill in the Diary alludes more than
once to his own friends and connections settled in the north of
Scotland, in Aberdeen and Banffshire. Mrs. James Milne is
here stated to have died in November 1771, and Mill, writing
in the beginning of 1772 (see Diary), records that his mother
died 'in November this year,' which necessarily means the preceding year, 1771. At Mill's ordination in 1743, the Rev. Mr.
Gray (of Nesting, ordained 1703), 'one of the oldest ministers
in the country,' remarked that 'my father was the first whose
head he had laid his hand on, as I would be the last' (Diary,
1753), which also entirely corresponds. The author of the
Diary invariably signs 'Mill,' but the two forms, Mill and
Milne, were at that time often used indifferently.[1] The name
as used by the Diarist has since become famous in the person of the historian of British India, and of his gifted son,
John Stuart Mill, who were of Forfarshire origin. I have
been unable to trace any connection between the families.

Dr. Scott in the *Fasti* is imperfectly informed as to Mill's
matrimonial history. He was not once, but twice married.
The marriage in 1754, which he notes, was not to Miss Young,
but to a Miss Thompson, whose acquaintance he made at
Edinburgh when Conjunct Commissioner that year to the

---

[1] Thomas Gifford of Busta, in his private Diary, referred to in the printed
evidence in the Busta case in the Court of Session (1833-1835), records the baptism of one of his children by 'Mr. James Mill of Lerwick,' in the year 1716.
This was our Mill's father.

General Assembly. She had two children, and died at Lerwick in 1758 (Diary). On July 29, 1765, he was married for the second time to Miss Ann Young, 'daughter to Mr. Robert Young, portioner at the Water of Leith,' Edinburgh. She it is who is mentioned as having died at Prestonpans, 1816. The first wife had some means, and the portion of the second was £200 sterling (Diary, 1780), a not inconsiderable fortune in those days for persons in their position. There are quaint, not to say ludicrous, passages in the successive courtships, fully narrated in the Diary.

The elder daughter, Helen ('Nell'), was married to George Tocher, 'Merchant in Aberdeen' (Diary, 20th November 1777), who died at New Byth in 1786, leaving her a widow with one surviving child, a son seven years of age. She survived her father, and, as 'Mrs. Tucker,' was his executrix in 1805. It is not known whether any descendants now remain.[1] The second daughter, Bell, died unmarried in 1798.

The notice in the *Fasti* shows that Dr. Scott was unacquainted with Mill's literary productions, with the single exception of his statistical account of the parish, which indeed is all that was known up to the present time.

It is not necessary here to dwell upon the details of Mill's life. He was seven years schoolmaster at Cullen (Diary, 1753), with the customary ambition in those days of stepping from the schoolmaster's desk to the pulpit. He thereafter acted as assistant to a minister at Pitsligo in Buchan for sixteen months. From this appointment he received the presentation to Dunrossness, Sandwick, and Cunningsburgh, in 1743, when about thirty-one years of age, and in the charge of these parishes the whole of his long life was spent, as is fully related, to near the end, by his own pen in the Diary.

---

[1] In the Diary, 1753, a cousin-german and a nephew 'who were my namesons,' are referred to.

A well-educated man, of vigorous intellect and strong purpose, his powers and influence were always exerted on the side
of religion, truth, justice, as his best judgment and conscience
directed. Narrowness of view and harshness of dogma were
almost unavoidable in his time and place, and should be interpreted rather as expressive of the spirit of the age in the circles
of the orthodox than as his own special characteristics. At
times he exhibits a breadth and a superiority to sect and
party prejudice that is as remarkable as it is praiseworthy.
His reputation for integrity and sanctity was high in his own
day, and still survives in memory in the district of country
over which his influence extended. He died in 1805, when
nearly completing his ninety-third year. Having apparently
no male representative, or near connections sufficiently interested, no tombstone has been erected to mark his resting-place.

In the belief that Mill's *Last Will and Testament*, if it
existed, would be of especial interest, I searched the Sheriff and
Commissary Court books of Shetland at Lerwick, and the
Register of Wills in the General Register House, Edinburgh,
but without being able to find any such document. Half a
century before his death, viz., in 1753, a Will was made, as
related in the Diary, when his means were destined for distribution in a variety of generous bequests, but this must have
been cancelled at a later date, when the claims of a wife and
family had to be considered.

The Inventory of the personal estate is recorded in the
books of the Commissary Clerk of Shetland at the instance of
his daughter, ' Mrs. Helen Tucker ' (' Tocher ' of the Diary), as
executrix ; whether nominated by will, or appointed *quâ* next-
of-kin, is not stated, but the presumption seems rather in favour
of intestacy. The amount, upwards of £2000 sterling, was a
considerable realised fortune at the time (mostly invested in
heritable security in Scotland), especially in view of Mill's
generosity in life, his expenditure on the manse property, and

the smallness of the stipend (£44, 10s. sterling, in 1739; £55, 11s. 3d. sterling, in 1793).[1] The glebe was, however, a valuable adjunct, and Mill's great age admitted of a prolonged period of saving. Each of his wives also contributed to the means of the family, and personal expenditure was not heavy.

Apart from the widespread belief in Mill's sanctity of character, there was a general conviction, transmitted by tradition to the present day, that he was familiar with Satan, with whom he had many strange encounters in bodily shape, and

---

[1] ACCOMPT of the Funds belonging to the Rev. Mr. JOHN MILL, Minister of Dunrossness, at his death on 13th February 1805.

Bond by Mr. Stewart of Allantown and Mr. Trotter of Castlelaw, ...	£500	0	0	
Do. by Mr. Ferguson of Pitfour, ...	500	0	0	
Do. by the Earl of Strathmore, ...	600	0	0	
	£1600	0	0	
Interest from 1st January to 13th February 1805, £9 8 5				
Deduct tax, ... 0 9 5				
	8	19	0	
	£1608	19	0	
Note by Mansfield, Ramsay, and Co., of 20th February 1803, ... £50 0 0				
Interest at 4 °/₀ to 13th February 1805, . . 3 19 2				
	53	19	2	
Do. by Do. of 22d November 1804, . .£200 0 0				
Interest at 4 °/₀ to 13th February 1805, . . 2 0 11				
	202	0	11	
Money found in the Repositories of the deceased, . . .	84	13	0	
Price of Stocking sold, and Arrears of Stipend paid to Mrs. Mill,	63	11	3	
Balance in A/c due by Wm. Wilson, Writer, Edinburgh, .	60	19	9½	
Value of Furniture got possession of by Mrs. Mill, the relict, .	30	0	0	
Do. by Mrs. Tucker, daughter of the deceased, . .	30	0	0	
Price of Furniture sold, ...£58 13 10				
Deduct expenses, ... 18 14 2½				
	39	19	7½	
	£2174	2	9	

Affidavit of the same sworn to by Mrs. Helen Tucker, daughter, executrix of her said father, at Edinburgh, 9th May 1806, before John Walker, J.P. there. Recorded in the Commissary Court books at Lerwick, 23d June 1806.

[N.B.—Beside the above personal estate, there was some house property in Lerwick inherited from his father, as mentioned in the Diary.]

over whom he had great influence and controlling power. It would appear that Mill himself not only believed in the existence of the malign personality, and in demoniacal possession, but had conscious recognition of his own personal dealings with the Arch-Enemy. See incidents in the Diary, 1754-55-56. Satan was not in his eyes the majestic hero of Milton. On the contrary, Mill seems to have regarded him with little deference, and to have treated him with scant courtesy, as when, on one occasion, he called the Fiend to his face 'a damned rascal for his lying impudence.' This was in 1754, when the medium of an interesting colloquy between them was a possessed female. It is something to be able to record that on these occasions Satan was not invariably a spirit of evil. Once (in 1755) he manifested himself as a truly benevolent demon—a woman possessed was saved from pains of parturition!

Not to multiply instances of intercourse with Satan, still, or till recently, in the mouths of the people, the following story related to me a number of years ago may be quoted. My informant stated, in the native dialect, that his 'father and grandmother and another person (whom he named) were present in the Dunrossness Kirk when Satan came in. He dared not come in at the west door facing east; but came in at the east door, and took his place at the table [Communion table]. Mr. Mill knew him, and began to speak in all the deep languages, last of all it may be in the Gallic [Gaelic],[1] and that beat him altogether. So he went off like a flock of "doos" [pigeons] over the heads of the folk out at the west door. Many of the people swooned.'[2] This incident may be supposed to have occurred in the ancient Cross Kirk, and it may be remarked by the way that the perception here of what is implied in the principle of orientation, which the narrator

---

[1] The language used by Mill on these occasions is sometimes quoted as Latin, sometimes Hebrew.

[2] Thomas Shewan's tale.—G. G., July 1876.

was found pretty clearly to understand, is of some interest so long after the close of the Catholic age in Shetland.

The more usual form in which the Enemy of Souls preferred to appear at this time was that of literally a 'black sheep.' In this way he often tried to lead or pursue persons to destruction (suicide)—usually by throwing themselves over the sea-cliffs. Mill, when near in such cases, was keen in detecting the fiend. He invariably broke his spell, forced him to a hasty retreat, and rescued the victim. This same power has also been attributed to Mr. Hugens,[1] one of Mill's predecessors (1720-1733).

Mill, indeed, had little fear of either man or demon. His whole life was a stand-up fight. The devil, the local heritors, the brethren of the Presbytery, parishioners, and servants, were all objects of antagonism, and at times of very spirited malediction. The malignity, laxity, and want of sympathy of the clergy was a source of constant bitterness; and on one occasion he felt it his duty to embark on a heresy hunt (1777), which only fell through by the perjury, as he regarded it, of certain clerical witnesses whose zeal for orthodoxy was not equal to his.

No portrait of Mill is known to exist. The only description of him now obtainable has been given to me by my venerable father, ninety-three years of age. It is only the recollection of a child of seven years (in 1804), but may be quoted as the testimony of, doubtless, the only person now living whose eyes have beheld him.

'He seemed to be upwards of eighty years of age. He was tall, slender, straight, and healthy-looking. Hair still dark. Dressed in knee-breeches and black silk stockings. Wore a broad-brimmed cocked hat. His manner of addressing the

---

[1] Walter Hugens, A.M. Translated to the parish of Sandsting and Aithsting, 1733. He had a family of fourteen sons and six daughters.

people was direct and uncompromising—" Ye sinners of
Cunningsburgh," etc. He had a fine sonorous voice. I
remember, when about nine years of age, hearing an elder
of the church tell the story that when he was inducting
the Rev. David Thomson he said to him, " O Davie, Davie,
it were more meet to mak you a soldier than a minister." [1]

The late Mr. Bruce of Sumburgh informed me that when
Mill was urged by his friends to seek an augmentation of his
stipend of £50 per annum, he replied, ' Hoot, man, I have more
than I deserve.' [2]

These references to Mill personally may be closed by the
following apt reminiscences. The first was contributed to the
Shetland Times (October 1, 1887) by R. M., son of an old
native of Dunrossness, who says :—

' Mr. Mill seems to have been a man of considerable attain-
ments, but very homely in his attire and manner, and of great
kindliness of heart. If he had one penny in his possession, it
would go to the first needy person he met. In later life he
was persecuted by his brother ministers on account of his friendship for the itinerant evangelist, Captain Haldane, and especially
for allowing him to preach in his church. Like many good
men of his time, he had a firm belief in the personality of the
devil, and of his active hostility to, and interference with, good
works. He was often heard talking aloud with his (to others)
unseen foe, but those who heard him declared that he spoke in
an unknown tongue, presumably Hebrew. After one of these
encounters, the worthy man was heard muttering, " Well, let
him do his worst; the wind aye in my face will not hurt me." [3]

---

[1] The Rev. David Thomson was inducted to the parish of Walls and Sand-
ness in 1787.

[2] Letter dated 22d March 1880.

[3] This was in response to a threat of the devil, that wherever he, Mill, went,
he, Satan, should be a blowing ' wind in his teeth,' in consequence of which Mill
was unable ever after to get passage out of Shetland.

At one time Mr. Mill preached strongly against over-indulgence in eating and drinking, and thereupon he made an attempt to strengthen his doctrine by living upon water alone. He carried this on until one day he fainted in the pulpit, and was thought to be dead.[1] On regaining consciousness he rebuked the people for making such a great outcry, reminding them that there was greater cause for crying that day in a certain place they wot of. Regarding his fasting, it is told that on one occasion he was to preach at Tingwall. The day before he duly took his "pig" of water, and walked up to Lerwick [a distance of sixteen or eighteen miles by footpaths], to sleep all night in the house of a friend. Next morning he was up right early to walk out to Tingwall, and was leaving without any breakfast. His host, however, placed his back against the door, and swore he should not leave till he ate and drank. On his return to his friend in the evening, he confessed that his "cursed" meat and drink had done him no ill. Another tradition refers to the burning of the manse of Skelberry. The minister and his wife shut up the house on Saturday, to spend the night and Sunday with Mr. Sinclair of Quendale. While the services were being performed [in the Cross Kirk near by], a messenger arrived at the church with word that the manse was burning, and the officer mounted the pulpit steps and delivered the news to the preacher, who said, "Hoot, man! let it burn. It's either fire from heaven, or an enemy has done it."[2]

These stories are thoroughly characteristic, and have every appearance of truthfulness. The narrator, R. M., heard them and many others suchlike from his father, who was probably living near Mill's day. The story of the burning of the manse, in 1751, is well preserved, after a lapse of nearly 140 years.

---

[1] See Diary, 1801.
[2] See the account of the burning of the manse, Diary, 1751. The cost of rebuilding it, and the offices, etc., was upwards of £200 sterling, paid by himself.

The next is from an old lady, deceased, who was in her twelfth year when Mill died. It is communicated to me by her son :—

'It was customary for Mr. Mill to mount the pulpit with his cocked hat tied under his chin, and a bunch of flowers in his hand. He had a daughter, a Mrs. Tucker, who was long a member of the Tabernacle congregation, Edinburgh.[1] Once the precentor gave out: "Prayer is requested for George Shewan o' the Myres, who is dangerously ill." The minister leaned over the pulpit, and enunciated deliberately: "George —Shewan—o'—the—Myres ill! Why, I saw him hale and weel on Thursday; more meet we pray for Thomas Smith o' Boddam." He usually went through the parish mounted on a native pony, with Hector, his man, following. On one occasion a little black dog kept in their wake, and raised sundry doubts and fears in Hector's mind. The venerable octogenarian said, " Tuts, man, du needna fear; it's me he wants, no dee " (*i.e.* it is me he—the Devil—wants, not thee).'[2]

Passing from personal reminiscences, Mill's writings deserve to be briefly noticed. These are :—

1. The Diary. MS.
2. His printed work on 'The Holy Catholic Church.'
3. Account of the Parish of Dunrossness (*Stat. Acc.*), etc.
4. Speeches delivered at the Lord's Table, etc. MS.

1. THE DIARY.—This is a small quarto volume, not quite uniform in size, but as near as may be $7\frac{1}{2}$ inches in length by

---

[1] This was the church (Baptist) of which Mr. James Alexander Haldane, her father's friend, was pastor.

[2] Memorandum from James Catton Goudy, London, Feb. 1885. This story of the devil in the shape of a black dog is oft repeated.

6 inches in breadth. The beginning, relating the earlier part of his life up to 1738, is lost; after this there is an unbroken narrative on 59 leaves, written on both sides, or 118 pages, ending abruptly in the entry of 1st January 1803, some leaves at the end, as at the beginning, being lost. The handwriting is clear, neat, vigorous, to the end. It is understood to have been in the possession of the Sumburgh family since Mill's decease, and is now printed for the first time.

The work, strictly speaking, is not a 'Diary,' that is, a record inscribed from day to day. It is a narrative generally descriptive of the occurrences of the day, but for the first thirty years it is retrospective. It is usually concerned with local and personal affairs, but is also at times largely occupied with the review of public life and national events at home and abroad. The title assumed for it is, however, the most simple and convenient, and it has the sanction of precedent in some well-known instances of autobiographic memoirs.

In the Diary there is no lack of heart-searching and faithful dealing with himself; but in the main it may be said that his tone of mind and whole life are vigorously objective. He is a practical man, living in the present, and the past has no charm or romance for him. His memory and information might have brought us back to immediately post-Covenanting times and the heartburnings of the Revolution Settlement. But while we regret that he, with so much knowledge, is almost absolutely silent as to the past, we may have the assurance that he is all the more a faithful exponent of the facts and feelings of his own day, which should make the work all the more intrinsically valuable as a record of eighteenth-century life and history.

It is not necessary here to enter into any detailed notice or criticism of the Diary, which is before the reader *verbatim*, and, as nearly as may be, *literatim*. A few of its more prominent features need only be referred to.

As already mentioned, the loss of the introductory portion
has deprived us of the account of his family, his birth, education, and early history, which must have been there recorded.
The narrative is entire from shortly before his appointment
to the parish in 1742, with the loss of a single leaf in 1771.
It is nowhere stated that it is intended for publication, but
Mill's literary instincts, and the fact of his having published
a work of merit, make it more than probable that its being
submitted to the public eye, either in his lifetime or afterwards, was in his mind. The careful revision of the text,
and the amendment or deletion of passages that might be
open to objection, are indications in favour of this supposi·
tion.

Up to 1770 the Diary seems to be personal history in
retrospect; it then becomes a continuous record, steadily
kept up at convenient intervals, embracing the whole current
of his private life and the working of the ecclesiastical
machinery in the parish, with a spirited sketch, enlarging as
the narrative advances, of contemporary public events.

The story of his life in Shetland opens under circumstances
of some dejection. The leading families in the district were
disaffected, if not hostile, to him, to his Church, and even to
the Government. The Revolution Settlement had left most
of them attached to the Episcopal communion, as is distinctly
brought out in the Visitation Registers of Hunter, the last
minister of that persuasion, from which extracts are given in
the APPENDIX. The state of religion and morals in the parish
was also unsatisfactory. The kirk was in ruins, and, until a
new manse could be built, he had to content himself with
residing in the house of a Jacobite laird, Sinclair of Quendale, to whom he had a marked aversion.

The erection of a manse, which was burnt in 1752, and
rebuilt, engaged his early attention. The church not only
required to be renewed, but it was even destitute of Com-

c

munion cups, which, with other causes, prevented the observance of the Sacrament for a period of six years after his
ordination. It is not said by whom, or in what manner, the
cups were at last provided. Four are now, however, in use,
and they are thus described by the Rev. William Brand, the
present minister :—

'The cups are two and two alike, and all very similar ;
only two are slightly higher and narrower than the other two.

The lower and wider ones are without any lines round the
rim, which is just a very little turned out. The other two
have an incised line immediately below the turn out of the
rim ; then immediately below that, two lines quite close to
each other ; and about a quarter of an inch further down, other
two quite close, and all very small. On these two cups there
are on the bottom the letters A.B.M.S.'

By the courtesy of the Rev. Thomas Burns, author of the

valuable work, *Old Scottish Communion Plate*, now in the press, I am enabled to give drawings, by Mr. Alexander J. S. Brook, of two of these cups, which are of silver. That ornamented with incised lines bears the hall-mark of the city of Hamburg, but the date cannot be fixed. It is also difficult to say what the letters A.B.M.S. represent. The other cup is stamped with the name-punch of James Welsh, who was admitted to the Incorporation of Goldsmiths of Edinburgh in 1746.

Mr. Brand adds that there are two very large black pewter-like plates, unfit for use, lying past as lumber; and a baptismal basin, also quite useless. The two large (probably collecting) plates are doubtless of the old customary Nuremberg make and pattern.

The Communion cups in use at the Church of Sandwick, as I am informed by the Rev. C. Nairne Baldie there, bear the date '1854.'

The old parish church, the Cross Kirk of Dunrossness, long in a decaying state, was allowed to go to ruin; and, after prolonged contention with the heritors, the present church was erected about fifty years after Mill entered upon the charge (1790-1791). Encroachments upon the glebe by neighbouring proprietors were also cause of continuous irritation, as entries in the Diary, and especially the extracts in the APPENDIX from the Records of the Presbytery, abundantly show.

Mill's career having been spent almost entirely in the district of which he had the spiritual oversight, the Diary discloses little of personal incident or variety of experience of very striking kind, beyond what was usual and natural in the circumstances of the time and place. His whole life and energies were devoted to the wellbeing of the people and the advancement of genuine religion among them. The 'Renewal' of his 'Covenant Engagements,' 1770, and the reflections on the recurrence of successive birthdays and on other occasions, exhibit a devout consecration to the high aims which were ever before him. In the denunciation of sinners and backsliders, constantly recorded in the Diary, he seems almost to wear the garb and to wield the pen of a Hebrew prophet; in his efforts at self-mortification and conflicts with Satan he reminds us of a saint of the middle ages; while his hatred of Popery, Prelacy, and all systems of supposed abounding error, bears the flavour of a stern and zealous Covenanter. These characters interblended, combined with the worldly astuteness of a modern business man, go to make up the personality of our author as he appears before us in the pages of the Diary and in his other writings.

His pastoral duties at home were varied only by occasionally officiating in other parishes, and by visits to the south as Commissioner to the General Assembly. These visits must have been regarded as formidable undertakings, usually occupying six days or more either way, and beset with risks of shipwreck, of capture by the enemy, or of disaster in other forms. It was often the course, on such occasions, even within the present century, to land at Peterhead on the way south, and pursue the journey to Edinburgh by road.

Communication between Shetland and Scottish ports was at this time unfrequent and uncertain. Cured fish was exported mostly to Germany, and, strange as it may seem, domestic supplies were for the most part received directly from Hamburg (see Diary, 1773 and *passim*). The news of public events in the same way often reached Shetland by long and circuitous routes. The battle of Saratoga, fought in October 1777, was only known to Mill in February 1778, and in 1790 his supply of newspapers for six months reached him at one time.

Allusion has already been made to Mill's encounters with the devil, and to demoniacal possession as fully believed in. In the same way, the Divine judgment following upon blasphemy or other offences was regarded as the simple and natural consequence; indeed, those who crossed the minister in any unbecoming way seldom escaped Divine retribution.

Mill was a keen supporter of the Government. The Jacobites and the exiled Stuart family he held in abhorrence. The disloyal, the Irish rebels, the mutineers in the navy, and the rebellious American colonists, are all reprobated in the Diary. The pressgang, enforcing recruits for the navy, he commended, though the people regarded it with aversion and fear.

The Diary abounds with sad tales of the sea. Ever and anon disastrous shipwrecks are recorded on those pitiless rockbound shores; and indications of the propensity, on the part of natives, to share in the spoils of the deep on such occasions are not wanting. Disasters to fishing-boats, with loss of life, are also of frequent occurrence, then as now.

Smuggling, which was extensively engaged in, was under the ban of the Church; but a tasting of duty-free gin seems not to have been despised even by ecclesiastics. On one occasion recorded in the Diary (1753) the offence was not in partaking of a 'dram,' but in doing so without asking the Divine blessing upon it!

The movement for Catholic Emancipation in 1779 encountered, as is well known, a bigoted opposition everywhere; and in Shetland the rejection of this measure seems to have given satisfaction. 'Black Popery,' as conformity to Catholic usages was termed, was repugnant to the Diarist, and his anathemas against the system are unsparing. The scheme for sending missionaries to 'the heathen,' which has since been developed into powerful denominational organisations, was in its infancy towards the close of the century, and glimpses are given of the earliest efforts of its promoters.

So early as in 1785 a movement appears to have been started in Scotland in opposition to the Patronage system, which however was not abolished for nearly a century later. To this movement Mill gave his hearty concurrence, though, in his earlier days, he was not averse to using influence, on his own behalf, with my Lords Findlater and Morton, in respect of any suitable living that might turn up.

The state of Education in the islands, as in remote places generally, must have been very backward. Details as to this are given under the proper head.

Dancing was regarded as a carnal pleasure, but his eldest daughter Nell, before being placed at school at Edinburgh to 'learn to make her own cloaths and see more of the world,' had been instructed in Shetland in such accomplishments as were useful to a gentlewoman, namely, 'sewing and working of stockings, writing, arithmetic, *dancing*, church music, etc.' (Diary, 1768).

The Diary records a curious survival of the old Scandinavian form of local judicature into the second half of last century. Originally, in Shetland, as in Norway, every district or parish had its court, presided over by the parish Foud (*Norse*, Foged). Under the Stewart Earls a violent and too successful effort was made to overthrow local institutions and to assimilate everything to Scottish forms. In this way, in the preceding century, the 'Fouds of ilk parochin and yle' were gradually superseded by a functionary bearing the Scottish name of 'Bailie,' and in the course of time the parochial courts fell into abeyance. That however of Dunrossness lingered long, and the Court-book of the parish, 1731-1735, Alexander Sinclair of Brew, Bailie, is preserved in the Sheriff Court at Lerwick.[1] So late as in 1756 Mill refers to a court held at Dunrossness by this same Alexander Sinclair as the 'magistrate.' What appears to be a circuit, rather than a local, court is also held in the district at the time by Sir Andrew Mitchell (of Westshore, Bart.).

The narrative is all through a little mixed. Anti-climaxes, descents from the sublime to the ridiculous in the same breath, are of frequent occurrence. For instance, in 1797, after descanting at large on the progress of the war with the French and Dutch, he (on the same line in the MS.) proceeds to relate the virtues of 'Lignum's Anti-Scorbutic Drops' and 'Brodum's Restorative Nervous Cordial.' Indeed, even at the most solemn moments, there is a quaintness, an unconscious humour, all his own, that is delicious.

When we turn from the local and personal we find his accounts of public events clear and of telling interest. Many incidents, not to be found in ordinary historical books, are carefully chronicled, and the facts of contemporary history are shown, not as they present themselves to us at this distance of time, but as they shaped themselves in the public eye at the moment. He witnessed the rising of 1745, the revolt of the Colonies, the consolidation of our power in India, the outburst of the French Revolution, and the beginning of the great drama which followed, with Napoleon Bonaparte coming to the front as the leading figure. The bearing of all this upon British interests was fully impressed upon Mill's mind; and Shetlanders, far off

---

[1] See Paper by Sheriff Thoms, *Proceedings* S.A. Scot., vol. xvi. p. 157.

as they were, were by no means indifferent spectators. The islands participated directly in the events and consequences of the war. Many Shetland sailors, voluntary or impressed, were in the service, a good deal of money was circulated in the islands in connection with naval and military preparations, and brilliant captures and recaptures were made on the coast, sometimes by natives. (See Diary, 1779-1794.)

Remarkable indications are given of public-spirited efforts for maintaining the war. Even in a poor country like Shetland, voluntary contributions were made, Mill himself, with other parishioners, having subscribed a sum of ten guineas yearly while the war should last (Diary, 1798).

His bodily vigour and assiduous attention to duty continued until he was far advanced in life. In 1793, when in his eighty-second year, he visited the Fair Isle, twenty-five miles distant, in an open boat. Here he · remained two weeks, preaching, catechising, baptizing children, and exercising the discipline of the Church.

In April 1796, when eighty-four years of age, the first unmistakable signal of failing powers was given, when he was struck with apoplexy, which unfitted him for five months for public duty. Again, in 1801, he was suddenly seized with a fit of weakness, and fell down in the pulpit, but recovered.

In 1803 the Diary abruptly terminates, with the entry of January 1st, by the loss of the closing pages. How long it may have been continued thereafter it is now impossible to say. The Kirk-Session Minutes were penned, for most part, by him up to 8d February 1805, when the pen literally dropped from his hand. The date of the following Sunday, February 10, had been inserted in anticipation, but when the day arrived he was unfit to pen its record, and death, long delayed, came at last and relieved him from his labours on the 13th of that month.[1] Having been born on February 23d,

---

[1] In the Notes at pp. 125, 129, the death is stated erroneously to have occurred on the 15th of the month, instead of on the 13th.

1712, he was thus within ten days of completing his ninety-
third year.

It is difficult to say, in perusing the Diary, whether we
are more impressed with the earnestness and moral stature of
the man, or with the transparent truthfulness and candour
of the record.

2. THE HOLY CATHOLIC CHURCH, etc. ; Edinburgh, 1773.—
More than a dozen years ago I was endeavouring to elicit items
of olden-time story from a weak-witted, but withal well-
informed, parishioner of Dunrossness, in the course of which
he alluded to ' Mr. Mill's book ' as a printed work of which he
was the author. I was incredulous ; but when he afterwards
brought to me a worn and soot-stained fragment, consisting of
140 pages, which he insisted was the veritable volume, I took
it from him for a consideration. That this old country minister, in an out-of-the-way district, had appeared in the arena of
letters as the author of a theological work in the last century,
seemed a delusion, a fiction of tradition imposed upon an ignorant native. But in going over the Diary some years later, I
found, to my amazement, the author's account of his printing
at Edinburgh, in 1773, a volume on *The Holy Catholic Church*,
more than once afterwards referred to. This led me to search
in the University, the Advocates', and other public Libraries,
but no trace of Mill's name as an author was to be found in
the Catalogues of any of those collections. The quest was
almost given up as hopeless ; but some time afterwards a con-
sultation with Mr. Bruce of Sumburgh ensued ; and, though
the work was altogether unknown in his family, or to the
oldest parishioners, he inserted an advertisement in the Shetland papers, which resulted in his obtaining from Mr. James
Irvine, schoolmaster of Nesting, and forwarding to me, an
anonymous work on *The Holy Catholic Church*. It bore the
required date, 1773, and proved, on comparison, to be the
completed counterpart of the fragment in my possession. The

mystery was now solved—the book had been issued anony-
mously. Its full title is as follows:—

THE

HOLY CATHOLIC CHURCH

OF

CHRIST,

DELINEATED

IN HER FAITH AND PRACTICE,

AGREEABLE TO

THE WORD OF GOD AND SOUND REASON.

OR,

A V I E W

OF

THE LEADING DOCTRINES AND DUTIES OF
CHRISTIANITY, DIGESTED UNDER PROPER HEADS.

WITH

A SACRED HYMN ANNEXED TO EACH ARTICLE,
BY A MINISTER OF THE ESTABLISHED CHURCH.

EDINBURGH:
PRINTED BY JOHN REID, FOR THE AUTHOR.
SOLD BY WILLIAM GRAY, AND OTHER BOOKSELLERS.

M DCC LXXIII.

It is not quite consonant to the purpose of the present
work to give a detailed account of this book. But it may be

explained that it is an octavo volume of 341 pages, containing
an entire system of Divinity, a summary of Christian faith,
duty, and practice, in public, social, and domestic life; with
forms of prayer, and portions of hymns, or suitable pieces of
poetry, interspersed with the text in every chapter. He admits
that 'there is little of the author's' in this poetry, most of it
being compiled from Watts, Young, Milton, and Blair, and it
is therefore difficult to form an opinion of his powers of metrical
composition. But the work itself seems to be of much more
than ordinary merit, though its tone is somewhat gloomy and
severe, and its dogmatic asseverations at times worthy of St.
Athanasius.

Chapter lii., 'Of Hell, or the Everlasting Torments of
damned Sinners,' presents a picture of endless woe drawn with
great vigour, and appallingly realistic in form and colouring.
In Chapter xlv. his doctrine on the subject is trenchantly sum-
marised in a few words :—

'As the tree falls it must lie. Thus all, whether high
or low, rich or poor, learned or unlearned, Jews or Gentiles,
Papists or Protestants, must in a little time be eternally saved
or damned,—triumph for ever in heaven, or fry for evermore
in hell,' etc. (p. 225).

Mill was an earnest loyalist, hating the Stuarts, the Jacobit-
ism of his day, Popery and Episcopacy, and his views on these
matters come out incidentally in Chapter xlviii., on 'Persecution
for Conscience Sake.' The 'bloody race of Stewart, being
Papists,' got their just deserts. Mary, 'a woman of a proud
and crafty wit, and an indurated heart against God and His
truth, insisted in the same steps of tyranny and treachery (but
with greater aggravation) that her mother walked in, and was
served according to her desert. For after that her darling
Davie Rizio, the Italian fiddler (whom most men then supposed,
and do still suspect, to be the father of King James VI.), received
his due reward in her presence . . . she never rested till she

and Bothwell contrived the murder of Darnley; and then she
married the murdering adulterer, the said Earl of Bothwell
. . . and afterwards she was beheaded by Elizabeth,
Queen of England.' Then follow the sufferings of the
Covenanting era, graphically described, but no word of pity
or sympathy for the hapless Mary, or any not of his way of
thinking.

While denouncing persecution, his own tendency is to
vigorous denunciation of other forms of religious thought. He
was as yet no disciple of the doctrine of Toleration, which had
been enunciated by Locke a considerable time before this, as
witness his somewhat bitter attack on Sandeman, the founder
of the sect of the Sandemanians, pp. 267 *et seq.* But before
the close of his life his sympathies and sentiments were greatly
broadened, and his hearty reception of Captain Haldane and
the Rev. William Innes, the well-known evangelical preachers,
when not only the ministers of Shetland, but the whole Church
of Scotland, were bitterly hostile to them, should ever be
remembered to his credit.

Apart from questions of creed and forms of thought not
quite in harmony with modern phases, though distinctly
characteristic of his own age, there is much to admire in this
truly remarkable work, as a faithful and vigorous exposition of
the theology and highest religious principle of the day. Pity
it is that the only complete copy of it known, at any rate in
recognised association with the author's name, is the acciden-
tally acquired one in my possession.

It has been stated that the book, though full of religious
poetry introduced at suitable places in the text, affords no
certain evidence of the author's powers of versification. Here
however is an undoubted example, a tribute to the memory
of his first wife, inscribed on a page of the MS. volume,
'Speeches delivered at the Lord's Table,' to be afterwards
noticed :—

(Elizabeth Thompson, 3ʳᵈ Daughter of Baillie Thompson,
Edinburgh), who died February 9ᵗʰ 1758.

In her was Christ the hope of Glory form'd
And Love to Jesus all her Bosom warm'd
Fair as the Morn, her bright Example shone
It's force attractive as the Magnet Stone
In each Relation of her Mortal Life
The Duteous Daughter and the Lovly wife
The tender Mother and the Mistress kind
The obliging Neighbour and the stedfast Friend
To Social Graces all her soul was turn'd
And Social Actions all her life adorn'd
If humble Souls and Souls of heart Contrite
If patient Souls and Souls to Christ unite
If souls that follow peace and Sanctity
If souls that Mercy love and Charity
If such Dear Souls commence Eternal Rest
When loos'd from Flesh, then hers is ever blest.

Sic mihi contingat vivere, sic mori.

3. ACCOUNT OF THE PARISH OF DUNROSSNESS.—This is a
valuable contribution from Mill's pen to the topographical
literature of the district. It is of importance to the present
volume, as affording a contemporaneous description, carefully
and accurately done, of the place where the scene is laid, besides completing the view of the Diarist's works. It has
been thought well for these reasons to include it among the
papers in the Appendix, although it is already in print,
in vol. vii. of the old *Statistical Account of Scotland* by
Sir John Sinclair, Bart., 1793, in which it is lost to sight,
practically unknown. It is stated in the Diary that the
queries were received from Sir John in September, and that
the *Account* in reply was forwarded to him in October 1790.
It is curious that he states in it that the new church was
built 'a few years ago.' In point of fact the foundations
were only marked off 2d June of that year, and the church
itself was not opened until the following year, 1791. There

may however have been subsequent revision, as the volume did not appear till 1793.

Mill, unconscious of the charm which venerable objects of antiquity impart to a district, omits, in the *Account*, and in his other writings, all reference to the local antiquities. Most prominent of these are the BROUGHS, or circular towers of the Picts, of which so many remains were around him, and which cannot be passed without notice in any description of the district. The Castle of Mousa, in his northern parish, Sandwick, is the most perfect example in existence of this class of structure, and one of the most ancient and most interesting architectural remains in Great Britain.

The other ruined Broughs in the 'Ministry' of Dunrossness, Sandwick, and Cunningsburgh may be enumerated, thus:—

At Aith (?)	in Cunningsburgh.
„ Burraland	„ Sandwick.
„ Levenwick	„ Do.
„ Clumlie	„ Dunrossness.
„ Scousburgh	„ Do.
„ Lunabister	„ Do.
„ Waterbrough	„ Do.
„ The Brough	„ Do.
„ Voe	„ Do.
„ Broken Brough	„ Do.
„ East Shore	„ Do.

The Brough of Mousa was cleared out and carefully overhauled nearly thirty years ago. It is fully described by Sir Henry Dryden, Bart., in the *Archæologia Scotica*, vol. v. Part I., where plans and sections are given showing the remarkable arrangement of staircase and galleries intersecting the main wall, which are the specially characteristic features of Brough buildings. The only external aperture is the entrance, 5 ft. 3 in. high, by 2 ft. 11 in. wide, on the ground-

CASTLE OF MOUSA, SHETLAND.

From a Photograph by G. W. Wilson and Co., Aberdeen.

[p. xlvi

level, on the side opposite to that shown in the sketch, which
is reproduced for this volume, from a photograph.

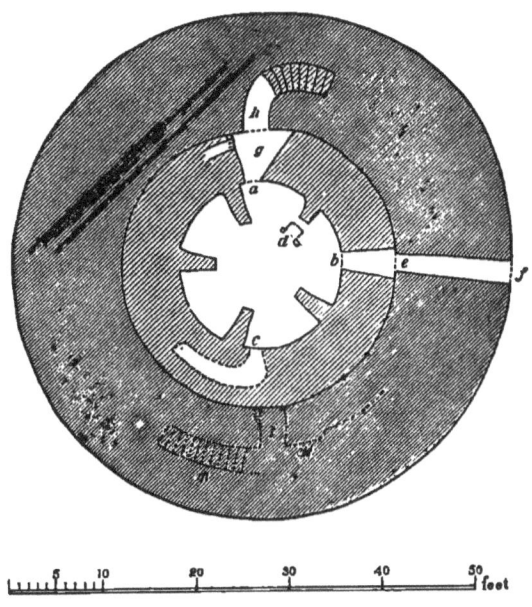

Brough of Levenwick—Ground Plan.

None of the other Broughs in the district, except those at
Levenwick and Clumlie, have been touched by the explorer.
The excavation of the former was the work of successive
holiday seasons[1]; the latter, hidden in a grass-grown mound,
was brought to light only last year.[2]

---

[1] Brough of Levenwick. Paper by the Editor, *Proceedings* of the Society
of Antiquaries of Scotland, vol. ix. (1871), p. 212. *a, b, c*, openings to inner
court; *d*, fireplace; *e, f*, entrance passage through main wall; *g*, triangular
space in front of staircase; *h*, stair to first gallery; *k*, termination of first gallery;
l, window looking into interior court; *m*, stair to second gallery.

[2] Brough of Clumlie. Paper by the Editor, *Proceedings* of the Society of
Antiquaries of Scotland, vol. xxiii. (1888-1889).

These Brough remains are not only, as has been remarked, the most prominent of the local objects of antiquity, but they are deeply impressive memorials of a prehistoric art and civilisation in these regions, of which we know but little otherwise.

The ecclesiastical antiquities of the district show but scant remains. They are referred to under a subsequent head —'Churches and Church Sites in Dunrossness, etc., with their Dedications.'

The circumstances, generally, of the parishes at the time when Mill's *Account* was written (1790) are so fully and distinctly set down by him as to require no further comment.

There is one feature to which it is proper to refer before concluding this notice of the descriptive Account of the parishes, viz., the Place-Names, especially the minor designations, several of which occur in the Diary.

The major place-names, those of villages, hills, lochs, water-courses, are necessarily all more or less stereotyped, and not easily eradicated. But apart from these, every knoll or hillock, every patch of waste or cultivated ground, every enclosure, every standing stone, every rock, creek, cave, or crevice by the sea-shore, bore its own descriptive name, almost always in expressive Norse.

As the old village settlements remained with little change from age to age, this minor nomenclature was preserved from generation to generation down from Scandinavian times. But with the gradual breaking up of village communities by the discontinuance of the run-rig system of cultivation, and the formation, instead, of separate detached holdings with changing occupiers, the old continuity of life and feeling and local knowledge has been greatly impaired; and in this way the minor names are rapidly disappearing, as they have already almost entirely disappeared in most of the mainland districts of Scotland.

The preservation, therefore, of as many as possible of those descriptive names of olden time is of importance; and an effort with that view was made a number of years ago, which resulted in the compilation of a large, but still necessarily incomplete, list of the place-names in each of the three parishes, besides Fair Isle and other places. Since then, the completion of the Ordnance Survey maps, on the large scale, has proved an important step towards the preservation of these names, especially those along the coast, and has made it less necessary to introduce such a list here. The minor names in one small district will serve as an illustration of the usually minutely descriptive character of these names in the older neighbourhoods; to attempt an enlargement of the list, so as to embrace even one of the parishes, would require a treatise by itself.

MINOR PLACE-NAMES IN CLUMLIE (Columba-lie) DISTRICT,

PARISH OF DUNROSSNESS.

Name.	Probable Old Norse form.	Meaning.
Virdifell	Vördu-fjall	Ward-hill.
Helliberg	Hellu-bjerg	Flat rock (by the sea).
Trimihew	Thrym-haugr	Stone of noise (do.).
Kamer	Kammer	A room, chamber (do.).
Trublcton	Troll-böl-tún	Haunt of the fairies.
Lingard	Ling-gardr	Heather farm.
Hwy yard	Hvi gardr	Enclosed yard.
Finglirty yard	Fönguleigr-teigr-gardr	The yard in good condition, rich.
Bugardsty yard	Bu-gards-teigr-gardr	Town yard.
Krintop	Kring-topt	Round-about toft.
North Lays	Nord leigur	North slopes.

d

Name.	Probable Old Norse form.	Meaning.
Nether Gairds	Nedr-gardr	Lower field.
Breiddal	Breid-dalr	Broad dale.
Mogidal	Miovi-dalr (?)	Narrow dale.
Runtie-gate	Hraun teigr gata	Rough-place road.
Trottaknowe	?	?
Fjalsas	Fjalls-áss	Hill-side.
Hoolan-haigree	(A knoll on the east side of Hallalee, demolished by the formation of the public road about 1850).	
Ramnagio	Ramnagiá	Gio (or creek) of rams.
Murigarth	Myri-gardr	Moory town.
Yaback	Hjá-bakki	High bank or ditch.
Stoorishon	Stori-shon	Big pool (near house of Braefield, now drained).
Fits	Fitjar	Ground at margin of loch.
Vills	Vellir	Fields.
Natshag	Nauts-hagi	Cattle-pasture.
Markidal	Merkju-dal	Merkdale.
Tarridal	Therri-dal	Dry dale.
Stigadie	?	?
Rings	Heidr-engjar (?)	Outfield heath.
Smerrilee	?	?

It only remains to add that the three parishes which united formed the 'Ministry' of Dunrossness, Sandwick, and Cunningsburgh, under Mill's charge, are the larger portion of the southern promontory of the mainland of Shetland. The extent from Quarff on the north to Sumburgh Head, the extreme point to the south, is about 16½ miles in length, with an average breadth of 2½ to 3 miles, at certain points less or more. Cunningsburgh is the northmost of the three parishes, and Dunrossness the most southerly, Sandwick lying between. Fair Isle, midway between Orkney and Shetland, 25 miles distant from either group, is also included in the Ministry. It is upwards of 3 miles in length, and nearly 2 miles broad.

The population at last census is quoted as :—

Dunrossness, ... 1818
Sandwick and Cunningsburgh, . 2308
Fair Isle, ... 214

For the better understanding of the district, in illustration of the Diary and of the *Account of the Parish*, the reader is referred to the copy of the Ordnance Survey map reproduced for this volume.

4. SPEECHES DELIVERED AT THE LORD'S TABLE, begun 1743.— This, the last of Mill's literary relics, is a small manuscript volume, containing twenty - four 'Speeches,' with a few 'Addresses' of a less special character. It is explained in a note that the speeches 'were then intended for the Sacrament [1743], yet was it not celebrated until 1749 by reason of the Unfitness of the people for that solemnity, and want of Utensils, etc.'

A part of the volume is set apart for a list of the *Number and Names of Communicants in Dunrossness Minis- try*, 1749.

The list embraces sixteen districts, from Fladabister on the north to Sumburgh Head, the extreme southern point of the country, comprising the entire area of the three united parishes of Dunrossness, Sandwick, and Cunningsburgh, which formed the 'Ministry' under Mill's charge. The total number of communicants is given as '567,' which may be assumed as that for the year when the roll was first completed, 1749; but there are numerous interlineations and additions which largely increase the number, and show that the roll is not limited to that year, but is a continuous record till probably an advanced period, if not indeed applying to the entire course of Mill's incumbency. It is thus of doubtful value, either as a matter of church statistics or as a test of population, so far as details go, because an accurate list of the communicants in the different districts for any one year cannot now be safely deduced from it, and the list has therefore not been transcribed for the present work. But some of the points brought out are noteworthy.

Taking the list as a whole, covering a somewhat extended period, the proportion of the sexes is fairly maintained in the aggregate, Dunrossness proper (excluding Sandwick and Cunningsburgh) showing 244 males and 232 female communicants. But there are some curious variations in the detail. For instance, in the district of Tolb, the female communicants are exactly double the males, *i.e.* 26 to 13 ; while in South Voe the males are more than double the females, being 11 to 5 ; and in St. Ninian's Isle, now uninhabited, and which would seem incapable of supporting more than one or two families, no less than 16 males, with 7 females, are presented. Scatness, with 6 males, has 20 female communicants; these in every case, as previously explained, extending over a series of years.

The state of the roll does not admit of a satisfactory comparison being made between its date and the present time, and the circumstances, besides, are widely different. In the Church of Scotland Year-Book, 1888, the communicants in Dunrossness are given as 424, and in Sandwick and Cunningsburgh, 413. To this must be added, in any estimate of church-membership, a considerable number for those attached to other Churches, while, at the date of Mill's Communion-roll dissent was unknown, except as regards the small remnant who had refused to accept the Revolution Settlement and still adhered to Episcopacy. Among these were the leading families in

the parish, namely, Sinclair of Quendale, Bruce of Sumburgh,
Sinclair of Brew, Sinclair of Goat, John Bruce Stewart of
Bigton, and some others, who were ministered to in private
by the Rev. Mr. Hunter, the last Episcopal clergyman until
the comparatively recent re-establishment of the Scottish
Episcopal Church in the islands.

The volume of Speeches, etc., is in the possession of Mr.
Bruce of Sumburgh.

To the four preceding works which have been described,
two in manuscript and two in print, and which are personal to
Mill as author, there might be added the *Records of the Kirk-
Session of Dunrossness*, which, during the entire period of his
ministry, were either penned by him, or, apparently, written
to his dictation.

THE selections from records and original documents printed
in the APPENDIX are of different dates, but they all afford
illustrations of local life and history in the times to which they
refer. Original matter of very striking importance in reference to a remote and obscure district like a Shetland parish is
not to be readily found, if, indeed, it exist at all; and it has
therefore been necessary to be contented with such materials
as were available. The extracts and documents quoted may
be noticed in order as follows, viz. :—

I.—RECORDS OF THE KIRK-SESSION OF THE PARISH OF
DUNROSSNESS, 1764-1805.

The Minutes of Session previous to Mill's incumbency are
not now known to be in existence. The earliest volume extends
from 1764 to 1841. Eighteen pages at the beginning are lost.
These doubtless recorded the proceedings from the date when
the book in use at the time of his settlement in 1743 was
finished to that of the first entry preserved, viz., 22d April
1764. From that time it is a continuous record (a few separate
pages lost), almost wholly in his own handwriting until near
the time of his death in 1805. It is a folio volume, 12 in. by
7½ in., much frayed at the edges, with only one of the boards
remaining, and the binding entirely gone. I am obliged to
the Rev. William Brand, the present minister of the parish, for
permission to make such use of it for the present publication
as might be deemed desirable, and I have accordingly, in the
APPENDIX, given a series of extracts illustrating the course of
ecclesiastical procedure, and the state of parochial economics
so far as these are touched upon.

The events of Mill's own life, and the principal occurrences
in the district under his care during the sixty years of his incumbency, are fully recorded in his autobiographic narrative;

and the Church records, confined to matters of purely ecclesiastical concern, are almost barren of incidents of general interest or importance. They may be said merely to chronicle the services of each successive Sunday, and the actings of the Session as a petty police and morals judicatory, supposed to be clothed with a certain sanction of divinity inherited from bygone times.

The unending burden of the record, here as elsewhere in Church Records of the period, is the old story of moral delinquency, which occupies alike the time of the Session and the pen of the Clerk, *ad nauseam*. Offenders, individually or in couples, are ever and anon presented, charged with the ' heinous crime,' which is often admitted, often stoutly denied, and condemned to undergo discipline as accords. To be ' rebuked and exhorted to unfeigned repentance, and to make public satisfaction for the scandal, *communi forma*,' was the fate, with varying degrees of severity, of these too numerous frail ones of both sexes. To stand before the congregation for twenty-six Sabbaths was the penal judgment in ordinary cases; in cases of obstinacy, or lapses for a second or third time, the judgment was sometimes extended to appearance in public for a whole year, with infliction of a fine suitable to the gravity of the case, after which the delinquents were ' rebuked for the last time and dismissed from discipline.' The fine was sometimes 10s. sterling, sometimes 15s., and occasionally as much as £12 *Scots*, *i.e.* about £1 sterling. There were instances in which the fine was remitted on account of poverty.

Antenuptial impropriety, though a constant subject of discipline, was treated as less heinous. Parties were at times dismissed from discipline after three, four, up to nine, appearances before the congregation.

On one occasion an alleged premature birth, caused apparently by the mother's having fallen from a horse, became matter of suspicion and inquiry. The parties were called before the Session to explain and exculpate (August 14, 1768).

Some respect of persons, especially when their purse admitted of a substantial fine being imposed, seems not to have been altogether disregarded. On 1st April 1804, James Hughson and Helen Aiken, offenders, having confessed and paid thirty shillings sterling, were dismissed for 'one day's appearance and publick Rebuke.'

For repeated offences, and especially persistent denials and contumacious resistance to discipline, parties were ordered to compear before the next meeting of Presbytery at Lerwick, twenty miles or so distant. Considering the trouble and difficulty of travelling such a distance, the interference with ordinary labour, and the disgrace which it involved, a judgment of this kind must have been a tremendous infliction, resembling the anathemas of the Church in the middle ages.

To those who, under strong presumptive evidence of guilt, persisted in denial, an 'Oath of Purgation' was administered, under the idea that, like torture, it would compel confession, and it no doubt was often successful in accomplishing this. A copy of the oath is nowhere given. It was evidently of great solemnity, not readily to be taken with an easy conscience. See APPENDIX, cases of 20th March 1764, and September 24, 1769.

After the death of Mill, the Session, under the presidency of the new minister, the Rev. John Duncan, came at length to see that the frequent appearances of offenders in public before the congregation were not attended with the beneficial results which were intended, and on 21st April 1806 they came to a resolution to modify the terms of public 'satisfaction,' as it was called. Appearances in cases of the most aggravated nature were reduced to four, and absolution from 'Public Scandal and Church Censure' in less offensive cases was to be still more easily obtained. Inquisition by the Session for

offences against the laws of morality, though greatly fewer
than formerly, continued in much the same way till after the
middle of the present century, though fines seem to have ceased.
With the advent of Dissent in the parish, this strictly *parochial*
jurisdiction gradually became circumscribed, as Church discipline formed, of course, an essential function of the congregational life of all the denominations in the district equally.

It may be noted here that the usual time when the Session
adjudicated upon these scandals was on Sundays, before or after
service. Occasionally meetings of the Session were held at the
manse; and on one occasion, the case being that of a frail
delinquent at Wilsness, near Sumburgh, the minister and two
elders proceeded to that place (17th August 1777), and, after
a Sessional meeting had been constituted by prayer, the case
was dealt with on the spot.

Blasphemy, including swearing and 'imprecating damnation' upon neighbours, appears to have been a too common
offence, which the constant exercise of discipline had little effect
in restraining. Offenders were not confined to the sterner sex,
females being frequently indicted, as will be seen from some
curious examples in the APPENDIX. In these examples somewhat singular eccentricities of imprecation are displayed, the
powers, in at least two instances, which are quoted, being im-
plored to send Satan down the throats of certain neighbours;
on another occasion Satan is asked to burn both the obnoxious
neighbour and her peats; and on another, a dog is the object
of an infuriated dame's malediction. With an intensely realistic view, prevailing at the time, of the presence and sulphur-
ous power of Satan, it is neither to be wondered at that his aid
was invoked in outbursts of passion, nor that the machinery of
Church discipline was set in motion against those who appealed
to his destructive agency, or prayed that others should be condemned everlastingly to his keeping. Heinous as the offence
was, the fine imposed was not excessive, sometimes one shilling,

sometimes a half-crown, or its equivalent, £1, 10s. *Scots*, and sometimes merely rebuke.

The *observance of the Sabbath* appears to have been carefully, indeed rigorously, guarded throughout last century, as it may be said it still is in the district, though nowadays the only restraining force is public opinion. In 1765 it was found that great scandal had been caused by a man and his daughter having rolled a cask of tallow from the seaside (where it had been driven ashore) on a Sunday evening. But this is not equalled in rigour of discipline by the treatment of an occurrence, so late as 1834, in the same parish of Dunrossness, when fines amounting to 30s. appear to have been exacted from parishioners who went out on the Sunday to some Davis Straits whaling-vessels, just arrived on the coast, to render the very benevolent help of taking ashore the chests of some of the crews belonging to the district, to save the labour of transporting them twenty miles by land from Lerwick. *Despising a public Fast-day* was reckoned approximate in scandal to Sabbath-breaking. For this offence one Peter Jamieson was summoned on 9th October 1787. He was dismissed without a fine.

The supreme anathema of the Church was, as in ancient times, *Excommunication*. It was only resorted to in extreme cases, where Church and Presbyterial censure were obstinately resisted and set at defiance.

The *nominations for the Eldership* seem, as might be expected, to have proceeded directly from the minister, as probably the best judge of fitness. If no relevant objections to the persons nominated were substantiated, their ordination to the office proceeded in the usual way. Most of the old elders being dead, the eldership was reconstituted on Sunday, 29th March 1772, when the following were ordained, viz. :—

For Bigton district—James Lisk, John Anderson.

  ,, Rerwick—James Laurenceson.

  ,, Scousburgh—William Sinclair, Walter Henryson.

For Scotshall—John Brown, William Stout.

„ Tolb, Scatness, and Willsness—John Strong, younger, and Laurence Young.

„ Noss—Henry Sinclair, James Mode [Mouat], and George Brown.

„ Hillwel—John Lesslie, senior, and John Arcus.

„ Lud and Cour—John Lesslie, junior, and John Shewan.

„ Garth—John Stout, Thomas Sinclair, and Magnus Irvine.

„ Skelberry—James Lesslie, senior, William Young, and John Sinclair.

„ Clumley—Robert Gadie and Gawn Gadie.

„ Southvoe—Alexander Scott and Malcom Halcrow.

„ Ringasta—James Lesslie, junior, and George Williamson.

In this way the whole parish was mapped out, under a complete territorial system, for Church supervision through the agency of a selected number of the most reputable and trustworthy of her communion,—that is, of the whole body of heads of families in the different districts of the parish, for Dissent was practically unknown.

The Elders above named are for the parish of Dunrossness proper. There is no record here at this time of those for the conjunct parishes of Sandwick and Cunningsburgh, which also formed part of the Ministry in Mill's time, and still indeed do so, though a separate minister is now provided, who officiates in the church of Sandwick. The Elders for these parishes are again named at a later date, at an ordination in 1791.

The duties of the Eldership are nowhere distinctly defined in the Minutes under notice, but were probably in no essential respect different from those usually attached to the office in Scotland. The Elders seem to have had an important charge in looking after the poor. The attendance of parishioners at

Church services, and at Communion seasons, previous to which tokens had to be distributed,[1] would involve continual attention on their part; while much of their time must necessarily have been consumed, and not very profitably, in the inquisitions in

No. 1.   No. 2.

DUNROSSNESS CHURCH TOKENS.
(1) D. K. (Dunrossness Kirk) 1749.   (2) D. K. 1797.

cases of scandal, which so largely predominated in the business before the Session.

The list of parishioners on the Poor Roll, and the distributions from time to time for their support, are an interesting study, and form a curious commentary on the state of matters now existing in country parishes under the Poor Law Act as contrasted with that formerly prevailing. From the particulars given in the APPENDIX, under the head 'Parochial Finance,' it will be seen that at the date of the first statement, January 1765, there were 20 paupers on the roll in the parish of Dunrossness, besides 4 widows, and 6 other persons who received trifling allowances. The poor of the higher class received £1, 10s. *Scots* each, or a half-crown sterling, apparently for a whole year; the ordinary poor received £1, 4s. *Scots*, or 2s. sterling; and widows £1, 16s. *Scots*, or 3s. each. The whole sum disbursed for the support of the poor from the Church funds reached only to about £3, 3s. for the entire year! It is proper to explain, in reference to this, that under the

---

[1] It is stated on one occasion (September 18, 1768) that the minister himself distributed the tokens at an afternoon service. Whether this was habitual or not does not appear.

old system the money given to the poor from the Church funds formed only a portion of their maintenance. The aid of relatives was first relied upon, and was usually ungrudgingly bestowed. This again was supplemented by door-to-door visitations by the poor themselves, who, in necessitous cases, were housed and fed by the parishioners, as they passed on from hamlet to hamlet, thus receiving entertainment from the better class of householders in rotation. This continued in practice down to perhaps thirty or forty years ago. It was not more burdensome to the 'ratepayers,' as householders are now termed, and was much more humane treatment of the poor than their enforced seclusion in district poorhouses.

At this time (1765) the salaries or allowances to parochial officials were not excessive. The precentor received 6s. 8d. sterling per annum for his services, the Church-officer, 5s., and the treasurer, 3s. 6d. The following year the precentor received a trifle more, namely £4, 10s. *Scots*, or 7s. 6d., but the Church-officer was reduced to 3s. 6d.

The sources of income were the Church-door collections, the fines imposed on persons amenable to Church discipline, and the charge for the use of the mortcloth at funerals, usually 6d. or a trifle more.

Funerals at the expense of the parish cost about 3s. in 1778.

It appears from an entry in 1767 that the Session had a supply of Books, doubtless Bibles and religious publications, on hand for sale. Of these there were sold to the value of £13, 18s. *Scots*, or, say, 23s. sterling, while a surplus stock, worth 10s. 6d., remained on hand.

On one occasion (25th March 1790) the Session made an advance to their officer of 15s. from the Church funds, repayable in one year. A small balance, termed the 'stock,' usually only a few pounds sterling in amount, was carried forward from year to year, and used as working capital for support of the poor, or any special demands.

Neither the Session Records, which were penned by Mill, nor his Diary, throw much light upon the state of education in the district at the time—the second half of last century and the beginning of the present. Such particulars as may be gleaned are given under a subsequent head, 'Early State of Education in Dunrossness.'

In 1818 the venerable official, the 'Reader,' whose office was suppressed by the General Assembly in 1581,[1] reappears upon the scene in the Minutes of this parish in the person of William Henry, so styled, who receives 15 shillings yearly for his services. He disappears from view in 1830, and was perhaps the last officially recognised 'Reader' in Scotland.

The ancient scourge of Leprosy was present in Mill's time ; at any rate, a subsidised pauper on one occasion was termed a 'Leper.'

A noticeable feature in these records during the second half of the century is the existence at the time, in the parish, of numerous family names, some of them known centuries before, but all which have now disappeared from the district. The following may be cited as examples, viz. :—

Grizel Blackbeard.	Helen Roeman.
Agnes Knarston.	Margaret Burleigh.
Christian Stott.	Marjory Grott.
John Archibald.	Sibrina Lamb.
James Macpherson.[2]	Christian Folster.
Elspet Ysmester.	Margaret Ratter.
Robert Marwick.	Helen Rich.

The majority of these are more or less well-known Orkney

---

[1] 'Anent Readers : Forsuamickle as in Assembleis preceiding, the office thereof was concludit to be no ordinar office in the Kirk of God, and the admissione of them suspendit to the present Assemblie : the Kirk, in ane voyce, hes votit and concludit farther, that in no tymes comeing any Reader be admittit to the office of Reader be any haveing power within the Kirk.'

[2] Macpherson. I was told by a descendant that the family derived from a refugee from the Jacobite 'Rebellion in Scotland.'

names, some of them probably those of vagrants who came and settled in the district, becoming ultimately chargeable on the Church funds, as most of the above persons were.

It was reported, traditionally, that a Dutchman, one *Gudrun* Funk, settled in the parish, whose son was Olla *Gudrun*. Olla's daughter was Isabel *Olla* or Ollie, who appears in the Poor's Roll of 1812.

In concluding this notice of the contents of the Kirk-Session records, it may be well to mention the state of the other local Registers. The following are in existence, and preserved in the General Register House :—

DUNROSSNESS, .   .   Births and Marriages from 1753.
SANDWICK and CUNNINGSBURGH,   Do.   „   1746.
FAIR ISLE,   .   Births from 1767 ; Marriages „   1789.

In DUNROSSNESS Register the Births are blank from May 1783 to April 1789, except 4 entries. The Marriages are blank from February 1756 to June 1790.

In SANDWICK AND CUNNINGSBURGH, the Birth Registers are irregular and defective from June 1782 to June 1785, and the Marriages blank from December 1782 to October 1786.

In FAIR ISLE Register about 37 families are recorded in groups, preceded generally by the entry of Marriage of the parents, with 15 transcribed entries of Births, 1767-1796.

The County Records of Shetland, preserved in the Register House, are as follows :—

PARTICULAR REGISTER OF SASINES—

ZETLAND, 1st July 1623 to 1st March 1672, volume 1 (prior to 1st July 1623) has been lost; volumes 3 and 4 are imperfect.

ORKNEY and ZETLAND (combined), 8th June 1661 to 5th December 1752.

SHETLAND, 11th October 1744 to 6th Feb. 1869.

COMMISSARIOT OF ORKNEY AND ZETLAND—
Testaments, 1611 to 1684, with Index.
Decreets, 1648 to 1668 (fragment).

SHERIFF-COURT RECORDS—
Sheriff Court of Orkney and Zetland, 1564, etc., and from 1612 to 1665.
Sheriff Court of Zetland, 1602 to 1604.

II.—EXTRACTS FROM THE RECORDS OF THE PRESBYTERY OF ZETLAND ANENT THE GLEBE LANDS OF DUNROSSNESS, 1737-1764.

These extracts have been given in fuller detail than was at first proposed, but they are not without importance as indicating the confused and dilapidated state in which, in many instances, the property of the Church must have come down from earlier times—apparently no distinct title and no clear definition of boundaries. The origin and history of the glebe cannot now be learned; but all goes to show that the 10 merks of land in Skelberry, originally intermixed—'runrig'—with the conterminous properties, formed the patrimony of the Church and the residence of the parish priest from the earliest time of a settled parochial system. The ground, like the revenues, in all likelihood suffered diminution at the convulsions of the Reformation, though it is true that in Shetland the transition was accomplished more smoothly than in most other places. As was common in many districts, the vicarage of Dunrossness passed into the hands of a layman, as shown elsewhere in the APPENDIX.

III.—ACCOUNT OF THE PARISH OF DUNROSSNESS, by the Rev. JOHN MILL, 1793.

This has already been noticed under the head of Mill's own writings, *ante.*

IV.—LIST OF PARISH MINISTERS OF DUNROSSNESS,
SANDWICK, AND CUNNINGSBURGH.

The laborious investigations of the late Dr. Hew Scott
have resulted in an almost complete list of the parish clergy
of Scotland since the Reformation being now available for
the student of ecclesiastical history in the pages of the *Fasti
Ecclesiæ Scoticanæ*. But the centuries prior to the Reformation
have no record of this kind. The clergy of pre-Reformation times are only to be discovered now and again, individually
or in small accidental groups, in charters and documents, in
occasional registers of Cathedrals or Religious Houses, and in
fugitive writings which may chance to have been preserved.

In Orkney the members of the Chapter of St. Magnus
had a better chance of surviving in record, and the names of
a good many beneficed clergymen connected with the Cathedral
have come down to us. But in Shetland, while we know that
the parochial divisions existed for ages before the Reformation
very much as at present, and while, as will be seen under
another head, the churches from the earliest times can, without
much difficulty, be identified, it is sad to have to record that
the clergy who had the spiritual charge of those parishes, and
ministered at the altars in those churches before many successive
generations of worshippers, have almost all passed into oblivion,
without leaving a trace behind. The only two pre-Reformation clergymen of Dunrossness whose names I have been able
to recover are—

Henry Strang, Vicar of Dunrossness, 1525.
Sir Nicol Wyschart, Do. 1546.

Both names occur in documents preserved in the Sheriff-
Court Office in Lerwick, and described in the *Proceedings of*
the Society of Antiquaries of Scotland.[1]

---

[1] *Notice of Ancient Legal Documents (Lay and Ecclesiastical) preserved
among the Public Records of Shetland.* By the Editor. *Proceedings* S. A. Scot.,
vol. xvi., 1882, p. 181.

e

The post-Reformation clergy of the united parishes are given in the APPENDIX. There is not much requiring to be added in reference to those names beyond the facts there noted. With the exception of Mill, the author of the Diary, and Thomas Barclay, afterwards Principal of Glasgow University, who were natives, they all appear to have been strangers to the country.

Malcolm Sinclair, designed 'Reader,' was presented to the Vicarage of Dunrossness in 1575, and continued in 1601. The name presents some ambiguity. Under the head of 'Ecclesiastical Revenues' of the parish, in the APPENDIX, this Malcolm Sinclair is stated, in a document of 1576, to possess 'the haill Vicarage of Dunrosnes,' he paying the 'Readers' at the different churches, Laurence Sinclair being then the Reader at Cross Kirk and the Fair Isle. In 1610 Laurence Sinclair, then designed 'Vicar and Titular,' is said to have 'set' the Vicarage to Malcolm Sinclair of Quendall, who also, in the previous year, 1609, receives from Earl Patrick a Discharge, printed in the APPENDIX, for the *Umboth*, or Bishopric revenues, of this and other parishes, which he is said to hold under tack from the Earl. It is not clear whether Malcolm Sinclair, the Churchman of 1576, 1601, and Malcolm Sinclair, this laird of Quendale, who held the Vicarage by the tack of 1610, are the same person. The laird was a person of some note in his day. It was he who received the shipwrecked mariners of the Spanish Armada in 1588, and whose tombstone, with the date 1618, still remains on the site of the ruined Cross Church at Quendale.

James Forbes, A.M., 1662 to 1682, has left his name on record in connection with a 'mortification' executed by his widow, of a small sum of land rent for the benefit of widows in the parish. Reference to this provision, which was attempted to be set aside by an heir, is made in the Diary (1756), when Mill stoutly asserted, and succeeded in maintaining, the rights of the beneficiaries. In 1786 Disposition was granted to John Bruce of Sumburgh by James Forbes, shipmaster, of the 'Pund of the Brecks adjacent to Voe,' in Dunrossness, under the burden of seven pounds Scots, payable yearly out of the rents of the room of Brecks when the same yields so much rent, to four of the most indigent widows, to be chosen in manner directed. It is understood that this small revenue (several times alluded to in the Kirk-Session Minutes) is now lost sight of from its original destination.

James Kay, A.M., 1682 to 1720, is the author of the valuable manuscript papers, preserved in the Advocates' Library, from which Sir Robert Sibbald obtained his description of Dunrossness in his book on Shetland, 1711 ; and from which also the paper in the APPENDIX, headed 'Feuds and Bloodshed in Dunrossness in the Sixteenth Century,' is now, for the first time, put in print. He seems to have been a man of learning and industry, and an earnest student of the history and topography of the district.

When to the above names are added those of John Mill and Principal Barclay, it may safely be affirmed that this far-off parish has had clergymen of whom all connected with it have reason to be proud.

V.—CHURCHES AND CHURCH SITES IN DUNROSSNESS, SANDWICK, AND CUNNINGSBURGH, WITH THEIR DEDICATIONS.

1. DUNROSSNESS.—There is nothing to be gleaned from the Session Records as to the old pre-Reformation parish church of Dunrossness, in which Mill officiated for nearly half a century. This was the 'Cross Kirk' or 'Cors-Kirk,' which stood for centuries on the Sand at Quendale, and which Mill on his presentation to the parish found 'in ruins,' as he, perhaps with some degree of exaggeration, expresses it.[1] Its state of disrepair

---

[1] The ruinous state of the church, want of manse, etc., had been complained

became, however, serious, and after much difficulty with the heritors, it was eventually superseded by the present church on the 'ground of Brew,' which was opened by Mill in 1791.

At a meeting of the Session on 31st January 1765, the minister acknowledged to have paid into the funds £2, 12s. stg. as 'the price of the Bell that was sent south.' This was, there is little doubt, the Cross-Kirk bell of the times of old sent to the melting-pot to be converted into cash. Certainly no sound of the church-going bell has been heard there since then.

According to Mill, the church was not provided with seats when he came to it (Diary, 1750). This was afterwards rectified, but while the church remained in that primitive state worshippers would come and go, providing their own resting-places, or standing during service. In this way the alleged incident of 'Jenny Geddes's Stool' about a century earlier, in the metropolis, became natural and easy in performance.

The title of 'Cross-Kirk' indicates its having been cruciform in construction, consisting of nave, chancel, and transepts, but no trace even of foundation remains to lend corroboration to this. The barbarous tastelessness of a neighbouring proprietor led to every stone being removed for house and farm-office buildings. There are preserved only a few tombstones, of which one, standing erect, is of some pretension. The inscriptions are weathered and decayed. The site retained its sacredness as the burying-place of the district for many years after the church disappeared, and, upon and around the sand-blown knoll upon which it stood, ghastly relics of those interments are still exposed to view, uncovered and protruding upon the surface in the wake of every succeeding blast.

---

of to the General Assembly by his predecessor, the Rev. William Maxwell, on 13th May 1740.

The dedication of Cross Kirk is not known with certainty. It might have been to the Holy Rood,[1] but a dedication to St. Matthew seems to be indicated in a paper of about the year 1610, on the Rentals of Benefices in Shetland, an extract from which is given in the Appendix, No. VI.

Brand, in his *Description of Orkney, Zetland, etc.*, 1701, makes only a passing reference to this ancient church, but Sir Robert Sibbald, whose work on Orkney and Shetland was published in 1711, gives an earlier and more particular account, as follows :—

'In the midst of this sand, (at the end of Quendal Bay,) stands the South Kirk of Dunroseness, called the *Cross-Kirk*, a Church prettie large and well replenished, but of no Magnificent structure, yet equall to (if not exceeding) the rest of the Countrey. This Church is surrounded with Banks of Sand, two or three paces distant from the Water, consequently no good Burial place, for, if it blow but an ordinary gale, many of the Coffins are discovered, and sometimes naked Corpses ; for all have not Coffins. To the South wall of this Church are affixed two Monuments, one very Large, and very curiously Cut, at the Expenses of Hector Bruce of Mowaness ; another (not so large nor so fine) belonging to Lawrence Sinclair of Quendale : there are other two, within the Church, standing upon Pillars, one pertaining to Robert Bruce of Soumburgh, another to Quendale ; besides these are no graved Stone Inscriptions or Monuments within Dunroseness.'

Low, in the course of his *Tour* through the Islands in 1774,[2] visited the Dunrossness Kirk, to which he briefly alludes thus :—

'The sand penetrates everywhere ; when I stept into the Kirk, observed it found its way thro' the minutest crannies,

---

[1] There is a place in the neighbourhood still called Corston, *i.e.* the town of the *Cors* or Cross.

[2] *A Tour through the Islands of Orkney and Shetland.* Published by W. Peace and Son (Kirkwall, 1879), p. 185.

covering the whole pews, and thus becoming very troublesome
in time of divine service, especially if the wind blows from
the sea, whence the sand shower seems to proceed.'

This account by Low is paraphrased, in an eloquent
passage, by Dr. Hibbert in his great book on Shetland,
published in 1822, but the passage contains little that is
really new.

The large, erect, and richly sculptured tombstone is in
memory of Barbara Sinclair, daughter of John Sinclair of
Quendale, who was married to Hector Bruce of Muness, in
the island of Unst, and died 22d May 1675. The inscription
is in Latin, and is now imperfectly legible. Another stone
commemorates Malcolm Sinclair of Quendale, previously alluded
to as possessing the lay vicarage of the parish, and as the
Malcolm Sinclair of the Spanish Armada incident. He died
Jany. 6, 1618. A third stone is inscribed, 'Hic jacet vir
illustris Iacobus Sinclarus de Quendale . . . . . qui obiit Jan.
29, 1636,' etc. etc.

The old Kirk of Dunrossness appears on one occasion to
have been profaned by a scene of murder. It is related in
a MS. in the Advocates' Library, volume 13. 2. 8, elsewhere
referred to in the present work, that in the reign of Queen
Mary, or shortly afterwards, in revenge for a quarrel, 'Henry
Sinclair of Sandwick, instigated by his wife, conduced his
man to stab Richard Leask, son-in-law to Oliver Sinclair of
Brew, which he did, as he was entering the door of the
Church, and so he died.' Vengeance, at the instance of the
friends of the deceased, followed, and the murderer was slain
'upon a Moor between Laxfoord and Lerwick.'

One other incident, perhaps a spurious one, may be quoted
under this head. It is an extract from an oration alleged to
have been pronounced within the Dunrossness Kirk. The
authority is the scurrilous but amusing work, *Scotch Presbyterian Eloquence Display'd* (1738) :—

'At first I begin with one [a Presbyterian Minister] I heard [of] from Zetland, who preaching on David and Goliah, he told the Hearers, "Sirs, this Davie was but a little Manikine, like my Beddle Davie Geddies there; but Goliah was a meikle strong Fallow, like the Laird of Quandal there; this Davie gets a Scrippie and a Baggie, that is, a Sling and a Stone in it; he slings a stone into Goliah's face, down falls Goliah, and David above him: After that David was made a King; he was keeping Sheep before; in Truth he came very well too, Sirs: Well said, Davie! see what comes of it, Sirs. After that he (commits sin) with Uriah. Nay (said the beddle Davie Geddies) it was but Uriah's Wife, Sir. In faith, thou art right; it was Uriah's Wife, indeed Man, said Mr. John."'

Whatever touch of exaggeration may be in the narrative it is not improbable that it may have some claim to authenticity. The reference to the 'Laird of *Quandal*' (the ordinary native pronunciation of the name) is strongly confirmatory, but the beadle's name, Davie Geddes, is not suggestive of the native soil. There is no known minister of the parish who bore the name of 'John' since John Kingsone (1571-1574), but the name may have been used arbitrarily, or the preacher may have been a stranger—most likely an Aberdonian. Anyway, it is sad indeed that such stuff, a murder, and one or two small passages-at-arms between Mill and the devil, should be the only recorded incidents from the many centuries of worship within the walls of this ancient sanctuary.

The foundation of the new church was marked off on 2d June 1790, and it was completed the following year.[1] On 11th July (Sunday) following, it is related, in the Minutes of the Kirk-Session, that 'the Minister Lectur'd Ps. 44 from v. 17th

---

[1] Mill's initials, ' I. M.', and the date ' 1790,' are carved upon the lintel of the north church-door; on that of the east door is simply the date, ' 1790.'

and Preach'd Text ut supra at a Tent adjoining to the Wall of the new Church Building on the ground of Brew.' At this point the old church vanishes from our view for ever.

The Manse and Glebe appear to have been, from the earliest known times, at Skelberry, as at present. In a MS. volume in the Advocates' Library (35. 3. 11), apparently of the seventeenth century, it is stated that the Glebe is so situated, and that it consists of '10 merks of land of Danish extent worth only per annum 44 lib. Scots.' These ten merks were mixed up, runrig, with the adjoining lands, and to ascertain and properly define them was a matter of anxious investigation by Mill, as papers in the APPENDIX sufficiently explain.

When Mill was presented to the parish, the manse, as well as the Kirk, appears to have been 'in ruins.' A new manse was built in 1751, and furnished in 1752, but burnt down the same year, and rebuilt by Mill, as appears from the Diary, at his own expense, shortly thereafter. The present manse is said to have been built early in the present century. It was repaired and enlarged about the years 1862-63.

2. *Sandwick.*—Reference is constantly made in the Diary, and in the Kirk-Session Minutes, to the 'North Kirk,' in which Mill officiated every third Sunday, or as frequently as weather and other circumstances permitted. This was the church of Sandwick, the immediately adjoining parish on the north; it also served as the place of worship for the inhabitants of Cunningsburgh, the most northerly of the three parishes which formed the Ministry, the church of that parish having been allowed after the Reformation to fall into decay.

The church of Sandwick is a modern structure, and no trace or knowledge of the ancient church seems to be preserved, except that its having been dedicated to St. Magnus is indicated in the paper on Shetland Benefices printed in the Appendix, No. VI. Sandwick ceased to be a separate charge

in 1593, and continued directly under the minister of Dunrossness until 1833, when it was made *quoad sacra*, with a
resident minister as at present.

3. *Church of the Fair Isle.*—A small place of worship, suitable, doubtless, for the requirements of the place, seems to have
existed here from early times.   Its dedication is not known,
but a small revenue, known as 'St. Peter's Stouk,' existed of
old.   Receipt and discharge for the yearly amount, viz., 'seven
Angel Nobles,' was granted by Earl Patrick Stewart to Malcolm Sinclair of Quendale in 1609.   See copy in the Appendix,
No. xi.   As mentioned in the Diary, the isle could be visited
by the minister only at rare intervals, but of late the Church
of Scotland has endeavoured to maintain a catechist able to
read sermons and be otherwise useful in the absence of an
ordained minister.

Besides the above churches which were in Mill's time, and
have been for a long period before and after his day, under the
charge of the incumbent of this extended ministry, several other
churches, or cells, or district oratories, were in existence within
the bounds from early ages to times comparatively recent.   All
these have been swept into oblivion, leaving only such traces
as may be recovered by the archæologist.   The sites are :—

4. *The Church of Cunningsburgh.*—This church, situated
at Maill's Ayre,[1] has long since disappeared, but the site,
enclosed by a stone wall, is still preserved as the burying-
ground of the district, where

> Each in his narrow cell . . .
> The rude forefathers of the hamlets sleep.

The Free Church and manse now stand close by.   Relics of
early occupation, both in Pagan and in remote Christian
times, have been brought to light on this spot.   Polished

---

[1] *Maill's Ayre* : i.e. *Mels-Eyrr* (Old Northern), beach of a sandbank.

implements, etc., of the stone age,[1] a fragment of an Ogham-inscribed slab,[2] and a monumental stone bearing an inscription in Runic characters,[3] have in recent years been brought to light.

The reading of the Oghamic fragment is, as usual in such cases, obscure, but the Runic epitaph admits of no doubt. Though incomplete, it clearly commemorates one Thurbairn, the father of the person who inscribed it.

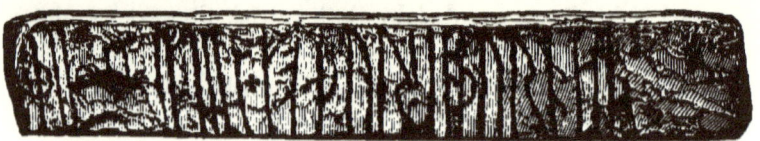

The reading is—

... RIS) ÞI ᛁᛁᚼ ᛁᚠᛁᛁR ✛ ᚠᛁᛈᛀR: ᛁᛁᚼ ᛈᛀRᚼᛁᛁR(ᚾ)

... RIS)THI   STIN   IFTIR   FOTHU'R   SIN   THURBAIR (N).

... rais)ed   this stone   after   father   his   Thurbair (n).[4]

The stone implements, the Oghamic fragment, and the Runic stone, are specially characteristic relics of three successive ages, viz., (1) the Pagan, (2) the Celtic Christian, and (3) the Scandinavian. The Celtic stage of Christian life, following upon ages of primordial Paganism, may be said, roughly speaking, to have terminated a thousand years ago, when the influx of the Norsemen gave dominance for a time to a new form of Paganism, the Norse, which, in turn, yielded to the higher forces of Christianity. These successive ages have thus left the strikingly characteristic relics, which have been referred to, upon this interesting spot.[5]

---

[1] Paper on Stone Implements from Shetland. By Professor Duns, D.D., in *Proceedings* of the Society of Antiquaries of Scotland, vol. xv., 1881, p. 241.

[2] Paper by the Editor in the *Proceedings* S. A. Scot., vol. xvii., 1883, p. 306.

[3] Paper by the Editor, *ibid.*, vol. xiii., 1879, p. 136. The stone was found by the Rev. Geo. Clark, F. C. Minister, Cunningsburgh.

[4] I am indebted for this drawing to the kindness of the Council of the Society of Antiquaries of Scotland.

[5] Another Runic and a small Oghamic fragment have also been found in the neighbourhood.

Extremely little is known of the Church of Cunningsburgh beyond the mere identification of the site. It only appears upon record in circumstances of neglect and disgrace, less than half a century after the light had disappeared from its altar, at the crisis of the Reformation. At a court held at Dunrossness, 7th July 1603, the following doom was pronounced:—

' David Leslie to mak repentance for misusing the Kirk of Cunnisburghe.

It is tryit that David Leslie hes maist schamefullie misusit the Kirk of Cunnisburghe, and placeit his guidis [*i.e.* cattle] theirinto, making the samen ane kow byre, for the quhilk he is decernit to mak his repentance in presence of the Minister and haill Congregatioune on Sonday nixt in sackclayth, and farder to pay xl ß. to the King for his offence ' (*Court Book of Orkney and Shetland*, General Register House).

The downward course to ruin no doubt rapidly proceeded after this, the parishioners having to repair for worship to the Church of Sandwick.

There is one old tombstone remaining in the churchyard. The inscription is made out with difficulty, but has been read:—

Here lies the dust of ane honest young gentlewoman called Anna Forrester lawful daughter of John Forrester, Aith, who died November 1691, aged years 11.

> The pious young
> Pass hence to glore
> While impious old
> Here lay up store.

The people have a tradition that the girl was killed by her mother striking her on the head with a bundle of keys, of which—the keys—they trace a representation on the stone. John Forrester, the father, designed ' lait Chamerlane of Zeitland,' was witness to a deed signed at Tow, Cunningsburgh, on 5th March 1684.

The dedications of the three parochial Churches appear to have been—

Dunrossness (Cross Kirk), . St. Matthew.
Sandwick, . . . St. Magnus.
Cunningsburgh, . . St. John [St. Paul ?].

The authority for these dedications, with the exception of that, alternatively, of St. Paul at Cunningsburgh, is a paper on the Benefices of Shetland, by the Rev. James Pitcairne, minister of Northmavine, which is preserved in the Charter House of the city of Edinburgh, and from which an extract is given in the APPENDIX under the head, 'Ecclesiastical Revenues,' etc.

The map of Shetland, prepared by Timothy Pont, and published at Amsterdam in Blaeu's Atlas in 1654, has the church in Cunningsburgh marked as *St. Paul's*. The same dedication is assigned to it by the Rev. James Kay, minister of the united parishes (1682-1716), whose account of these parishes, contained in MS. Advocates' Library, volume 13. 2. 8, was published by Sir Robert Sibbald in his book on Orkney and Shetland, 1711.

5. *St. Ninian's Isle*, on the west side of the promontory of Dunrossness; a retired and charming spot, approachable on foot at low water. The chapel here is referred to by the Rev. James Kay, in the beginning of the eighteenth century, in the MS. above referred to, as then existing. The Rev. John Brand, whose *Brief Description*, etc., was published in 1701, says :—

'To the North West of the Ness lyes St. Ninian's Isle, very pleasant; wherein there is a Chappel, and ane altar in it whereon some superstitious People do burn Candles to this day.'

In the year 1876 the Editor had the good fortune to dis-

cover, in the burying-ground surrounding the chapel site
(scarcely a stone of which can be said to remain *in situ*), a
monumental stone, now known as the St.
Ninian's Stone, bearing on one of its edges an incised inscription in Oghamic characters, and which is
now deposited in the Museum of the Society
of Antiquaries of Scotland.[1]

This precious relic of remote antiquity seems
to indicate an origin that may be safely attributed to the Celtic Church of pre-Scandinavian
times, that is, prior to the end of the ninth
century.

6. *Church at Ireland*, on the west of the
Dunrossness mainland, near St. Ninian's Isle.
According to Kay's *Narrative* (MS. Advocates'
Library, vol. 13. 2. 8), quoted by Sibbald :—

'Southward from Maweck lyes an Hill called
Ireland Head, from which toward South-east
lyes a village called Ireland,[2] where stand the
Walls and Steeple of an Old Kirk.'

We have thus the testimony of a trustworthy authority that one of those remarkable
towered churches, presumably resembling the
church of Egilsey in Orkney, and, as such,
akin to the towers of Brechin and Abernethy,
and to the round towers of Ireland, was standing at Ireland
(or Eyrrland) less than two hundred years ago.   An old

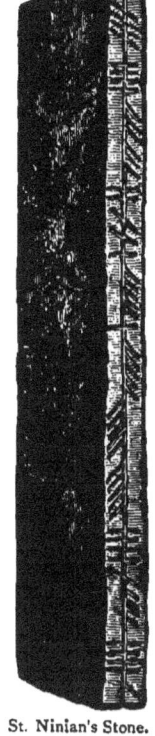

St. Ninian's Stone.

---

[1] The characters, which have been read . . . ESMEQQNANAMMOFFEST,
have puzzled the late Sir Samuel Ferguson, and other Celtic scholars, and
have not as yet been satisfactorily interpreted.   See Paper by the Editor
in vol. xii. of the *Proceedings* of the Society of Antiquaries of Scotland (1876),
p. 20.

[2] That is, *Eyrr-land* (Norse), a place adjoining a gravelly bank by the sea-
shore.

tradition, to which much attention need not be paid, existed in former times to the effect that three such towered churches, St. Magnus at Tingwall, St. Lawrence's in Burra Isle, and this church at Ireland, were built by three Norwegian sisters,—Tingwall by the eldest, Burra by the midmost, and Ireland by the youngest. The tower in Burra is stated, in the account quoted by Sibbald, to have been then five or six stories high. No knowledge of the dedication of the church at Ireland is preserved.

7. *Levenwick.*—All trace, all memory or knowledge, of a church here is gone, but the character of the site still occupied as the 'Kirkyard' of Levenwick, proclaims without much dubiety that here was the place of worship of the district, and the name would seem to indicate its attribution to the Celtic St. Levan.

8. *Clumlie.*—Here constant and unvarying tradition has pointed out the site of an ancient chapel, the surrounding ground still bearing the name *Kurkyfield*, i.e. Kirkfield. The only significant relic is one grave-slab, removed from the spot to act as a pavement stone in the village more than thirty years ago.

There is strong presumptive evidence in the name Clumlie, that the dedication was to St. Colum, or Columba, the father, co-ordinately with St. Ninian, of the Celtic Church of the outlying districts of Scotland. The name, by a simple and scarcely discernible transition, seems to modify itself from the Gaelic *Choluimcille*, in Skye, to *Columlie*—the town and loch of Clumlie, in which form it also appears in Orkney in connection with a church site which may, with some reason, be likewise assigned to St. Columba.

The site is one of special interest, the village of Clumlie, now mostly in ruins, having been built alongside, and latterly out of the material of, a Celtic stronghold (*Brough*, or round tower of the Picts) which has been in ruins for, it may be, a

thousand years, and the remains of which were only brought
to light by excavation last year.

In addition to the ancient church sites which have been
described, there is one other of equal interest in Burra Isle,
which is geographically in the same district, though not included in the 'Ministry.' The two contiguous isles of Burra,
connected by a bridge, lie along the west side of Mill's northern
parish, Cunningsburgh, and in the westmost of these isles,
anciently called. the 'Kirk Isle,' is the churchyard of Papil, in
which, as previously mentioned, stood a church with a lofty
tower, dedicated to St. Lawrence. The Rev. Hugh Leigh,
A.M., minister of Bressa, Burra, and Quarff, 1672-1714, reports
that its 'steeple will be five or six stories high ; though a little
church, yet very fashionable, and its *Sanctum Sanctorum* (or
Quire) yet remains.' [1]

It was in this churchyard, in July 1877, that the richly
sculptured slab, now in the National Museum, and known as
the Burra stone, caught my eye.[2]

The stone is 6 ft. 10 in. in length by about 1½ ft. in
breadth. Its sculpturings show a cross within a wheel, with
interlaced Celtic ornamentation. Beneath this, on either side
of the shaft, are figures of two ecclesiastics, bearing croziers
or *baculae*, two of them also having satchels. A panel below
bears a nondescript animal, resembling a dog or lion ; and at
the bottom are two semi-human figures, holding axes, and in-
serting their bird-like beaks into a human head between them.

The Burra Stone is, like the Ogham stones of St. Ninian's
and Cunningsburgh before noticed, a relic of the ancient Celtic

---

[1] Leigh's MS., printed in Sir Robert Sibbald's *Description of the Isles of
Orkney and Zetland* ; Edinburgh, 1711.

[2] Paper, *Notice of a Sculptured Slab from the Island of Burra, Shetland*,
in the *Proceedings* of the Society of Antiquaries of Scotland, vol. xv., 1881,
p. 199.

Burra Stone.

Christianity which is now shown, on indubitable evidence, to
have flourished in these islands before the advent of the Pagan
Norsemen in the ninth century. The district had thus a
religious history of a time and of a character of which Mill,
worthy man, had no conception, and which it would have been
perhaps a matter of some difficulty to induce him to realise.

VI.—Ecclesiastical Revenues of Dunrossness, Sandwick,
and Cunningsburgh.

Little need be remarked by way of explanation under this
head. The authentic extracts given show the gradual enlargement of the minister's stipend from the small sum of
40 merks, estimated at £2, 12s. 6d. shortly after the Reformation settlement (1571), to £262, with manse and glebe, at
the present day.

The smallness of the sum at the former date illustrates the
force of the saying attributed to Knox, anent the misappro-
priation of the property and revenues of the Church by the
greedy 'Reformers,' that ' twa pairtis were freely gevin to the
devill, and the third mon be devyded betwix God and the
devill.'

The extract dated 1610, in reference to ' The Just Rentelis
of the Benefices' of Shetland, is from a paper which I found
preserved in the Charter House of the city of Edinburgh,
among a large number of interesting documents relating to
the islands which were accumulated in the time (1641 to 1662)
during which the revenues of the Bishopric of Orkney were
held by the city under lease from the Crown.[1]

---

[1] The paper is printed in full by the Editor, *Proceedings* Society of Antiquaries of Scotland, vol. xviii., 1884, p. 291.

f

VII.—Earl Rognvald and the Dunrossness Man, an Unpublished Story of the Twelfth Century.

This story may not seem germane to the purpose of the present work, but if it violates the canon of unity of time, it certainly does not do so in respect of unity of place. It gives us a glimpse of everyday life in the parish at a time many centuries earlier than anything of a personal nature elsewhere recorded.

The story, which was found at Upsala by Professor Vigfusson, is a MS. fragment belonging to a more extended version of the *Orkneyinga Saga* than that now known; and not having been brought to light at the time, it was not included in the translation of the Saga. It will no doubt appear in the long-promised version by Sir George W. Dasent and Professor Vigfusson.

Earl Rognvald was a hero of a rollicking type, who travelled far, as a Crusader to the Holy Land and elsewhere; and many incidents of gallantry and drollery are related of him, quite in the spirit of the *ruse* he played upon the Dunrossness man on this occasion, and of the Skaldic stanza which followed. The occurrence, no doubt, took place when the Earl was shipwrecked in Shetland, as told in Chapter lxxix. of the Saga, where it is stated that he 'stayed a long time in Hjaltland.'

The fishing industry, and the movements of the people in connection therewith, are brought before us with great distinctness in this narrative, seven hundred years old, and are in no marked degree dissimilar from what prevailed in the district in Mill's time, or what still prevails there.

---

[1] *The Orkneyinga Saga.* Translated from the Icelandic by Jon A. Hjaltalin and Gilbert Goudie. Edited, with Notes and Introduction, by Joseph Anderson. Edinburgh : Edmonston and Douglas, 1873. Pp. 128, 129, 130.

I have made the translation from the original as given in *An Icelandic Prose Reader*, Vigfusson and Powell; Oxford, 1879.

VIII.—FEUDS AND BLOODSHED IN DUNROSSNESS IN THE SIXTEENTH CENTURY.

The narrative given in the Appendix is extracted from volume 13. 2. 8 of the manuscript collections in the Advocates' Library. It is from the pen of the Rev. James Kay, minister of the parish 1682 to 1716, and is contained in a 'Description of Dunrossness' compiled by him, previously referred to.

The two incidents of slaughter described are not recorded in any other document at present known. History and local tradition alike bear testimony to hostile incursions on the islands by Lewismen, but without sufficient circumstantiality of detail.

It is stated at some length in Macvurich's and Hugh Macdonald's MS. how, in the fifteenth century, Hugh Macdonald of Sleat and William Macleod of Harris ravaged the Orkneys;[1] and in 1461 Bishop William of Orkney, in a letter to the King of Denmark and Norway, complains of these marauders, under John of Ross, Lord of the Isles, coming to Orkney and Shetland 'in great multitudes in the month of June, with their ships and fleets in battle array, wasting the lands, plundering the farms, destroying habitations, and putting the inhabitants to the sword, regardless of age or sex.'[2]

Low, writing in 1774, repeats the traditional story of these incursions, and refers to the 'Lewismen's graves' at Sumburgh. The 'Lewis Scords,' indentations in the sand-heaps on the shore near Scousburgh, on the west side of the

---

[1] *Collectanea de Rebus Albanicis* (Edinburgh, 1847), pp. 306 *et seqq.*
[2] The document is printed in the *Diplomatarium Norvigicum*, vol. v. p. 605.

parish, have also been pointed out to myself by resident natives as a scene of slaughter and burial-place of those in- vaders. According to the local story, the male inhabitants from as far north as Cunningsburgh, hastily summoned, armed themselves with spears, pitchforks, and every other form of available weapon, and rushing upon the invaders inflicted an almost exterminating defeat. But the tradition is silent as to time or the names of the leading actors. Hibbert alone, upon what authority is not known, states that 'one of the Sinclairs of Brew' was in command of the Shetlanders;[1] and here he approaches to the narrative now given in the APPENDIX, where the cause of the struggle is said to have been enmity between Oliver Sinclair of Brew and William (Macleod) of the Lews, so late as in the reign of Queen Mary.

Oliver Sinclair of that day, usually designated 'Ollaw Sinclair of Havera,' was well known as the *Great Fowde*, or Governor, of Shetland. He it was who entertained Bothwell on his flying visit to the isles in 1567. But no such incident as is here related has been associated with his name. Nor are William and Hugh (Macleod) of the Lews easily identified. Roderick appears to have been the chief of the Lewis Macleods about this time. William (Macleod) of Harris, a usual name in that family, chief of the 'Siol Tormod,' was living till 1554. Hutcheon (or Hugh) cannot be traced.

Although, amid all the feuds of the Macleods, no other account seems to be preserved of the expedition to Shetland, so circumstantially related in the MS., it is to be supposed that the writer, living little more than a century from the time of the alleged occurrence, should have had reliable data for the foundation of his narrative. While therefore it seems at present to lack satisfactory confirmation, it deserves to be recorded here in view of the possibility of corroboration at some future time.

---

[1] Hibbert, *Description of the Shetland Islands*, 1822, p. 243.

The story of the struggle between Dillidasse and Sinclair
of Sandwick, resulting from the slaying of Richard Leask,
son-in-law of the same Oliver Sinclair of Brew, as he entered
the Kirk of Dunrossness, is also unknown but for this MS. of
Kay. The slaughter in revenge is stated to have taken place
near Laxfirth in Tingwall. Not far distant in the same
parish is a standing stone which has for long been regarded
as the scene of the death of Malis Spere, on the occasion of
his incursion in Shetland, as recorded in the Iceland Annals
in 1329 : but these events are involved in much obscurity.

Richard Leask, son-in-law to Sinclair of Brew, who was
stabbed, was probably a man of some consideration. Sir
David Sinclair of Sumburgh, in his Will, dated 1506,[1]
appointed Richard Leask one of his executors, along with
Thorrald of Bruch, who was probably the then laird of Brew.
They are described as 'discreit men'; and to Leask ('Richart
Lesk') he leaves 20 merks land in Cwndistay (?) and his
English ship—'my Inglis schipe with all geir.' Assuming
that Richard in both cases is the same individual, some clew
is given to the date of the story, which may probably have
been somewhat earlier than the reign of Queen Mary.

IX.—MINUTES OF COURT HELD AT SUMBURGH IN
DUNROSSNESS, 1602.

These Minutes are transcribed in full from a Court Book
of the Earl of Orkney, 1602-1604, preserved in the General
Register House. This Book has been made use of by Peterkin
in his 'Notes,'[2] and in the Miscellany of the Maitland Club

---

[1] Testament of Sir David Sinclair of Sumburgh, Captain-General of the
Palace at Bergen, and *Foude* of Shetland, dated at Tingwall, 9th July 1506.
Miscellany of the Bannatyne Club, vol. iii.

[2] *Notes on Orkney and Zetland*, by Alexander Peterkin, Sheriff-Substitute
of Orkney; Edinburgh, 1822.

(vol. ii.), in which places copious extracts are given both from this book and from the Court records of Orkney and Shetland of later dates. But this particular Court, held in Dunrossness, has not hitherto been noticed.

Earl Patrick Stewart was at the time at the height of his magnificent prodigality, sustained by the oppression and plunder of the islanders, which led to his ruin and terminated his career on the block. The Court, which was presided over by one of his deputes, John Dishington, very fairly exemplifies the reign of terror which prevailed. Real or imaginary mis-demeanours were charged almost promiscuously; and as the assize consisted either of creatures of the Earl, or of unwilling assessors terrified into acquiescence, fines, alleged to be 'for the King,' but really for the voracious exchequer of the tyrant Earl his kinsman, were imposed with rigour.

Many of the alleged offences are of a trifling nature—mostly small personal assaults, theft, petty slander by calling bad names, etc.

In one case, a couple of thieves, Adam Cromertie and James Barnetsoun (a Scotticised form of the native Scandi-navian name Berntsen), have their goods, geir, and lands (if any) escheat, and themselves banished *to Norway*. The direct-ness and frequency of the communication with that country (still apparently regarded as the fatherland) is shown by the order that the culprits are to be off 'in the first passage within the space of ane moneth'; and if they be again appre-hended with even the most trifling theft ('the walour [*i.e.* value] of ane ure'), they are to be 'tane and hangit be the crage quhill they die, in exempill of utheris.'

There are two cases of charge of Witchcraft—'turning sieve and riddle for a pair of scissors (scheiris)' and again, 'turning of sieve and the scissors.' In both cases the parties are sentenced to acquit themselves by the oath of compurgators —the 'saxter aithe,' or oath of six neighbours of repute,

or underlie the law for the crime. The result is not told, and
the method of divination is not more particularly described.

The slaughter of Matthew Sinclair of Ness, which has
sometimes been obscurely alluded to, but never distinctly explained, comes before the court in the shape of caution taken
for the appearance before my Lord and his deputes, at the
next head-court at Scalloway, of a number of persons implicated.
The case accordingly came up at the Court at Scalloway
on the 16th of the same month—August 1602,—when the
following persons were indicted for the crime, which is said
to have been committed on the 27th day of the month of
June bypast, viz.,—

Francis Sinclair of Uyea.

Robert Sinclair his brother.

John Bruce, servitor to Adam Sinclair of Brew.

James Sinclair, son to Laurence Sinclair of Gott.

Laurence Sinclair, son to William Sinclair of Ustaness.

John Lindsay, servitor to Robert Sinclair.

These were all found to be 'actuall doaris and Committaris'
of the said slaughter at Dunrossness, and having taken the
crime upon themselves, and being fugitive therefor, their
whole goods, gear, and lands were forfeited.

A curious and, one would think, not very relevant
question was brought before the Court by one David Reid,
who desired the 'Testimoniall' of the judge and the assize
whether two persons, Magnus Flett and Gellis Keillo, were
lawfully married, and whether Francis Flett were their lawful
son. The judgment was in the affirmative, whereupon David
asked 'Act of Court.' It does not appear upon what ground
he was entitled to make the inquiry.

The Court assumed jurisdiction over foreigners, who
presumably had something in Shetland to attach, as in the
case against Denneis Sueman of Brahame (Bremen), Herman
Sueman, Zanie Himmel, and Court Mair, a Dutchman,

deceased, in which judgment was pronounced in favour of the complainer, one Laurence Tulloch, a native residing in Skelberrie. Herman Sueman appears to have been resident, or to have had a place of business, in the parish, because a charge of theft was brought up at another time for fish stolen from his 'Skeo,' or drying hut (where hard, or 'stock,' fish was cured). But there is no doubt that at this time Dutch and Hanseatic merchants, the latter chiefly from Hamburgh and Bremen, were extensively engaged in the importation of Continental products and the exportation of fish from Dunrossness. One of these, Garthe Hemlein, of Bremen, then residing in the parish, and charged as 'airt and pairt' in the slaughter of 'Matthew Sinclair already referred to, is linked with a remarkable episode in Scottish history—the flight of Bothwell.[1]

The ancient compurgatorial system still prevailing at this time, as exemplified in the proceedings of this Court in the acquittance by the 'Lawright aithe,' the 'sexter' and the 'twelter aithe,' that is, the oaths of the *Lawrightman*[2]

---

[1] After the parting with Queen Mary on Carberry Hill, 15th June 1567, Bothwell, titular Duke of Orkney, betook himself to the northern isles, and was entertained in Shetland by Oliver Sinclair of Brew, father of Matthew Sinclair now murdered. Anticipating the pursuit by Kirkcaldy of Grange, Bothwell took advantage of Geert Hemelingk's ship, the 'Pelican,' then lading at Sumburgh Head, and obtained the use of the ship and crew under contract with Hemelingk, preserved in the Privy Archives of Denmark, and dated 'jnn Schvineborchovett,' *i.e.* at Sumburgh Head, the 15th August 1567. The Pelican was taken and detained in Denmark when the unfortunate Bothwell was seized, and Hemelingk had to make strenuous efforts to recover her from the Danish Government. A certificate of his honesty as a merchant since he came to Shetland, given to him by Olaf Sinclair of Bru, 'Kemener und overste principall van Hidtland,' dated at Lassefirde (Laxfirth), is also in the Danish Archives. The whole story is told by Professor Schiern in his *Life of James Hepburn, Earl of Bothwell*; Copenhagen, 1875. Translation by Rev. David Berry, F.S.A. Scot.; Edinburgh, 1880.

[2] The Lawrightman (*Old Northern* Lög-retta-madr, *Norse* Lögretmand) was a public official in every parish appointed to look after the rights and interests of the people, in contradistinction to the *Foud* (*Norse* Foged), who was the resident judge, or 'Bailie,' the representative of government.

of the parish, or of six, or twelve, honest neighbours, as
the case might be, is noteworthy.

The place-names which appear in the records of the
Court are scarcely distinguishable from their modern forms.
But while it cannot be doubted that the body of the present
inhabitants of the district continue to be of the same stock,
it is remarkable how many changes have taken place, and
how few of the persons or families named at this early period
can be traced down to representatives at the present day.
The following names are extinct:—

Blackbeird [1]	Cumming	Parkie
Butter	Jirga Bege (a woman)	Rattray
Cowpland	Keillo	Rendaill
Cromartie	Louttit	Stok
	Melling	

Some of these are still common in Orkney. There are
also some other names not now existing, but which are so
thoroughly Scottish as to seem temporary importations in
the train of the overlord and his dependants.

Most of the respectable natives tried to abstain from
appearing at these Courts, and five of those chosen for the
assize on this occasion were fined for non-appearance. The
following names of parishioners at the time (1602), either
members of the assize, or appearing elsewhere in the proceedings, may be noted:—

William Bruce of Simbuster.
John Niven of Scousbrughe.
Arthur Sinclair of Aithe.
Malcolm Sinclair of Quendale.
Adam Sinclair of Brew.
Laurence Sinclair of Gott.
Henry Sinclair of Sandwick (App. No. viii.).

---

[1] The Kirk-Session Records show that the name Blackbeard was continued
in the district so late as 1777 (Grizel Blackbeard, a pauper).

Bruce of Simbuster is now represented in the senior line by the family of Bruce of Sumburgh, and in the junior by the Bruces of Symbister. The other families named are all extinct, and their properties have been swallowed up in larger estates.

There is in existence, so far as known, one record, and one only, of the names and movements of the people of Dunrossness at an earlier date than this. At Courts held at Tingwall in 1576, the householders, or occupants of the land, in every parish of Shetland were summoned to give evidence in the trial of Laurence Bruce of Cultemalindie, the great Foude of Shetland and instrument of the oppressions of Lord Robert Stewart, first Earl of Orkney of the Stewart line. Of those appearing from Dunrossness, most are either patronymics, as Johnssoun, Magnusson, Symondsoun, which, in the usual fashion of Scandinavia, changed with each generation, or Christian names merely, as Olaw of Hellyness, Nichole of Clapwall, Magnus in Skelberrie, Thomas in Mawick. When a modern surname is given it is so vaguely connected with a place, or has no place-designation, that identification with modern residents is impossible. The only name in this the earliest list of Dunrossness people to be identified as still locally existing, is that of Gawane Gadie of Lougasettar, represented by Mr. Gilbert Goudie, Braefield, in the same neighbourhood.[1] But the variations in families and the changes in the occupancy of any given district in a period of more than 300 years could be scarcely less marked.

---

[1] The full particulars of the ' Complaints of the Commons and Inhabitants of Zetland,' 1575-76, and the Probations led thereupon, are preserved in the General Register House, and are printed by the late Mr. David Balfour of Balfour and Trenabie, in his *Oppressions of the Sixteenth Century in the Islands of Orkney and Shetland*; Maitland Club, 1859. Gawane Gadie's special ' Bill of Complaynt' appears (pp. 73, 81) to have been, with others, forwarded to the Regent's Grace and Secret Council, King James VI. being then in minority and the Earl of Morton in power.

Altogether, apart from the mere exhibition of legalised
oppression by Earl Patrick Stewart, the record of this Dunrossness Court of 1602 gives us a clear and telling picture of
many incidents of common life in a Shetland parish nearly
300 years ago, albeit presented in sinister and unsympathetic
circumstances. It is set before us in the garb of Scottish
law, and with the simulation of ordinary criminal practice,
through which we see the natives, in sullen helplessness,
moving across the scene, with names, language, and manners
that tell of foreign origin, and modes of life peculiarly their
own, all which continued to be reflected in the lives and
manners of the people in Mill's time, 150 years later.

X.—FEU-CONTRACTS BETWEEN PATRICK, EARL OF ORKNEY,
AND WILLIAM BRUCE OF SYMBISTER, OF LANDS IN DUN-
ROSSNESS. 1592-1605.

These deeds, preserved, in the shape of an official copy,
in the Charter-chest at Sumburgh, are of great local interest.
They explain the circumstances of the first settlement in the
district of a family ever since connected with it by large territorial possession. They also illustrate local conditions at an
important period—300 years ago,—when the ancient Scandinavian system was passing away, and a new era of laws, institutions, landownership, taking its place. We see the fishing industry actively prosecuted not only by natives but by
fishers from Orkney and Caithness. The references to the
' New Hall,' otherwise the ' House and fortalice of Soundburgh,' fix very nearly the date of the erection of the mansion
of ' Jarlshof' of the *Pirate*, now a ruin. But there is historical
ground, as well as archæological evidence on the spot, to lead
us to believe that this site was an occasional residence of the
Norwegian earls at a very much earlier date, if indeed it was

not that of persons of distinction long before the invasion of the Norsemen in the ninth century.

The land granted in feu is described as the '20 merks of Soundburgh, callit Kingis landis,' and other 4 merks, termed 'Provestis landis' intermixed therewith, still recognised together as the 24 merks of Sumburgh. The Provostry land, as explained in a footnote in the APPENDIX, belonged originally to the Dom Kirke, or Cathedral, of Bergen in Norway. Though included by the Earl in the feu, with warrandice against any pretenders to it from Denmark or Norway, some dubiety as to the effectiveness of the title is apparent, and it was not till sixty years later, namely in 1662, that the doubt was put at rest by a deed of confirmation granted by King Frederick III. of Denmark and Norway, but with an explicit clause of redemption, all as elsewhere explained.[1] So far as merely legal considerations go, this clause might any day be put in force, and the four merks be claimed by the sovereign of Denmark, as representing the ancient Church of Norway! The claimants from Norway are elsewhere referred to in Sumburgh deeds as the 'Lordis of Norroway.'

The Earl himself held the Earldom estate only by virtue of a revocable charter from the Crown, and he had therefore no right to alienate any portion of the property. But the time was a confused and troubled one both in Shetland and at the seat of government. The Earl was hard pressed for funds to maintain the princely state he assumed. Power was in his grasp, and he used it, and by these deeds Sumburgh for ever passed from the heritable dominion of the Crown as representing the ancient Earldom.

The lands of Sumburgh, which from early times were

---

[1] Paper by the Editor: Notice of a Charter of Confirmation by King Frederick III. of Denmark and Norway (1662), and other documents in the Norse Language relating to Shetland. *Proceedings* S. A. Scot., vol. xiv. (1879) p. 13.

part of the Earldom estate, were made over to Sir David Sinclair, son of Earl William St. Clair, by his brothers and sisters, the other sons and daughters of the Earl, by charter dated at Edinburgh, 3d Dec. 1498.[1] Sir David, by his Will, dated at Tingwall, 9th July 1506, bequeathed all his landed property in Shetland to Lord Sinclair, from whom the lands of Sumburgh would appear to have passed to the Crown, and to have continued as part of the succession to the Earldom until now finally alienated by Earl Patrick Stewart.

William Bruce of Symbister was a Fifeshire gentleman who came to Shetland as a connection and assistant of Laurence Bruce of Cultemalindie after the appointment of the latter in 1571 as *Great Foude* of Shetland under Lord Robert Stewart. He eventually retired to his native country, where his tomb remains in Crail churchyard, leaving his Shetland properties to his eldest son, and the Fife estate to a son by a second marriage. His grandson, William Bruce, third of Symbister and Sumburgh, left Sumburgh to his eldest son, Robert (1642), and Symbister to the second son, Laurence. The two families have continued distinct to the present day.

XI.—Discharge by Patrick, Earl of Orkney, to Malcolm
Sinclair of Quendale. 1609.

It has already been mentioned that this Sinclair of Quendale held at this time a tack of the vicarage of Dunrossness granted to him by Laurence Sinclair, 'Vicar and Titular.' The present deed shows that he also held, in the same way, various other Church revenues, which are detailed. A complaint by Mill to the Presbytery of Zetland in 1763 shows that Robert Sinclair of Quendale of that date still claimed to hold the vicarage of the parish.

---

[1] Charter, printed in Peterkin's *Notes*; Edinburgh, 1822.

The origin of the Sinclair family of Quendale is involved in an obscurity which is not likely now ever to be cleared. Tradition associates them with the ancient family of St. Clair of the Earldom; and Van Bassan, a Dane, quoted by Father Hay in his 'Genealogie of the Sinclaires of Roslin,' compiled in manuscript about the year 1700, gives a highly fanciful and untrustworthy account of their extraction and rise.[1] In the end of the sixteenth and in the seventeenth and eighteenth centuries, they were of first consideration in the islands. The estate was large, consisting in 1713 of

1311 merks land in Dunrossness,
309 ,, do. ,, Sandwick,
368 ,, do. ,, Aith, Cunningsburgh,

with the island of Mousa.

The following representatives of the family can be identified, viz.—

Malcolm Sinclair of Quendal, Lay Vicar of Dunrossness. Received the shipwrecked men of the Spanish Armada in 1588. Died Jany. 6, 1618 (Tombstone).

James Sinclair of Quendal. Died Jany. 29, 1636 (Tombstone).

John Sinclair of Quendal, one of the Commissioners for Shetland named in Act of Parliament 1661, and again in 1667.

Laurence Sinclair of Quendal, ditto, 1689.

Robert Sinclair, younger of Quendal, ditto, 1706.

Robert Sinclair of Quendale. Report by George Drummond, Accountant-General of Excise in North Britain, to the Commissioners of Excise, bearing that, having inspected the books of the said Robert Sinclair, then Cashier of Excise, he found him short £847, 2s. 9½d., applied to his own uses. Report dated 16th June

---

[1] *Genealogie of the Saintclaires of Roslin* (Edinburgh, 1835), p. 172.

1713, recorded 17th March 1718. This is the laird of
Quendal frequently under the anathema of Mill in
the earlier part of the Diary. He was alive in 1763,
and was succeeded by his son,

John Sinclair of Quendale. By this time the family
fortunes had become very low. Sequestration was
awarded, according to Mill, in 1750. A Scheme of
Division among the creditors was prepared, 15th May
1765, and the whole estate was exposed by public
roup, 26th February 1770. The larger portions were
bought by Mr. Bruce of Sumburgh and Mr. Grierson.

The Discharge by Earl Patrick to Malcolm Sinclair is
in my possession, gifted to me by the late Mr. Andrew
Smith, Lerwick, uncle of his Grace the present Archbishop of
St. Andrews and Edinburgh.

XII.—DIARY AND BAPTISMAL AND MARRIAGE REGISTER OF THE
REV. JOHN HUNTER, EPISCOPAL CLERGYMAN IN SHETLAND.
1734-1745.

This is introduced as a brief and fragmentary local
chronicle by a Shetland clergyman almost contemporary with
Mill, but of a very different school. After the Revolution
Settlement in 1688 and following years, the leading families
in Shetland appear to have maintained their adherence to
Episcopacy; and, though that communion was practically
proscribed, they retained the services of clergymen of their
own views under all the disabilities to which such clergymen
were subjected. Mr. Hunter was the last so retained, and
his Diary shows the families to whom his itinerant ministra-
tions were addressed, the baptisms and marriages at which he
officiated, and the donations he received for his 'encouragement'
and support. His position appears to have been a poor and

dependent one, though his patrons were not unmindful of his need of creature comforts, as his accounts show. His record is altogether profoundly different in style and spirit from that of his orthodox Presbyterian contemporary, Mill; but the facts noted, from which a few extracts as examples are given, are by no means devoid of interest.

Hunter was the author of a somewhat scurrilous and doggerel epic called *Laxo's Lines*, framed on the model of *Hudibras*, and not altogether suitable for publication. An abridged copy is in my possession.

Hunter was the last Episcopal clergyman in Shetland until the restoration of that communion at the consecration of St. Magnus Church in Lerwick in 1864. His residence at Dunrossness appears to have been at Sumragarth, but he was constantly on the move among the families who sympathised with him, and probably a good deal at Lerwick, then a growing town. 'St. Barnaby's Chapel' is sometimes alluded to. Certain indications would lead to the inference that this was somewhere in Dunrossness, but the Rev. J. B. Craven, author of the *History of the Episcopal Church in Orkney*, says that the chapel was in Lerwick, where its ruins are still to be seen 'below the present parsonage' (p. 130).

XIII.—Early State of Education in Dunrossness.

Neither Mill's Diary nor the Kirk-Session Minutes, which were penned by him, throw light upon the state of Education in the district during the time covered by these writings, viz., the second half of last century. All that can be gathered from occasional references is that a 'School' was in existence in the parish, locality not named, and also in the Fair Isle.

The consideration that a work professing to treat of

parochial life in any district during a former period, and
ignoring the state of educational arrangements at the time,
would overlook an interest of vital import, has induced me to
investigate the earliest sources of information available on
the subject.

So early as the year 1724 it had been resolved at a meeting
of heritors at Lerwick that a school should be established
in every parish, and funds provided for the purpose. The
effort was creditable to all concerned, but the attempt to
put it in force was only partially successful owing to the
poverty of the country and the apathy of individuals.
Education continued at a low ebb all through the islands,
and its state would have been still worse had not the Society
in Scotland for Propagating Christian Knowledge come to
the rescue.

The records of this Society, and the earliest Parliamentary
Returns bearing upon the subject, so far as known to me,
have been laid under contribution, and I believe that the
earliest information now attainable is embodied in the extracts from these and other authentic sources given in the
APPENDIX.

The facts disclosed show a state of Education poor enough.
The salaries of the S.P.C.K. schoolmasters, originally (in
1774) as low as £3 stg. per annum, were advanced in
1780 to £7 and £10, and in 1810 reached £14 and £15,
with sometimes a dwelling-house besides. The maximum,
£18, was attained in 1849. The cost of instruction was
usually about 2s. 6d. per quarter for reading, writing, and
arithmetic, beyond which the curriculum did not extend.
The attendance of both boys and girls seems to have been
considerable.

It is only just to Mill's memory to explain that he was
not satisfied with this state of matters. Whenever opportunity offered, as when he was a member of the General

g

Assembly in 1765, he laboured with enlightened zeal for having Education placed upon a proper parochial basis, but with indifferent success. There appears to have been but one parochial school in the three parishes, on the strictly legal footing, until the recent establishment of the School Boards under the Education (Scotland) Act, 1872.

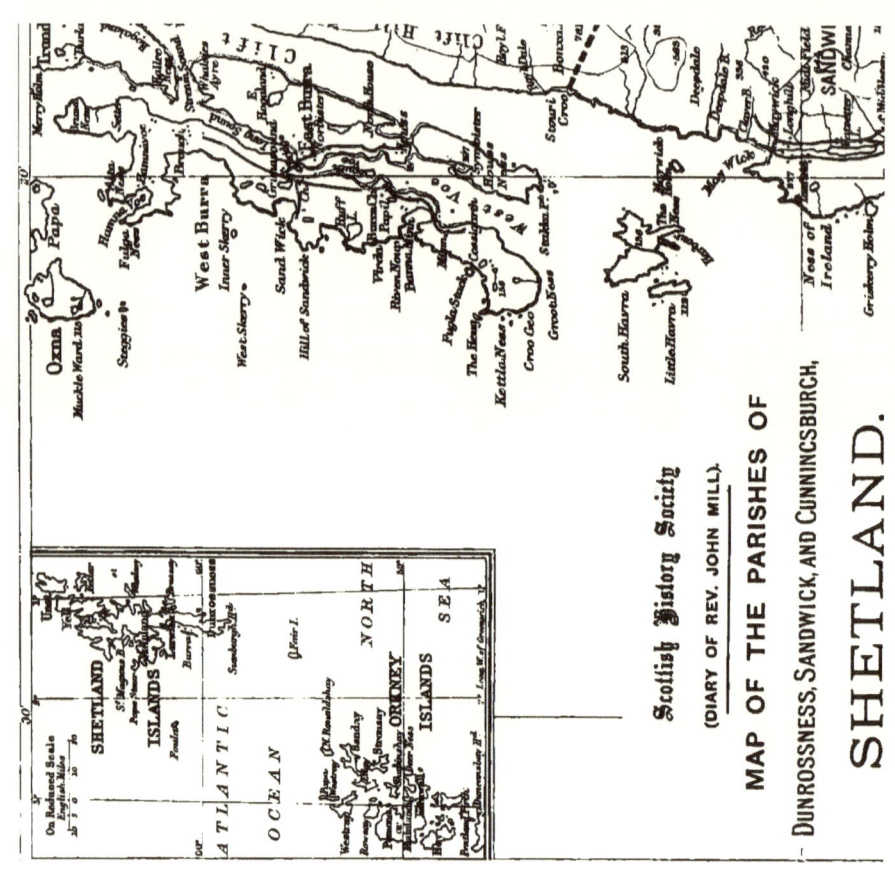

Scottish History Society

(DIARY OF REV. JOHN MILL).

MAP OF THE PARISHES OF

DUNROSSNESS, SANDWICK, AND CUNNINGSBURCH,

SHETLAND.

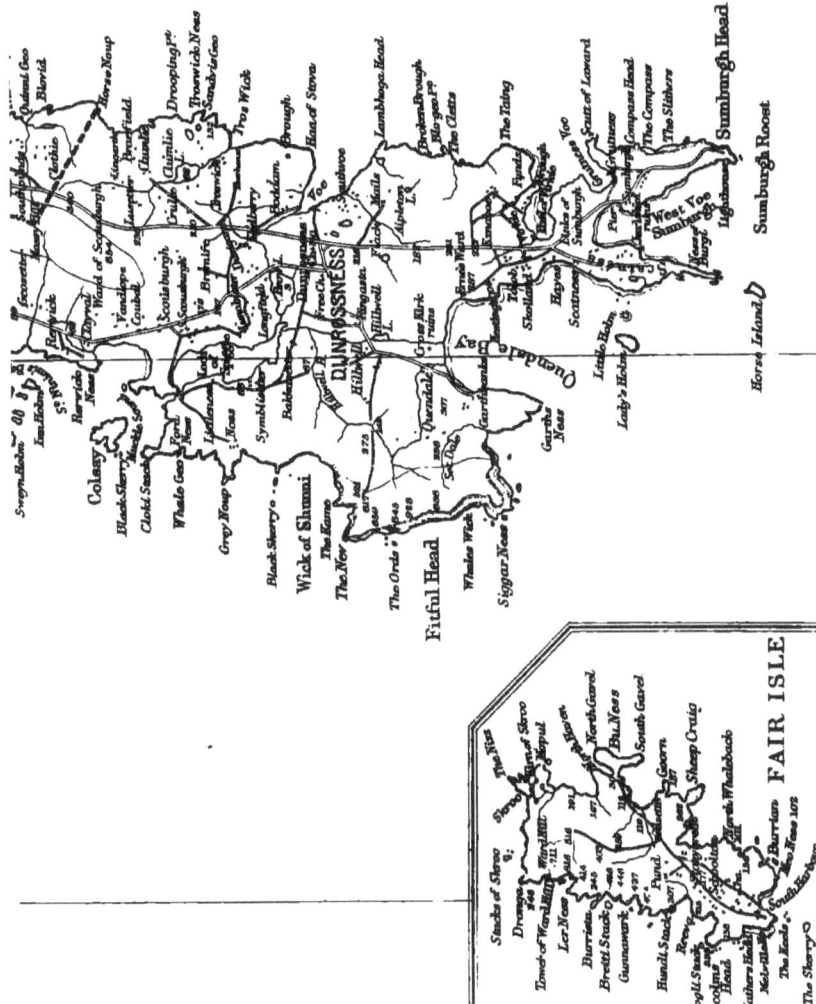

THE DIARY

DIARY

OF THE REV. JOHN MILL

1739]   [1740

. . . . ¹promise for this end. But being cast away on
the coast of England by a great storm when attempting to
return home in the month of April, this design miscarried,
for the Earl Morton,² going over said year to Zetland in
quest of wrecked money, settled another who had accompanied
him there with this view. Meantime I wrote a letter to my
Uncle's Relict, which she showed to his Lordship, giving an
account of his promise. But he put it off with this, that as
I was not present the Parish must be supplied with a minister,
and I should have the next settlement. However, having
demitted my charge at Cullen, and meeting with a brother-in-
law at Aberdeen on his return home from London, I made
a trip to Zetland with him in 1740, but finding another settled
at Lerwick³ I looked upon it then as a great disappointment,
but found afterwards it was rather a kind Providence.

---

¹ The introductory portion of the narrative is lost.

² The Earl of Morton was at this time lord superior of the islands, in possession of what remained of the land and revenues of the Earldom of Orkney
and Lordship of Shetland. This ancient inheritance had passed from the old
Norwegian Earls to their successors of 'the lofty line of high St. Clair,' and
from the latter to the Crown by the deed of excambion with Earl William St.
Clair in 1471. Lord Morton in the course of time obtained possession, in
virtue of successive charters from the Crown, and had thus the patronage of most
of the parishes. The Earldom and Lordship were acquired by Sir Lawrence
Dundas, ancestor of the Earls of Zetland, by purchase, in 1766, for £63,000.

³ The Rev. Thomas Miller, M.A., son of Thomas Miller, notary-public, Alyth.
Called to Lerwick 7th Nov. 1739. He died 1766.—(*Fasti Ecclesiæ Scoticanæ.*)

A

Having visited my friends and taken a view of the countrey, I returned in September by a vessel bound for Aberdeen, and had been thrust in by a cross wynd very providentially from Norway, as I knew of no other occasion. In my way to my friend's house from Aberdeen, I called at a minister's house who proposed my being assistant to the minister of Pitsligo in Buchan, who was then thought to be in a dying condition. My friends relished the offer, expecting to get me settled in the minister's place if he died, and the gentleman who had some connexion with my friends and nephew to the patron, being on his journey from Edinbro to the north, was addressed by the Gordons at Old Aberdeen proferring him a sinecure of £50 Ster. p. an. in their gift provided he obtained a presentation in favours of a friend of theirs, which he embraced and gave his promise, not knowing of the design formed in my favours. The minister recovered by means of a receipt I obtained from the Countess of Findlater, and lived many years after, whereby they met likewise with a disappointment. My friends had obtained the promise of an Itineracy of £25 per annum of the King's Bounty at Keith where severals of them lived and nigh to that; and, when my credentials were ready to be sent south upon my coming forth to the ministry, the Dutchess of Gordon[1] prevailed on the Managers to grant it in favours of another. However Providence so ordered that was settled before either of these young men.

During my 16 months' stay at Pitsligo, having the whole charge of the parish, and being oft called to preach at Sacrament occasions in the summer time, though it bore hard upon a beginner, yet wrought for good. Adversity tries men, and 'tis good to bear the yoke in youth. Meantime the Earl of Findlater[2] wrote me from London signifying that he had obtained the Earl of Morton's promise of a presentation to a Kirk in Zetland, and that I should repair thither with all

---

[1] Duchess of Gordon. The widow of Alexander, second Duke, who was implicated in the rising of 1715, and died in 1728. She survived till 1760.

[2] Earl of Findlater. Family of Ogilvy of Deskford, who possessed the title till it became dormant in 1811, on the death of James, seventh Earl. The reference here is to James, the fifth Earl.

convenient speed. But as I understood the Laird that paid
the stipend out of the tithes uplifted by him was such a tyrant
and oppressor[1] as obliged two ministers to remove to other
parishes by transportation, and glad to be rid of him through
bad usage, I wrote the Earl by post that I did not chuse to
go there, and would rather put up with a less income to live
in peace. Meantime Lord Morton's Factor writing me not to
fear going to Dunrossness, seeing matters were now put upon
another footing than formerly by a factory granted in favours
of young Quendal his son, who had a good character, and though
my Father's friends were anxious to have me settled among
them, yet, as nothing did then cast up, they advised me to go,
hoping to get me transported, which probably might have
been effected, to a parish vacant in 1745, where my principal
friend had an estate ; but no accounts could be got thereof
during the rebellion that brok out that year.

Though I arrived in Zetland June 1742, and preached to
the people of the parish all the winter, I yet was not settled
till April 1743, during which time I met with two Remarkable
Dangers and Deliverances. One evening discoursing with Mr.
Robert Scollay, Merchant in Lerwick, and smoking a pipe
of strong tobacco, all of a sudden my stomach turned, which
made me throw up, and while standing before the fire fell down
suddenly by a swerf[2] or stoppage of blood, as if shot throw
the head. Providentially a web of cloth (Mr. Scollay observed)
had been lien at the end of the room, and was brought up
and laid upon an arm chair that day at the fireside, which
saved my head from being crushed in the fall upon that chair.

Another time, going from Lerwick to Cunningsburgh in
a boat, the side of the boat was laid under water by a sudden
flan[3] off Bressay Head, and the man who managed the sail had
not the presence of mind to let it go. Finding the water

---

[1] A tyrannical heritor. This was Sinclair of Quendale, representative of an
ancient family now extinct, specially referred to elsewhere in the Diary, and in
the Introduction and Appendix.

[2] *Swerf*, Old Northern *Svarfa*, used reflexively as *to be turned upside down*.

[3] *Flan*, the usual Shetland term for a squall. Old Northern *Flan*.

rushing in about my leggs, I cried out 'Lord preserve us!'
It pleased God the boat suddenly recovered, otherwise, in less
than a minute's time, we had been all drowned. It was a
rebuke for my presumption in going with the boat when dis-
suaded by some gentlemen, and one of these a friend.

I found one of my Kirks in ruins[1] and no manse, which
obliged me to put up with quarters in the house of a gentleman
disaffected to Church and State,[2] which with a numerous and
extensive parish occasioned a struggle with many difficulties for
several years; during which time I was seized with a sciatica
pain in my left thigh which oft deprived me of night's rest and
rose to such height as made me cry out. How terrible must the
case of the damned in hell be that are racked in soul and body
to eternity. This falling out on a Saturday night, at my
quarters in the north parish,[3] I was not able to preach the next
day, and desired a messenger going to Lerwick to send me one
of the surgeons belonging to the Man of War that lay in Bressay
Sound. He said, though they might know how to dress a green
wound yet were probably ignorant of the nature of my trouble,
which made me cheerfully resign to Providence to continue or
remove it, as seemed good in His sight. The same night the
Lord put it into my landladies head to desire me try some
warm thing. I asked her meaning. She replied, it was to
clap a hot bath of earth under the place affected. This
looked so feasible that I bid her bring it, which done I fell
asleep, and when I awaked found a sensible abatement of
the pain. By repeated hot baths I was put into a sweat
that lasted 48 hours, wasted the substance of my body,
coloured my day shirt that covered a scarlet vest with the
dy, and made my bigg coat which I lay down with, as if it
had been washed in the sea. However it proved a mean of
recovering to such degree that I preached next Sabbath,
and though much of the root of the disease remained, yet

---

[1] Cross-Kirk at Quendale, the former parish church of Dunrossness. The
present church was opened in 1791.
[2] Sinclair of Quendale.
[3] The North Parish, *i.e.* Sandwick, which with Cunningsburgh was, and still
is, included in the 'Ministry' of Dunrossness.

(blessed be a good and gracious God) didn't hinder the discharge of any part of my function, which was my greatest fear. However it keeped me for two years in a weak and infirm state; and when two Swedish East India ships were wrecked, the one at Lerwick and the other in this parish,[1] in the latter end of 1744, I quitted my room to accomodate some of the stranger gentlemen at Quendal, and betook myself to a closet without fire, whereby the cold revived the trouble again, and seized me in a violent manner at my quarters in the North Parish, a second time, which disabled me for work several weeks.

Meantime young Quendal payd me a visit and proposed the drinking of tar water, which at first seemed whimsical, but as the former cure had no effect at this time and being persuaded that Providence had put it into his head, I was satisfied to make trial, especially as I found that Bishop Barclay in his receipt mentions tar water as a remedy for the sciatick —and caused my landlord prepare some of the Norway tar accordingly; and, what is very remarkable, I found a sensible abatement of the pain. Every Sabbath morning, being about the same time of that day, I was seized with a severe fit of it, till such time as it went off. However I continued drinking the water all winter, and in the beginning of the Springtime, my skin struck out in a sudden ruff—a sensible vigour in my constitution ensued, which I had not felt for a long time, attended with a strong appetite, and after purging away of the noxious humour, was as clean and whole as ever, and never felt the least tincture of the distemper since, except a little dindling[?] by extraordinary colds that I ever knew any affected with that distemper ever got free of it.

I desire to kiss the rod that smites. He does not afflict, nor grieve the children of men willingly, nor for His pleasure, but people's profit, to make them partakers of his holiness that they may share in his happiness. And blessed be his great and glorious name who was pleased to open my eyes to

---

[1] A ship of Stockholm, wrecked on the west side of the parish. Tales are still told of the quantities of spirits and other stores clandestinely seized by parishioners.

read in my sin the punishment; nay, and made it a means to
mortify and cure me in some measure of a secret lust that
had too much prevailed to God's dishonour and my own
hurt.

In the latter part of the year 1745 the rebellion broke
out in favours of a Popish Pretender.[1] They got the better
of a small number of troops at Preston Pans. The action at
Falkirk seemed a drawn battle. In the beginning of 1746
they went to England, and took in their way the town
and Castle of Carlisle, which success in the beginning so
flushed the Jacobite party, and drew many forth to their
ruin (that otherwise would not have joined their army);
their strong confidence everywhere boasting as if it were a
gained cause gave me strong hopes that God would blast
their designs, which was done in the Battle of Culloden,
by means of the Duke of Cumberland in April thereafter;
for 'tis the glory of the Most High to pour contempt on
vain men who speak as they would have it without regard
or submission to His sovereign pleasure, letting them know
that wherein they dealt proudly He was above them; and
instead of over-throwing our happy Constitution in Church
and State (as they designed) served only to settle it on a
surer basis.

In the year 1747, being chosen one of the Commissioners
to represent the Presbytery in the General Assembly, I
went for the north to visit my father's friends at same time,
and preached oft there, as also at Edinbro and Glasgow;
as my sermons were taking with the generality of hearers,
the vain heart began to swell, and though not sensible of
it, yet met with a severe rebuke of Providence when, preaching and praying in the Tolbooth Church at Edinburgh,
I was put into great confusion and disorder, which several

---

[1] The Rebellion of 1745. Some of the leading families had Jacobite leanings,
but Shetland was too far from the scene to be seriously involved. The Scandinavian temperament had nothing in common with the Highland enthusiasm for
the Stuart family.

took notice of. The light of a large window flashing in my
face, with the gayety of the congregation, so unusual, might
have some influence; but I took it from God as a just judgment, and it proved a mean of making me more cautious
afterwards, to throw off all base slavish fear of man, to set
myself to act withal as under God's eye and seek his honour
and not my own.

I waited long for an occasion homeward and as two ships
were making ready I let the 1st go off, because of some graceless passengers, choosing rather to take passage with a ship
belonging to my own parish. But I soon repented of this as I
was several weeks detained by cross winds, and the indisposition
of the ship master, who behaved notwithstanding in a rude
manner obligeing me to ly upon my own trunk in the Cabin,
while he keeped his own bed. But 'tis observable that in his
passage to Hamburgh that same winter, the sea broke into his
cabin. Upon his return the vessel was wrecked in the harbour,
and himself carried off the stage. He called for me on his
deathbed, and told me in a very unconcerned manner that all
behoved to go the same road. True, said I, but men don't
die as beasts, for there will be a remarkable difference and
separation 'twixt saints and sinners at death and the great
day.

In the year 1750 Quendal's estate was sequestrate. This
family had been inveterate enemies to the Gospel and its
ministers, and though they are suffered to prevail for some
time for a scourge to the wicked, and to exercise and try
the faith and patience of God's saints, yet the vengeance of
Heaven overtakes them at last; their memories rot and perish
with themselves. Thou puttest away the wicked as dross.
This Robert Sinclair of Quendal cast a careless account,
saying he would get his own time of it, but found himself
mistaken. He had keeped me from Kirk and Manse hitherto
and obliged me to preach in the open air during the
Rebellion, saying I should not pray against his King; nor
get a Kirk till he pleased; but I said I wou'd have a Kirk
when God pleased, whether he would or not; and so it
came to pass soon after, and was built by his own son

too,[1] where he met besides with one of the greatest affronts of his lifetime. He sat down at this Kirk of Sandwick on the mast of a wrecked ship, threatening to carry it off by force. Meantime the magistrate came with a party, obliged him to rise, and carried it off; and, for his further mortification, one Horrie whom he had oft employed as a publick Notary in his drunken fits to keep off his creditors from getting their just debts etc., being appointed as factor on his sequestrated estate by the Lords of Session, this occasioned a bitter enmity and bone of contention. My stipend had been poorly paid before and little better now by this factor who had on many occasions discovered a malignant temper and hatred of Gospel. My sister told me he was going through Lerwick with company, drinking the rents and tythes, and that if I didn't go to him [I] would get nothing. I told her I would make him come to me; and having called a messenger to give him a charge of horning, he came in all haste, and paid a good sum; and being assured that if he did not pay me pointedly at every term, I would give him a charge and cause him pay interest for the same, which made him more tame and friendly ever after, according to the nature of the spaniel tribe, that are more acted [on] from a principle of fear than conscience or fear of God.

By this time an horning was executed at my instance against the heritors, both for Kirk and manse; and very providentially a large vessel from Norway loaded with wood for Irland, was put into Quendal bay by a cross wind and by a great storm driven ashore and wrecked below the Ness Kirk, which is never plenished with seats to this day, though the people would have cheerfully paid for them. The wood was sold off for profit. However the Kirk of Sandwick and manse of Dunrossness were built with wood [out of it].

The Kirk should have been built first, but as I had a booth to preach in [I] preferred the manse, which was built in 1751 and furnished in 1752; but more suddenly burnt down on a Saturday night in November said year when I was at Quendal. But as no fire was put on that day, and nobody in the

---

[1] This new kirk was the church of Sandwick. The new Dunrossness church was not built till forty years later.

house that night, the kindling of the fire is like to remain a secret. The servants in the kitchen were awaked Sabbath morning by the crackling of the slates, whereby I lost to the value of £130 sterling, by computation, of books, cloathes and almost all sorts of furniture new, eatables and drinkables, besides extraordinary charges laid out on the Manse. Rebuilding the Manse, together with the office houses, garden dyke etc., all paid out of my own pocket, amounted to the sum of £200 stg. and upwards. Many condoled my loss, but I told them a man never lost much till he lost his soul, which was an irreparable loss ; whereas, if I was spared, God would soon make up this loss in like or better things ; and blessed be his worthy name, I found so to experience.

It pleased God to shake the rod over my head (as it were) and give warning, to show how loath he was to inflict this heavy stroke ; for having one night got a fire in the closet to prevent my books and cloathes being damaged by the damp air while I was drinking tea in a room below, a stone at the back of the chimney gave an explosion like the fireing of a gun, and drove the fire with the iron grate on the loft floor, which I took for something falling in the garret by the mice ; but seeing a bright light through a crevice in the loft, and calling to mind the fire in the closet I immediately run upstairs, and finding the diningroom filled with smoke, and some English blankets on fire that had been set to dry, nay, and some of the floor burnt through, I got all quenched by the tongs, (which blistered my hands with the excessive heat) without any further damage at that time. And tho' this made a little impression, yet it soon wore off, and I went on frowardly, still sinking gradually into a worldly frame, and little sensible of the great need the best Christians have of applying to the Lord Jesus Christ dayly, and living in a close dependence on the Grace treasured up in Him, for mortifying indwelling corruptions and strengthening weak graces to carry on a work of sanctification through the whole course of our lives. When this awful and alarming providence aroused me out of my slumber it pleased God in great mercy and tender compassion to set His Holy Spirit at work for circumcising my carnal heart, for tho' sin was already beat down from the higher faculties of the soul, yet had taken strong root in the affections, which I was not then aware of.

His first operations seemed to resemble the ticks of a pendulum clock, giving at first one, and thereafter two or more touches at the same time, which, though a little uneasy, and my body so weaken'd by excessive fasting that I could scarce walk, yet was glade the Lord condescended to take so much pains upon a polluted worm, for rectifying mistakes and reforming all disorders of soul, tending so greatly to its prosperity and its advancement in the spiritual life, that I would not have exchang'd conditions with most people I saw, even in elevated stations of life, when matters were at the lowest pass. Hence that gracious promise was fulfilled to blest experience—He makes all things, even the most cross and grating to flesh and blood, work together for good to them that love God etc. This is a great mystery to the blinded graceless world, who call such things by the names of enthusiasm, fanaticism and New lights, without knowing what they say or affirm, as natural brute beasts speak evil of the things they don't understand; for as the Apostle speaks, the natural man understands not the things of the Spirit of God, and are looked upon as foolishness, because he is a fool himself. The wisdom from beneath is earthly etc.; the wisdom from above is pure etc., they are quite opposite.

Meantime the Providence of God brought reasonably to hand several treatises saved from the flames, that proved of great use, namely Goodwine's Child of Light walking in darkness—Allan's Godly Fear—Carmichael on Mortification, which doctrine I was much a stranger to at this time. But no sooner did the Lord open my eyes and heart than prevalent sins came flying in my conscience like so many fiery serpents, which galled it exceedingly, and convinced me to purpose of the great subtilty, deceit and strength of indwelling sin which wars against the soul. The Lord was pleased to draw me to himself with the chords of Love, by means of His Blissed Word when I was about sixteen or seventeen years old, as commonly such as are free of gross sins are. But presuming too much upon my being in a justified state, reconciled, pardoned and freed from condemnation etc., made me grow

presumptuous and secure, hereby abusing the grace of God,
if not to licentiousness, yet to too great freedoms and want of
caution 'gainst spiritual enemies, which provock'd the Lord to
lay me at this time under a strong Law-work, whereby I was
made sensible what an evil and bitter thing 'tis to depart from
the living God, and prove guilty of such base ingratitude for
numberless distinguishing mercies. This consideration grieved
me to the heart, that I should be so long in Christ, and yet so
little of the good work carried on that I seemed rather for
some time past to have been razing the foundation. Repent
and do thy first works, lest I come and spue thee out of my
mouth, was very applicable to my present case, and I felt so
much of the gall, bitterness and wormwood of Sin that, had
my body been burning in a fire, I would have made no account '
of that in comparison of the hell I felt at this time in my
conscience ; yet was absolutely necessary to make one stand
more in aw of offending so good and gracious a God for the
future, that I might walk more tenderly, strictly and conscien-
tiously before that God in whose hands are our breath and
all our comforts. Thou wast a God that pardoned our
iniquities, though thou tookest vengeance on our inventions.

In this condition I went for Fair Isle May 1753, in order
to administer the Sacrament to that people, which I could
never get the itinerant minister to undertake. A Dutch
fishing Vessel took us on board, together with our boat, in
Quendal Bay, and brought us within a few miles of the Isle,
and then put out our boat etc. The wind and tide was
contrary, the night coming on and a mist forming on the top
of the Isle. I was seized with a strong fear, as if the Lord was
going to cast us away, which made me entertain constant
discourse with the boatsmen on pious subjects ; and growing
cold, I desired them to put me ashore at the north harbour
which lay nearest.

Upon landing I began to muse, on my way to the houses,
and was suddenly filled with a rapture of heavenly joy, which
made me cry out in praise to my kind and gracious Saviour,
the sweet and lovely Jesus, who had hereby dispelled all my
doubts and fears, and given such courage and strong confidence
in Him. After walking almost the length of the Isle, I came

to the largest Village, and finding the people in bed, knocked
at one of the doors where smoke ascended from the fire, which
to my great surprise proved the Kirk Officer's house, who got
up in all haste, and conveyed me to the baillie's house, where
I lodged. I first examined all the people, and then the communicants, and preached about 19 times during the twenty days
I remained there, yet was wonderfully upheld and carried
through—blessed be His worthy name who increases strength
to them that have no might.

Though I was never in such a weak habit of body, having
made my Testament a little before, and bequeathed most of
my substance to pious uses, considering as I had my All from
God, [I] should devote it to His service, especially as I had no
children of my own at this time, therefore bequeathed £100
ster. to the Society for Propagating Christian Knowledge;
another £100 ster. to the Grammar School at Lerwick, the
place of my nativity, which also stands much in need ; £20
ster. to the Poor of Cullen of Boyn, where I was Schoolmaster
for seven years, and £20 to the Poor of my own Parish,
besides what I left to a cousin german and a nephew, who
were my name sons, and would still be desirous to have something to leave for these, or such like pious uses, over and above
providing for my own, in a competent measure.

Upon my Settlement in April 1743, I found the people
generally rude and ignorant. Mr. Gray, one of the oldest
ministers in the countrey, came to my ordination, beyond all
our expectations, and contrary to his friends' inclinations, as
he was valetudinary. He told me as he advanced he found
himself gradually mending. My father was the first whose
head he had laid his hand on—I would be the last, and was
persuaded it was the work of God he came about. He kept
up pretty well for several years after this. What knowledge
my people had of the principles of religion from the Catechisms
was mostly by rote, which induced me to procure many
copies of Crawford and Vincents for helps to understand them,
which, through the divine blessing, together with hearing
of sermons and examinations brought both young men and
maids to such degree of knowledge that they could scarce be

put out upon any practical question of Divinity in whatever
shape it was proposed. They understood the sense and meaning, and several, 'tis hoped, live in an habitual practice of these
truths. Nay, some discover'd the Spirit of God had been at
work with them, which cheared me not a little, in hopes of
further success, the want whereof had thrown a great damp
on my spirits, least all the pains taken should be in vain,
and their souls lost and undone for ever. This made me defer
the Sacrament of the Lord's Supper for six years, though I
had other discouragements from the want of house, communion
cups, tables, and other utensils necessary. But as there seems
to be an unusual stir among the people upon such occasions,
which probably may flow also, in some measure, from the
solemnity wherewith the ordinance is gone about, therefore
am resolved to give it as oft as possible, while any good effects
are discovered thereby.

Among the first celebrations of this ordinance a young girl
came to my room with tears in her eyes, saying I didn't
know her; she meaned, as to the state of her soul, which she
described in such a plain and ingenuous manner as made me per-
ceive she had been with Jesus; and what is very remarkable,
while I was employed in examination work, some time after this,
being obliged to take a different route from what I intended,
and go by a bridge, because of a swell in the burn, providentially the same girl saw me, and came running and signifying
her gladness in meeting with me, to solve her doubts concerning
her spiritual state, because she found her heart more wicked
and vile than ever, and therefore concluded it was worse with
her than formerly. I told her that had been my own case,
but herein she was in a mistake, for at conversion we see more
dimly, afterwards more clearly, like the man whose eyes Christ
besmeared with clay. Sin rises at first view, like molehills,
but afterwards like mountains, when our inbred corruptions
are further stirred up by fresh measures and degrees of grace
and light in the understanding. I asked her how she came to
discover these evils she was ignorant of before; as blind
sinners, who are dead in trespasses and sins, are utterly
insensible of the plagues of their own evil hearts, as was
evident of her graceless neighbours, who made no complaints

of this nature; which served not only to stop her mouth but yielded her no small comfort upon due reflection. She was afterwards matched with a young man of the same stamp, who had both an eye herein to the Apostle's direction of not being unequally yoked with unbelievers.

This young man foresaid made a complaint to me at an examination, in the year 1753, upon a neighbour for taking the name of God in vain, and imprecating damnation upon him. But though the crime could not be made out by proof, yet being persuaded of the truth thereof, I gave him a private rebuke, and warned him of his great danger, unless timeously prevented by genuine repentance, which he promised to set about; and afterwards desiring to have his first child baptized, I asked him if he had repented in good earnest of the foresaid heinous crime. He replied that he had, according to his ability; and as the house where he stayed lay in my way to the North parish I called on the Saturday, and again put the same question previous to the baptism of the child, before all the people present, and he made the same answer as before. After the baptism he brought a dram, and offering to take it without a blessing asked, I checked him. The fellow trembled, and was in great confusion, which made me suspect he had lied in saying he had sought pardon from God, and was adding sin to sin rather. After leaving the house, I was informed that, soon forgetting what had been told him, he gave loose reins to daft mirth; and going out, was suddenly struck dead at the peat stack.

Next morning one came and told me that the man whose child I had yesterday baptised was lying a corpse, which coming fresh to remembrance during the sermon, I laid the whole matter, as it stood, before the congregation, warning all thereby to guard against that heinous sin, as they would wish to escape God's righteous judgment.

In the year 1754 the manse being again repaired, at my own proper charges, least the walls should go to wreck, as I knew my heritors wouldn't grant a farthing this way, unless compelled by law, and the issue of a process was uncertain. Besides, the patron had promised to make me up from the vacant stipends, which were upwards of £2000 Scots. As I didn't choose to keep house alone, and finding none suitable to my inclinations here I proposed to look out for one at Edinburgh etc. where I was chosen to go as Commissioner to the General Assembly.

However I did not neglect my native countrey, and made suit to some who seemed of the best kind, but was mistaken in them. One of them was addressed by one of the best estates in the country, who drew her to balls and daft mirth. But he and all his Brothers were cut off by a sudden stroke,[1] yet this awful providence made little impression. She ventured to match with a worse, both as to character and estate, though I warned her of the danger, and finding her resolute, said she might take her swing. She wanted to be a Lady, and get Madam at any rate; but finding little pleasure in it, soon repented of what she could not help. She had convictions; but finding all in vain, it made me weep, that, being so nigh, [she] should come short of the Kingdom of God. Nay, she discovered so much of the disposition of the Old Serpent that, perceiving my wife's pious inclinations, she pressed hard to get her dance with her and daft companions at Lerwick, saying there was no harm in it, though her constitution was then broke, and only a little before her death. My wife told her she might be doing, if she had freedom to dance, but she had none. Another I addressed proved meantime with child to a relation. She afterwards married though her friends were against it, and would have preferred me before him, yet reckoned myself much obliged to her for rejecting the proposal, as I would not for the whole world she had embraced it.

As 'tis harder to know women who are more upon the reserve than men who act more openly in the world, the conduct of those two bred a disgust indeed, but had this good effect, that I was more apt to distrust my own judgment, and

---

[1] The reference here is to the four sons of Thomas Gifford of Busta—John, Robert, William, and Hay—who were drowned by the upsetting of their boat in crossing Busta Voe, on 14th May 1748. The text shows that the writing is retrospective, both as regards this incident and the subsequent reference to his wife.

commit myself to a Kind Providence for direction in an affair
of this nature, desiring He might blast my proposals, or not,
as He saw cause for the future, chusing rather to have one
truly good and gracious than for money, which the blind graceless world seeks mostly after in bargains of this kind. Therefore a disappointment of this kind afterwards gave me little
or no concern, though I met with them in the north, when
visiting my friends, and at Edinburgh, and Glasgow. The
greatest objection I found was the great distance, and leaving
their friends.

In 1754, assisting at Sacramental occasion at Cumbuslang,
preached to about 8000 who behaved decently all the time.[1]

The minister that was conjunct-commissioner from the
Presbytery was married before me, and this proved an introduction to my marriage with a young lady who came to visit
us, when I was Bridgroom's best man (as they are called).
We conveyed her home, and had an invitation to drink tea
with her in the afternoon, which we accepted, and by frequent
converse together discovered such a tincture of real piety, and
finding she had one of the best characters from well disposed
people who knew her, I condescended at length that my
brother's wife should make the proposal, which she was so very
eager for, and gave her the preference to her own friends, who
were indeed well-looked ladies ; but she said they were too
much set upon the gaieties of the Town, and would not suit
my temper and manner of life so well as Miss Thompson.[2]
This appeared so ingenuous and disinterested as served to
confirm me in the choice, and soon found to experience, blessed
be His worthy name, I was not disappointed. Besides, this
match proved a mean of bringing me into acquaintance with
several pious and judicious christians, of different states and
conditions in life, which has been a great comfort to me since,

---

[1] This is suggestive of the great Cambuslang revival. But that movement
was some years earlier. The sentence is an interlineation, and the date may be
a mistake.

[2] She was a daughter of Bailie Thompson, Edinburgh.

and of great use in the common concerns of life, as none but
those of this stamp are much to be trusted where the world
is concerned.

After preaching at South Leith, one of the minister's wives
there being under great trouble of mind, and, desiring to speak
with me, she employed a gentlewoman of my acquaintance to
invite me to afternoon's tea at her house, desiring to converse
with me anent her spiritual state, I found her in great agonies
of conscience, almost at the brink of despair, though formerly
she had been a professor, and as she fancied in a hopeful
way. She applied all the threatenings (as usual in such cases)
to herself, but could take no comfort from the promises.
I recommended besides several books suitable to her state,
and met with her afterwards at a fellowship meeting at
Edinburgh, where most that were present, both young and old,
talked freely of their experiences, which made her cry out—
'Tis well with you, but oh! I'm in a lamentable condition!
Thus she continued for some time, till the Lord's time came
to give peace. When He gives quietness none can hinder,
and when He hides his face etc.

In this Society I met with an old experienced Christian,
one Mrs. Keil, who had gone through various trials, and
seemed to have Scriptures at hand suitable to each. She caught
me by the sleeve after coming out from preaching in the
College Kirk [1] at Edinburgh, where I was providentially called
to preach (through sudden indisposition of the minister who
was to have preached), by an application in the forenoon,
a little before I entered the pulpit of the Trone Church, to
preach there. It pleased the Lord to carry me through with
much spirit and liveliness, and the Sermon seemed to have had
a good effect upon this exercis'd Christian, who was very urgent
to have me with her that night, or the next day, to a fellowship meeting, which I did not chuse to do with a stranger
in a strange place, and therefore told her I was going off to-
morrow for Glasgow. But upon my return and marriage, my

---

[1] The Collegiate Church of the Holy Trinity, Edinburgh, founded by Queen
Mary of Gueldres in 1462. Taken down, for the formation of the east railway
approach to the Waverley Station, in 1848.

wife and I, being called to the above meeting, found her there.
I know of no better method to keep up the true spirit of
Christianity and mutual edification than by these sort of meet-
ings : as iron sharpens iron etc.

Being called at this time to preach again in the Tolbooth
Church during the indisposition of both ministers, I found to
comfortable experience, the great advantage of relying on
Divine aid, aiming at His honour and following his conduct,
for my sermon had the approbation of all the hearers.

We had long waited an opportunity of returning home.
At last a small vessel offered, and as I was anxious to be at
my charge, determined to risk all. My dear wife would by
no means stay behind, though her friends were averse to
going at this season of the year, and though her comrades
and friends seemed resolute against her going at first, yet,
when it came to the push they proved the reverse.

We set out in the end of December 1754 and had as fine a
passage as if it had been in the height of summer ; and O
what a signal mercy it was, considering the poor women were
unaccustomed to sea voyages. While others were talking of
risk and danger, I was not only serene and composed but
enabled to look with contempt on winds and waves as being
persuaded they had no power over me, but what was given
from above.

I left my wife at Lerwick till the manse was got in order
for her reception ; supposing a married state would ease me in
a great measure of worldly cares. But I soon found it rather
increased them. The charge of repairing the manse straitened
a little, but we soon got over it. The greatest plague was
with cross-grained naughty servants, being thievish and mischievous, and liker wild beasts than Christians. My wife
being of a delicate constitution couldn't bear the fatigues of a
labouring and obstinacy of such wretches as neither feared God
or regarded man. However, providentially, I was put upon a
better method of setting of my land in halvers and keeping
only one servant in the house, whereby I had more profit and
less trouble. I endeavoured through grace to deal faithfully
with the consciences of all sorts, which was not without effect,
though not in a saving manner. I found a strong stress laid

upon ordinances, especially the Sacrament of the Lord's Supper, as if it was a charm to save them, though they lived in sin ; and the strongest arguments tending to prove the contrary, that it rather increased and aggravated their guilt, yet can't beat this delusion out of their heads. Nay, though God struck a healthy young man suddenly dead, who presumed to come to the Lord's table while he was living in whoredom, as afterwards appeared, and the people were publickly warned to take heed of sinning in like manner.

Meantime Satan raged exceedingly, and got actual possession of two poor women and a man. One of the women was mute, and made no answer to what I said ; and a friend asking her quietly the reason, she said Satan would not suffer her to speak, which indeed I suspected. Then Satan seemed to make use of her tongue and said — The pulpit was upon the South Side of the Kirk. I said it would continue there as long as God pleased. He said I made lies upon him, for which I called him (as indeed he was) a damned rascal for his lying impudence, and that I spoke the truth, which he cared not for. While I spoke to the poor woman, he said I had no business with her,—that she was Satan's. I told him he could be assured of none till they were actually damned. While I was praying, he contradicted, saying—Grant not that. But at last became mute after a few sentences. The poor woman came to her senses and was much concerned when they told her she had spoken rudely to me, not being aware that it was more the speech of the enemy of souls than hers. Another poor woman was much in the same case, and during the possession brought forth a child without any sense of pain.

A school master in the parish came to me about the same time with a written account of his conversion, as he supposed ; and indeed it looked so like the thing, and being of a regular walk and seemingly tender conscience, that I took it for granted, till such time as he called for me at a countrey house where I was catechising the people, among whom he stood some time, and then retired and lay down upon a bed, where I found him ; and asking how matters stood, he spoke of a great weight of heavenly joy. I said he was one of the happiest people on earth,

if that was true, for it was a rare attainment, and that only
of some of the most eminent saints. Then he said the Spirit
made a second attempt to enter in at his mouth, which if he
had done [he] could not have borne it. Here I perceived a
delusion and that Satan had all the while been deceiving the
poor man, by transforming himself into an angel of light. I
asked him how he could imagine that the Spirit of God behoved
to make His way in at our mouths, and warned him to guard
against such delusions. Some days after he came to my room
in a great fright; with his Bible under his arm, and told me he
could get no rest in the night season, and heard one walking
on the roof of the house above his head ; that he heard the
report of a gun fired at his ear and saw a black swine behind
that attempted to take hold of his heels. Whereupon I
advised him to watch and pray, for that Satan was seeking
advantage against him ;—that the Bible was not a charm to
keep him away, but of itself only a dead letter; 'tis not
Christ in the Word, but in the heart, that destroys his works.
The evil spirit at last got possession, and that to such a
degree that he was like to do mischief to his poor wife and
children, which obliged the people to take and bind him, yet
would he then reprove, swearing ; and when it pleased God to
remove the Evil Spirit, he came again to his senses, and was
sensible how grossly he had been abused. I told him pride
and self-conceit lay at the bottom ; that Providence had let
loose the Enemy to humble him, and would be a great mercy
if it had this good effect upon him. Yet notwithstanding of several repeated checks of this nature, Satan seemed
still to keep possession, and he goes on in his self righteous
manner.

After my settlement, being informed of a piece land that
had been mortified for behoof of four poorest widows in the
parish, and that one James Forbes, a shipmaster, had seized
the said fund for his own behoof, I gave in a complaint to the
Sheriff, Sir Andrew Mitchell,[1] in a court held at Ness Kirk,

---

[1] Sir Andrew Mitchell of Westshore, second Baronet. The title became
extinct on the death of his brother, Sir John, about 1786.

where Forbes foresaid compeiring pretended he was nearest
heir to Mr. James Forbes,[1] minister, whose relict (who left
that deed of mortification) was only a liferentrix and had no
power to do so. To this I replied that the deed was legally
done, and never quarrelled before, which supposed she was invested with full powers, and that the nomination of the widows,
and payment of the fund had been in the Session's possession
time immemorial. Notwithstanding of this, the Court members
joined with him and looked on it as a gained cause. Nay,
and some of the elders connected with his friends sided with
him, but soon repented of this, as he took both lands and moss
over their heads, and put the poors' money in his own pocket.
But noways daunted or discouraged with these puffs and
blasts, I was determined to prosecute the affair to the utmost,
rather than suffer the poor widows to be deprived of what
they had such a good title to ; and therefore laid the matter
as it stood before the Procurator of the Church, who wrote
me in return that I was in the right. The Knight, seeing
this letter, said—Advocates would be of different minds ;
whereupon I called for the Messenger, and desired him to
prosecute the affair before the Sheriff Court, till it came to an
Interloquitur, and then I would write for an advocation, and
bring it before the Lords of Session, who I hoped would do
justice. Forbes, being informed of my design, and suspecting
it would go against him came in all haste willing to agree
upon any terms I pleased, which, for peace sake I granted,
upon the old footing of uplifting the yearly rent of 7 pounds
Scots' money from the tenant and paying in the same at
Candlemass to be distributed by the Session. Otherwise, he
should have no further concern with it ; and though he has
oft failed yet can't get it out of his hands for want of
right magistrates. Nay, though I prosecuted the Factor on
Quendal's sequestrated estate for an arrear of stipend, before
the then Chief Magistrate, yet he made many wretched
shifts to put it off from time to time to create trouble and
charges ; and when he found I would have it another way

---

[1] Rev. James Forbes, A.M., minister of Dunrossness 1662-1682. See
INTRODUCTION.

in spight of him pretended then to find I was in the right,
and offered to pass decreet in my favours for principal and
interest etc.

About the year 1756 I found a strong spirit of envy and
malice running against me, the Devil stirring up his poor
blinded slaves to create trouble by an attack not only upon
my character but property. The Laird of Symbister and
Bigton,[1] during my absence, caused serve an edict for riding of
marches, in consequence of which they perambulat the ground
covered with snow and held a court in a private manner. The
magistrate, namely Alexander Sinclair of Brow,[2] for a belly-
full of drink, passed sentence in Symbister's favours, who forthwith sent his tenants to labour up the ground in dispute,
though I protested against the judge as incompetent in matters
of property, and his sentence therefore to be null and void.
Moreover, I caused labour the ground, sowed it and cutt
down the corns in spight of him. And as the Creditors
on Quendal's sequestrated estate were equally concerned, I
insisted that they should either renounce their claim, or
join in the prosecution before the Lords of Session. But
Symbister dropping his claim I keep'd possession of the arable
ground.

'Tis remarkable that my dear wife died in Lerwick in
1758 when about to repair to the physicians at Edinburgh
to cure a swelling after the birth of the second child. The
swelling rose gradually from her leggs, notwithstanding all the
means that could be got, till it came to her vital parts, and then
cutt her off. Mr. Gilbert the minister of Bressay,[3] who married
a little before me, went south with his wife to gather up some

---

[1] John Bruce Stewart of Symbister. Married Clementina Stewart, heiress
of Bigton in Dunrossness, and assumed her family name.

[2] Alexander Sinclair of Brow, last parochial Magistrate or 'Bailie' of Dunrossness.

[3] Rev. Francis Gilbert, ordained minister of Bressay, Burray, and Quarff,
1752. Died on the passage from Leith to Shetland, 2d May 1758, aged thirty-
four.

Legacies left by her father and aunt, which lifted them up to their ruin, for he died upon his passage home, and she soon followed him ; so that in about four years after the Captain died also, and none remained alive who came in the Cabin in 1754 save myself. Vanity of vanities etc. I was under great apprehension concerning my wife during the birth of her first child, which made me earnestly supplicate a throne of grace in her behalf. It pleased God to relieve her soon, and she recovered so well as to nurse the child Nell, who met with several. remarkable deliverances, during her infancy ; for being one day in the garret, she tumbled down the stair without hurt. At another time awaking from sleep and none in the room, she got up and tumbled headlong over the bedside upon a stone floor, yet without harm. A third time, sitting hard by the tea Kettle then boiling on a choffer, the Kettle turned suddenly over, and scattered the water around her, which caused the mother to give a shriek, and immediately I pulled her up and thereby providentially saved her from hurt. Upon her mother's departure for Lerwick, the Lady Quendal took her along and though she went up and down a large dark turnpike stair daily, yet it pleased God her foot slipped not, which otherwise might have endangered her life. When my wife took pains before the birth of the second child, as I couldn't bear to hear her cries, I went to Quendal and put up the Lady for her assistance, which yet I repented of and should rather have staid at home, and held up her case to a good and gracious God, who had formerly delivered her by means of a poor old woman who was the best that could be got at that time. But the ignorant Creature having taken a table Knife, and made crosses over the bed after the childbirth, according to her superstitious custom—the remains of Black Popery, my wife bid her be-gone with her devilry, and couldn't bear to hear of her after-wards. She got the best midwife in the country, but didn't succeed so well, trusting possibly too much in the instru-ment.

It grieved me much to find so little stir among the dry bones, the generality here and elsewhere being so immersed in the body and world that the most rousing sermons and awful alarm-ing providences make no impression on their blind heads and obstinate hearts, though a pestilential fever that began in 1758 raged for several years, which, together with the Smallpox in 1761, carried off upwards of 200 young and old; yet alas made but little impression. In February and March said year by a long tract of snow and severe weather numbers also were cut off, horses sheep and cattle. Great scarcity of victual ensued, while the sea yielded no fish; and by reason of a great drought, the cows yielded little milk, whereby the inhabitants were generally brought to great straits, as a just judgment for abuse of plentiful seasons by gluttony and drunkenness, which oft broke out in scandalous uncleanness of all sorts. Nor was any suitable improvement made of such awful dispensations in any serious and hearty concern for salvation and preparation for the Day of Judgment and Eternity—every one looking about them how breaches might be made up in the loss of husband, wife or child etc.

In May said year 1761, two Dutch vessels stranded at Sandwick, mistaking it for Bressay Sound. A number of persons went on board one of these vessels and in a violent and forcible manner carried off to the value of £50 Ster. worth of goods; which the Admiral[1] at first threatened to punish them for. But taking £60 Ster., for two Admiral Courts relative to the wreck, took no more notice of the plunderers. Affliction was added hereby to the afflicted. But as the Sacrament of the Lord's Supper was to be celebrated at that Kirk soon after, and this affair had given just scandal; in order therefore to separate 'twixt the clean and unclean, I put two boats' crews upon oath, who had been employed in the salvage of the goods, and found clearly proved that about 40 men had been concerned in the forsaid plunder. The Session appointed them to stand before the Congregation in different parcels, and be rebuked for the scandal; which they all did, except 8 or 9, who stood out till they were summoned before the Presbytery, who so far took part with these rogues (who were the most criminal, and

---

[1] The Admiral, *i.e.* the officer acting as Vice-Admiral of Shetland in the custody of wrecks, etc. Admiral Courts = Courts of Admiralty.

had made the first attack upon the Vessel), that they thought
proper to dismiss the affair altogether at first as being incompetent judges, till I appealed from their sentence to the General
Assembly for redress ; which made them deal with the delinquents to submit to a Presbyterial rebuke, which they accordingly did accept of, and, for peace sake, I dropped the appeal,
on condition that the Clerk should give me an extract of
this sentence to be read next Lord's Day, from the pulpit of
Sandwick, which was done accordingly to their further shame
and disgrace.   O the wretched stupidity and sottishness of
sinful mortals !—' Who hath believed our report ?'—Till such
time as the Spirit of God awakens the sleepy conscience, and
changes the curst nature of man, neither word or rod makes
any impression, yet though Israel be not gathered, God will be
glorious, and the reward of His faithful ministers will never
be the less ; and bless'd be his glorious and worthy name, who
encourages me to depend go on and wait His good time for
the spiritual blessings promised in these latter days ; and that
amidst all struggles with a body of sin and death He is
pleased sometimes to bless me with the light of His reconciled
countenance, etc.

In the year 1762, being chosen Commissioner to the General
Assembly, I landed at Peterhead, and payed a visit to my
friends in the north, where I preached ten Sabbaths running to
the universal satisfaction of the hearers ; as also at Edinburgh
and Sacrament occasions at Newbottle etc.   What success
attended these sermons I know not ; but as I aimed at God's
honour and good of souls, by striking a blow at the root of sin,
by preaching up the spirit of Christianity and power of real
holiness ; found to blessed experience that promise made good
that such as honour God He will honour etc.   Though alas !
many will commend a sermon yet continue still in the gall of
bitterness etc.

I went to Dysart the beginning of September, thinking from
thence to take passage home.   But the wind proving contrary,
and fearing the vessel would not get out when the wind proved
favourable, with her salt cargo, they sailed again for Leith
harbour, whereby very providentially I had access to converse

with and hear publickly the famous Mr. Whitfield[1] four different
times, first on these words And they that were ready went in to
the marriage, and the doors were shut; second And we know
that we are passed from death to life; third The Scribes and
Pharisees murmured saying, This man receiveth sinners and
eateth with them; and 4th Genesis 1st and 2nd, And the Earth
was without form and Void—the drift of all tending to lead
sinners to Christ and promote pure and undefiled religion,
without regard to party notions, that so many lay stress upon
and show a mighty zeal for. He is a plain and affectionate
preacher, and discovers a singular talent in keeping up the
attention of the hearers and moving their passions. As I
had a strong desire to see, hear and converse with such a
worthy man, so have reason to bless God who ordered it to my
great comfort and satisfaction. Good people esteem, love and
speak well of him as they do of all God's faithful ministers;
but the profane herd of all sorts hate, ridicule, bely, and slander
him, and such like out of mere enmity and malice. Thus the
promise is fulfilled in all ages, I will put enmity betwixt thy
seed and her seed etc. Upon the fourth day of September, on
our return, the sailors gave out early in the morning that they
were off Mousa; and thus, when we were thinking of being
soon in our desired haven, I was suddenly roused by a sea which
broke through the cabin window, and poured upon my head,
which I took up as a warning to get up and consider our
danger. When I came upon deck, the mariners were calling
to one another to get the ship off shore and save our lives.
By the moonlight I supposed a little cloud to be a rock at first,
and so nigh that we were in danger of going ashore forthwith;
which made me dart up sudden ejaculations to the Lord to save
us, and thereupon called upon the rest of the Crew below to
come upon deck; but the hellish blasphemies of the cursed tars
damning one another put me in greater fear than the danger

---

[1] Rev. George Whitfield, one of the principal founders of the Methodist
Church. Born at Gloucester in 1714. Died in America in 1770. The place
where he preached in Leith Walk was till lately known as 'Whitfield Place.'
It was on an earlier visit to Scotland, in 1741, that the great revival at Cambuslang took place.

we were in; and had it been dark, as it was very providentially moon and morning light, they had all perished in the
tideway of North Ronaldshay, and probably none of our lives
had been saved, and these had gone to hell with its language
in their mouths. The main-sail was entangled and couldn't
be got hoisted, till some got up the shrouds and set it to
rights again, which had occasioned so much stir among them.
Then I perceived to lie off the quarter-deck, a good way off,
the northmost isle of Orkney, lying low in the water. The
tideway made a foul sea, and might have broke a weaker
vessel; the wind shifting at same time we got clear of both
North Ronaldshay and Sanday, and got a safe harbour in the
isle of Stronsay before breakfast; and this deliverance was the
more remarkable that, though we had several shipmasters and
a double crew on board, they were so infatuate as to mistake
their reckoning, and ignorant of the place we were in till
clear daylight discovered it. Besides, the wind soon rose
so high that we might have missed both countries for some
time at least. After four days' stay among a kind and hospitable
people, we loosed again, and reached Lerwick in seventeen
hours time. O that men would praise the Lord for his kindness and wonderful deliverances to the sons of men. Before
I left Edinburgh I was engaged in courtship with a Knight's
daughter, who had the character of a pious young lady;
but as our acquaintance was short, we agreed to delay the
marriage till next Spring, but before that time another minister
nigh Edinburgh made offers of the same nature, which were
accepted of purely on this account to be nigh her friends.
Two other young ladies equally agreeable were proposed by
my friends, then, but I chuse to be true to my engagements.

In January 1763, a large three masted vessel commanded
by one Captain Ferguson from Burrowstoness, and bound for
America, was by a storm driven into Sandwick bay in the night
time and stranded below the Kirk, and had she gone to either
side, had run a great risk of losing their lives, whereas all were
saved and provisions too. One Swan in P'thead [i.e. Peterhead]
was mate. Said year having bespoke a Saw Stock from Quendal
for putting up a little stable for my riding horse etc., while

masons were putting up the walls, one came and told me the
Saw Stock was rotten and couldn't serve my purpose, which
obliged me to take horse and try if anything could be got for
roof, doors etc. at Quendal or Symburgh. In my way one came
running about another business, and telling him occasionally
of my design [he] answered, he could supply me with all
ready made, which was the more remarkable that I knew not
where timber was to be had at that time. Thus should we eye
God in all providential dispensations respecting ourselves or
others—the secret of the Lord is with them that fear Him,
while those that regard not the operation of his hand are
justly reputed a blind and stupid generation.

In the year 1764 one of the King's yachts from Leith was
wrecked, through mistake of the pilot, upon Fitwil [*i.e.* Fitfell]
head. Reid, the Captain, and crew etc. met with a miraculous
preservation, being put upon a sand beach having a ridge of
rocks on either side—the entry being narrow, and in the night
time in darkness.

Said year, the man and his family who laboured one half of
my glebe growing still more rude and insolent that I couldn't
get a servant keeped in the house, [I] was determined to put
him off, and had warned him, though I knew not where to
find another to supply his place. Meantime Providence so
ordered that one came enquiring if I would accept of one to
labour my land, and we soon agreed to terms etc. etc. In the
year 1765 I went Commissioner to the General Assembly with
a view at same time to obtain redress of grievances by encroach-
ment made on the priviledges of my glebe by some Lairds ; and
to have the affair brought before the Lords, and plead on the
Church funds, and also for getting schools in the Parish upon
a Legal footing ; but was remitted to the ordinary Courts to
commence the process, which was setting me to the Long
Sands ; yet the Committee appointed for such matters discovered their partiality in granting sums for carrying on
processes to augment stipends, but would grant none to defend
the Church's property.[1]

---

[1] See INTRODUCTION : Extracts from Minutes of Presbytery *re* Glebe Lands.

Being afraid my Children would be spoiled thro' want of proper discipline, and as I couldn't take them home without a helpmeet to have them under my own eye and inspection, Providence furnished one suitable to my taste. July 29, 1765 I was married for the second time to Miss Ann Young, daughter to Mr. Robert Young, portioner at the Water of Leith, by Mr. John Erskine minister of New Greyfriars, Edinburgh. 'Tis remarkable that she was proposed to me in 1754, before I was first married ; and with this view, one unknown to me desired her mother to admitt a visit, but she said she would rather bury her daughter at home than let her go at such distance ; therefore keeped her in close dependence that she might stay with her till death ; but now when it came to the push in good earnest by my own addresses Providence overruled her by the unanimous concurrence of some friends she most confided in. It was further noticeable that she and another agreeable young lady were proposed three years before, and [I] was urged by my friends at Edinburgh to make my addresses to her, which I would not do then, being engaged with another. But Providence made a better choice for me in reserving her to this time, giving a stronger proof of her affection which was founded on better grounds than the former,—of no less worldly advantages as to friends and means, and, what I valued most, a person of substantial piety. We set out from Leith, August 10th, put into Stonehive [Stonehaven] the 13th, where we lodged agreeably in one Doctor Lawson's. Before we got into harbour a boy was thrown overboard by the sail, but getting hold of a rope was saved ; but next Sabbath morning I reproved him for singing a common Song. He forgot that it was the Sabbath day. We took a view of Dunnoter Castle, in ruins, that about a century ago had been a prison to good Christians, persecuted by the Malignants of those days, who ruled the roost. Our Landlady said she would have shown us the Whigg's Vault had she been with us, but we found it without her direction. In this little town were two Episcopal clergymen, the one jurant the other non-jurant. The curse of God sooner or later falls on all persons and places, enemies to the Gospel and true Christians who are the excellent ones of the Earth and substance of the land. We loosed from Stonehive

the 17th do. dropped anchor at night in Peterhead Bay, and
on the 20th current landed in Bressay Sound, when through
thick fogg we were just to the west of Bressay and as the wind
was against, were in danger of being driven to Norway, had not
kind Providence changed the wind, and dispelled the fogg.
Soli Deo Gloria.

In 1766, no sooner had we settled at home than one of my
principal Heritors wrote me a letter signifying that I behoved
to complete the Kirk of Sandwick, otherwise they would make
me liable for damages; in answer to which I told him that
though the Horning for the Kirk and Manse run in my name,
yet as young Quendal, as heritor,[1] had undertaken the work,
and the money had been paid in to him, the law might take its
course : whereupon they applied to the Presbytery for a Visitation of both : and being informed of their threatenings and
combinations to do me mischief, I applied at same time for a
Visitation, being determined to have recourse upon them for
reparation of the Manse, Garden Dyke, office houses, done at
my own charge, Communion Cups, and everything I wanted,
which the law entitled me to. When they found this, matters
were compromised—they agreed to pay in the remainder of their
sums, the undertaker to complete the work, and I was to prosecute outstanders upon the Horning ; and finding the few
members of Presbytery they were closely connected with were
so partial as to do their business, but pretended they had no time
for mine, I dropped the prosecution, chusing, for peace sake,
to lose all my expences which I had expected out of the vacant
stipends, and which indeed the Earl of Morton had promised
to grant, both by word and write, upon the sale of Quendal
estate ; but then put me off with this, that Quendal had paid
no vacant stipends, and that I behoved to have recourse upon
my Heritors. Thus I found the Psalmist's words true that
Great Men are a lie. However I regretted this the less as the

---

[1] The estate of Sandwick at this time belonged to Sinclair of Quendale
(Sandwick 309 merks, formerly in the family of Sinclair of Sandwick, with the
island of Mousa in addition ; Aith, Cunningsburgh, 368 merks, formerly
Sinclair's of Aith).

burning of the manse and furniture etc. had, in the course of Providence, turned more to my spiritual advantage than it was all worth. Nay, and blessed be His worthy name, who has made me up more than all the worldly loss in temporals likewise. One thing I must remark particularly, that God over-ruled the Lairds' designs beyond their intention to issue in a thorough repair of the Kirk of Sandwick, which otherwise, through Quendal's indolence etc. had gone to wreck etc.

In 1767 I preached at Lerwick on Rev. 16 & 15, after the death of their minister Mr. Millar, which they seemed very well pleased with, though formerly they had been much displeased when preaching on Psalm 24 & 4, the application making their consciences reel and fall on them. But I was not much moved by their frowns or smiles, it being my highest ambition to please God.

As this parish lies in a corner by itself at a distance from others, I find most of ministers loath to give themselves the trouble of coming this length to supply in absence, or assist at Sacraments, especially as the most convenient season for dispensing this ordinance of the Supper is after the time of far-fishing is over in August. The nearest ministers being engaged soon for the Sacrament at Walls, and finding I could scarce make out wine or assistants, and having also the ordination sermon on hand for a successor to Mr. Millar at Lerwick, obliged me to drop it out for a season, which the Parish seemed to take amiss, as most look upon it as a charm, confers some good thing, and puts away old scores of their sins. Nay, such as seem to make least conscience of duty and walking according to the laws of God are most eager to partake of this ordinance. This is a fearful delusion which they are oft warned of, yet there's nothing but Omnipotence can drive it out of their heads etc.

In 1768 being elected a member for the General Assembly, my wife accompanied me to see her aged mother, and other relations, as also Nell, my eldest daughter, whom we settled with the Miss Scots, a minister's daughters of good reputation,

to teach her to make her own cloathes, at least, and see more of
the world, as she had got already what this Country afforded
as to sewing and working of stockings, writing, arithmetick,
dancing,[1] Church music, &c. We staid only three weeks at
Edinburgh, and returned again by the packet, being about six
days on our passage going south, and as much in our return ;
but met with a violent gale of easterly wind which put us nigh
the coast of Caithness, when the storm increasing, upon the
14th day of June, Tuesday, the shipmaster laid about for
Peterhead, and coming nigh it about six in the afternoon, it
proved so thick and dark that we couldn't see the town, and
therefore were obliged to stand to sea all night, and if Providence hadn't ordered it so that the wind shifted a point into the
north, our lives had been in great danger by the ship's going
ashore. But it pleased a good and gracious God that the
storm abated about two of the clock in the morning, and we
got to breakfast next day in Peterhead, loosed on Thursday
and reached Bressay Sound on Sabbath morning the 19th.
Soli Deo Gloria.

After my return I found John Bruce of Symburgh had
marked out a pund[2] on my priviledge, for setting two tenants
upon, and accordingly builded two houses for them.

In 1769 I went for Fair Isle in the beginning of June, and
having examined the whole youth of the isle, and also young
communicants, the Sacrament of the Lord's Supper was celebrated on June the 11th and Providence favored with a proper
opportunity of returning once and again, upon the morrow
after the Thanksgiving Day, Thanks to God for all his mercies,
especially for His unspeakable gift, for of Him and through
Him and to Him are all things : to whom be glory for ever and
ever, Amen. There seemed to be some good christians there.
One woman, in particular, told me something of her experi-

---

[1] His daughter's being instructed in dancing is discordant with his previous
expression of views on the subject.

[2] *Pund* : the term in Shetland for an enclosure usually taken in, by a dyke,
from the hill, or from commonty ground ('Skattald').

ences, and a considerable number of them accompanied me
to the boat, at my departure, with singular expressions of
affection.

O MOST blessed and glorious God, Thou alone art worthy   **1770**
to be feared, adored, and admired by all thy reasonable RENEWAL OF
creatures as the First Cause, the greatest and best of Beings, MY COVENANT
as the Author of my being and of all those mercies I enjoy in ENGAGEMENTS.
common with others, but especially for thy matchless love in offering Jesus Christ, thine Only Begotten Son, and all the benefits
purchased by His blood, for poor wretched sinners of mankind
who shall accept of him as the free gift of God, and the Pearl
of great price, who alone can bless and make them happy in
time and through eternity. I desire to bless and magnify thy
Great and Glorious Name for thy distinguishing mercy and
love in separating me from my mother's womb and calling me
effectually by thy grace out of that woful and wretched estate
of sin and misery wherein I was plunged, and lay with others
quite insensible and secure till Thou wast pleased to open the
eyes of my understanding to see my sin and danger, translating
me from darkness to light, and from the power and slavery of
sin and Satan into the glorious liberty of thy dear children,
shedding abroad thy love into my heart, and thereby giving
that sollid and substantial peace and joy that infinitely sur-
passes all the carnal joys and pleasures of the most prosperous
worldlings ; yet must acknowledge to thy glory, most gracious
and merciful God, and also to my own shame, that though I
was thus called, and that early, about 15 or 16 years old, from
a state of vile nature, enmity and rebellion into a state of
Grace, favour and friendship with Thyself, yet I wretchedly
and foolishly run out and run away from thee, and that not
only when I knew thee not, but even after Thou wast pleased
to reveal Thy Son in me ; and would have run away endlessly
and eternally from Thee through the force of temptations and
strength of indwelling corruptions, if thy grace and mercy had
not prevented by hedging in my way as with thorns, sanctify-
ing word and rod for reclaiming me from the error of my ways.
And though thou wast pleased to take to thyself my pious

C

father during my infancy, yet stirred up friends to take care of my education, and in thy good time to put me into the ministry to preach the everlasting Gospel of thy dear Son, and setting me over two large congregations, among whom I have been employed for the space of twenty-seven years nigh, but alas! with little success, and have just cause to make the prophet's complaint: Who hath believed our report? etc. And though I have cause to fear that 'tis owing to manifold breaches of Covenant engagements, and defects in a faithful and diligent exercise of the duties of my office, yet can appeal to the Searcher of all hearts, who knoweth all things, that I love Him above all, and that 'tis the sincere desire of my heart to be found faithful to Christ, to my own soul and those committed to my care. Thou Lord knowest also that the dishonour done to thy worthy name, not only by my own failings and short-comings in duty and elsewhere, but the scandalous outbreakings of all kinds of sins among all ranks of persons, through the parish and whole country, grieves me to the heart, and makes rivers of tears flow from mine eyes; and at the same time, that there is nothing my soul so earnestly pants and longs for as to behold Thy power and glory displayed in Thy Sanctuary, by the saving operations of Thy Holy Spirit, in His awakning, convincing, and converting influences on perishing souls, and that 'tis my highest ambition to have the approbation of Heaven by a faithful and conscientious discharge of all the duties I owe to my God and my father's God, to my flock and family, to my neighbours and self; and for this end I desire to bind myself afresh, by dedicating and devoting both soul and body, and all I am and have, to the glory of Thy great Name, resolving, in the strength of Divine grace, to cleave close to the Lord Jesus Christ in every state and condition thou seest best for me, whether of prosperity or adversity, and to walk before Thee in holiness of heart and practice all the days of mine appointed time on Earth, cost what it will; and in testi-mony hereof, have subscribed these presents at Manse of Dunrossness this 3rd day of February 1770 years.

JOHN MILL.[1]

---

[1] Up to this point the writing of the Diary seems to have been mostly a retrospect over past years. It now seems to assume the character of periodical jottings at more or less frequent intervals.

Three of my nearest neighbours among the clergy, moved with envy, malignity, and wrath against me for reproving some things that were scandalous in their conduct etc. being met in Presbytery, they shewed their teeth and enmity by appointing me to supply in a vacant parish about 23 miles distance, in the month of January, when it was with difficulty that I could supply my own people, tho' one of these members was within three or four miles of said parish Kirk, and the other two ministers about as much more from Sandsting; but I wouldn't go till they all went first. Symburgh enclosed two punds more upon the priviledges of my glebe land, and set two more tenants upon the same, without asking my advice, hereby wasting the Scatteld [1] and cutting off my moss and pasturage, though he had only a just title to little more than two thirds of the same; and in the former pund set out to two tenants, in 1768, he had a title only to one half of the same; but as it might cost me more than its worth in the prosecution, upon advice from Edinburgh I dropped the same, as the Church would grant me no assistance.

Though there is little stir among the dry bones, yet, blessed be His worthy name, I discovered two young people whom the Spirit of the Lord seemed to have wrought upon; they were lately joined in marriage together, had been both last occasion partakers of the Lord's Supper. Some months after, the woman died after childbirth, and her husband came in great concern, acquainting me with the circumstances of her death; how she minded secret duty, wept bitterly, was afraid of un-worthy communicating, and had sore struggles with Satanical suggestions before her exit; and he seems to be an exercised Christian himself.

---

[1] SCATTELD, more usually and more correctly SKAT-HALD (which is pure Norse, a *holding*, or possession, for which *skat*, tax or rent, is paid)—the common pasturage to which a district has right. The district possessing a Skathald is itself sometimes conveniently denominated a Skathald, as 'the Skathald of ————.' The term probably originated from unenclosed and unappropriated land (*Almenning*) being regarded as public property vested in the State as represent-ing the community, and therefore subject to tax, or rent, from those using it Occupied land in Shetland, the direct property of its owners, recognised no Superior, in the feudal sense, and paid no Superior duty.

Some years ago, a countrey man in the northmost part of this ministry couldn't rest in the night-time and was at last prompted by the Enemy of Souls to drown himself. Soon after, another, decayed in worldly circumstances, was tempted to do the same about the middle of the ministry; and a third man, in the south part, turned dumpish, and acted the same fearful tragedy this year. A boat was cast away by the sudden rise of a surge, which rushed upon the sail, and overset her, in sight of other boats, who saved one man, and other two perished, father and son; and, what was most remarkable, the father used not to go to sea, but was employed that day, instead of another son who used to go with the boat. This wretched old man was observed to be often grumbling and crying out against bad weather, and here he perished in good weather.

Of five cows, when three of them were to be cut off for the badness of their teeth, and I knew not how to have their room supplied, as they were turned both scarce and dear, and a greedy fellow was seeking a high price for one, an honest well-wisher came and offered me a better and cheaper cow; another did the same, and a third I exchanged for one of the old cows to be a mart, and all these three were but seven years old, and among the best like cows in the parish. Deus providebit.

There seems to be a common work of the Spirit of God on many, convincing them of the necessity of a supernatural work of Grace in order to their eternal salvation, that engage to diligent attendance on ordinances, which I have discovered in severals on sick beds, yet seem to rest there mostly; but a woman I saw lately in these circumstances, upon hinting the absolute necessity of being renewed and sanctified, cried out—'Lord, take me not off this earth till I know it to experience' etc. [*a leaf lost here*]

*   *   *   *   *

. . . as to refuse the principal gentry in the countrey access to him; but when it suited with his worldly interest, and to acquire it, he stuck at nothing, however mean and sordid; when his haughty treatment of the Lairds had so far exasperated them as to [induce them to] enter into a combination against him, and lodge a formal complaint to the Commissioners of Customs, it was found by deposition of witnesses that he

had been acting diametrically opposite to the very design of his
office in smuggling and offering to act in concert with others
for carrying on a clandestine trade to cheat the government,
for which he was deservedly broke in 1768, and is now reduced
to Bankruptcy, wherein the Scripture is fulfilled, that 'Pride
goeth before destruction and a haughty spirit before a fall.'
He died soon after, and left nothing to his poor family but
hatred and contempt.[1]

In 1772, the months of January and February were very
cold, by a continued frost and snow, whereby many out-liers[2]
(as called), sheep and horses, were cut off. The meal and malt
rose high, and what was brought to the country sold for
4s. 6d. per lispband.[3] I smote you with blasting and milldew
etc. yet have ye not returned to me, saith the Lord. My
mother died in November this year, aged 84.

1772

In March Lady Symburgh[4] was so bad after childbirth
that she was thought to be a-dying, and when my wife and
daughter went to see her, Symburgh sent a servant to let her
know when nigh the house that her visit would not be accept-
able. This piece of kindness was the more astonishing, as she
keep'd naughty creatures about her, whose company seemed
more agreeable to their vitiate taste. However Providence so
ordered she grew worse. Upon this, which made them send an
express desiring to pray publicly on Sabbath for her soul;
and said night another express came for some rice to be
applied to the body. Being afterwards sent for to see her,
I sat by the bedside, and spoke a deal to her, which she took
in good part, and after prayer, she was desirous of another
visit, and wonderfully recovered.

---

[1] The loss of a leaf here has caused an interesting narrative to perish. What
is left seems to indicate that the ruin of the ancient family of Sinclair of Quendale
is referred to.
[2] OUTLIERS : animals not stabled, or kept under cover, but finding food and
shelter for themselves.
[3] LISPBAND, or LISPUND, a native weight in Orkney and Shetland, originally
12 lbs., but raised gradually, as a means of extortion, to 18 lbs. Scots measure.
[4] It was common to style wives of leading heritors 'Lady,' in this way.

· May 1st.—After musing on several texts of Scripture which I judged might be instrumental of gaining sinners to Christ, on going to the window I perceived a bright and livly image of the sun in the garden mould before the window, the like whereof I had never seen in my life. Retiring from the window for a little, it resembled a burning coal, and approaching nearer to the glass, it appeared with as bright lustre as the sun and cast forth splendid rays around in like manner; which made me trust and hope that the Lord would please yet, through my poor endeavours, make the Sun of Righteousness arise with healing under his wings on some dark minds, and shine on some earthen hearts etc. This may be ascribed to a natural cause, or to fancy and enthusiasm; but if we may not believe our senses when mistakes are guarded against which might mislead them, we should believe nothing if it flowed from a natural cause. This would probably fall out more than once, which it never did before or since.

Having some time ago formed a scheme of leaving something that might prove beneficial to the souls of men after my decease, I took some pains to write my sentiments on the principles of religion and Christian liberty, as to faith and practice founded both on Sound Reason as well as on the Scriptures of truth, confining the same to as narrow limits as possible, to make it easy [of] purchase, and for promoting a Catholick spirit of true Christianity, which is confined to no party. Having thus completed my design in two or three years, I carried the manuscript to Edinburgh last year, and put it into a judicious minister's hand for perusal; and after exchanging some letters on the subject, he committed it to a printer, a sensible good sort of man, who undertook to put it in a proper dress, and accordingly printed a thousand copies thereof for £50 ster. Jan. 1773, which I reckon the best bestowed money that ever I laid out, if through God's blessing (to whose good Providence I do heartily commit it) the little book shall prove a mean of gaining but one soul to Christ Jesus, Amen.[1]

---

[1] His published work, *The Holy Catholic Church*. Edin. 1773. See IN-TRODUCTION.

In the beginning of this year the vessel by which I com-   **1773**
missioned for house necessaries was suspected to be lost, as she
had gone from this country about the middle of September
last, and some ships arriving from Hamburgh [1] brought accounts
that she was not come there long after; but she cast up towards
the latter end of January. After suffering much damage by a
storm, they got in to Norway, and from thence to Hamburgh.
' O that men would praise the Lord for His goodness ' etc.   O
for a grateful heart for kind Providences. I never lost any
commissions to this day.

A young horse was missing for some months, and though the
officer called him at the Kirk,[2] no accounts could be got of
him, till a man in this village [3] who had gone in quest of one
that had strayed from him, and in seeking his own horse he
providentially lighted on mine, and brought him home without
his own horse—the greater the mercy that horses can hardly
be got for money, being scarce and dear.

Against the middle of April, the straw was quite exhausted
by the missmanagement, or rather knavery, of a servant; and
being exceedingly scarce that it couldn't be got for money,
was apprehensive least my cattle should perish for want. Yet
by the good Providence of God, it was, and oft, sent by the
people gratis to the door, and when in most need; and at
last got as much hay to purchase as served, and some lispunds
of oats also, which I could not procure before at any rate.
Glory to the rich Provider of all etc.

In June the ground in many places looked black, which
made severals sow the ground a second time, supposing the
seed to have been destroyed by the story (?) worm, which
seemed indeed to have been nipped, but not quite destroyed,
for a sudden heat and drought having destroyed the creature,

---

[1] Supplies received in Shetland from HAMBURG. This well-known custom
in last century seems strange, but is easily accounted for. Then, as for centuries
before, and as is still the case, the larger portion of Shetland cured fish was
exported to Continental markets, chiefly through Hamburg. Intercourse directly
with ports in Scotland was intermittent and uncertain.

[2] Called at the Kirk : the then best available method of public advertisement.

[3] This village : Skelberry, where the Manse and Glebe are.

the seed sprung where none was sown afterwards a second
time and produced a crop, though late.

In August, the Sacrament of the Lord's Supper was
celebrated at the Ness Kirk ; but O ! there 's a great restraint
of the Spirit.

About the beginning of October a large vessel from Boston
in New England and bound for Burntisland, having one Smith
for master, and Parker the owner, with his lady and four
children on board, was driven by stress of weather, about ten
of the clock in the night time, upon the west part of Fair
Isle, 'twixt two rocks,[1] by which merciful and wonderful
interposition of Providence they were all saved, being about
twenty souls, with their provisions and some of the cargo.
Next day the ship went to wreck etc.

On the 24th of said month, an English vessel of 400 tuns
from Norway, load with saw stocks, was driven by a storm
of westerly wind on the rocks of Havra,[2] when the whole
crew perished in the nighttime. About the same time also, a
vessel from Leith, with 260 emigrants for North Carolina, was
by stress of weather put into Vela Sound in Walls. The
smallpox at same time carried off severals, and some of their
children crammed in the hold were said to be stifled to death
and thrown overboard into the sea, before they landed ; after
which the vessel was driven from her anchors, and so damaged
that they could not, for several months, put to sea again. The
people were dispersed through the several parishes for subsistence according to the Sheriff's decreet. They went back for
Leith in April, and the project for America thereby miscarried.

1774   In May 1774 [*paragraph of* 12 *lines deleted*].

*   *   *   *   *
In the beginning of June I went for Fair Isle, and celebrated
the Sacrament of the Lord's Supper there alone, where is a

---

[1] The wreck of the *Lessing* from Bremen to New York in 1869, and the
saving of the crew and emigrants on board, was in precisely similar circumstances,
—between two rocks, at the *Sheldie Cave*— a miraculous preservation.

[2] Havera (*Hafrey*, isle of oats ?), a small island on the west side of Sandwick,
the middle parish of Mill's ministry.

remnant of 'real Christians,' and in general so warm hearted to their minister that they came in a crowd to the boat at my departure to shake hands and bid me a solemn farewell, besides some presents they made of fish, barley etc.

On the 21st of said month a strong gale of wind arose that carried of a small sloop from this parish that for many days was amissing; but at last she cast up again ; and said day three boats with sixteen men were lost at the North Maving[1] fishing, whereby 'tis said that sixty children were left fatherless ; yet these awful Providences are little considered and improven, or the operation of his hands regarded.

Some time before a considerable quantity of Hollands gin, etc., was found lodged in the Church of Nesting and carried off by the Custom House yatch [i.e. yacht], and the vessel, belonging to Lerwick merchants, that brought the liquor run the risk of being condemned and burnt ; and though they smarted formerly in a severe manner for this clandestine trade, yet so strong is the greed of gain, notwithstanding it drains the money and debauches the countrey, they know no measure in bringing home more tho' the yatch soon returned and took much more from severals in Lerwick. Some was retaken from the Custom House.

In the month of October an Hamburger loaden with ry from Archangel was much damaged (by stricking on the rock called the Unicorn from the name of that ship wherein the Laird of Grange struck in pursuit of Earl Bothwel[2]); but getting into a creek in Nesting parish, the ry proved of great service to poor people, who had full liberty to take thereof, which, after being steeped in fresh water, they dried etc. for use. About the same time an English vessel from Archangel loaden with oil and rye was wrecked at Noss in Bressay and little saved but the men's lives. Two Danish vessels got in with difficulty, and a vessel from Holland loaden with wheat from Archangel had lost her rudder in the storm, and was

---

[1] North Maving : parish of North Mavine (*Nord Maveid*).

[2] The UNICORN ROCK, not far from the north entrance to Bressay Sound (Lerwick). The incident is authentic, as fully attested at the time. The *Unicorn* had on board Kirkcaldy of Grange and Bishop Adam Bothwell (1567).

dragged into Lerwick Bay by boats. O that men would praise the Lord for signal preservations etc. The master's name was Van Ross of Scotch parents in Zurick [Zuyder?] See.

1775   In January 1775 a large ship from Copenhagen of 20 guns (Nicolas Moram, master) stranded by a storm at Sandwick, nigh the Kirk, having sugar and tea, silks and calicoes etc. supposed to be worth in all £20,000 Libs. Ster. The ship wrecked and cargo mostly damaged. This is the fifth ship lost there within ten years' space. She was bound for Santa Crux in America.

March 11th. In return from the Presbytery at Lerwick to the north parish, we were in great danger from a strong blow of wind that was like to oversett the boat, and a heaving sea that keeped a man often throwing out the water, yet would they not lower the sail. But praise to a good and gracious God who brought us safe to land.

In said month I met with a very agreeable surprise from my eldest daughter Nell's putting into my hand a written account of her conversion, which seemed to be genuine and true; and it was the more remarkable that not long before she was much given to dress, diversions, and encouragment of young frothy men to make suit to her, which she seems now to be grieved for, and to look down [upon] with a holy contempt and disdain.

I was no less surprised with an account my sister wrote me in April of three Greenland Captains[1] who frequented her house, and savoured much of real piety, and bought each of them a copy of the 'Holy Catholic Church';[2] and her remark on it was just and true, that God has his remnant sometimes among the worst of people, as these rough tarrs seem to be.

In June I was no less surprised to find that the servant maid, aged 23 years, was under a real work of the Spirit of God, by getting a distinct view of all her sins, and says it

---

[1] Greenland Captains: commanders of whale-fishing vessels, calling at Lerwick to complete the complement of their crews.
[2] *The Holy Catholic Church*: Mill's own printed volume.

began with observing the great change she saw upon my eldest
daughter to the better; and though she met with opposition
from some of her nearest carnal friends, who imputed it to
melancholy etc., yet she seems resolute to hold on in the way
of holiness.

'Tis remarkable that when I had no prospect of any
slaughter beasts a kind Providence furnished soon three of
these, two whereof—an ox and cow—I put to the grassing.

A dangerous rebellion broke out in America by our
Colonists etc.

August 12th. About ten of the clock at night, while sitting before the fire, a spark of lightning came down through
the chimney, which surprised me a little, after which frequent
flashes shone on the windows and loud peals of thunder
followed, but no harm ensued. Some days before this, the
Collector of the Customs being in this parish made a seizure
of gin, which being transported to Lerwick and lodged in a
house, the Greenlanders then in the harbour, instigated
by the owners, broke open the door, and carrying it away,
the Collector, attended with other Custom House officers,
came upon them, and stabbed one of them in the thigh,
which obliged them to drop their prey; so hot are people
upon their lusts and idols that they fly in the face of
Government itself and stick at nothing for gain.

August 27th, the Sacrament of the Lord's Supper was
celebrated at Sandwick, which I was obliged to set about
alone, being disappointed of two of the nearest clergymen
who dreamed that I could not do without them, and thereupon turned very saucy, under a groundless pretence that I
showed not such respect to their wives as they deserved. But
like draws to like. They supposed they would get their bellies
stuffed nearer home, and go on with an empty form while
the blind lead the blind, and is the main drift. But blessed
be his worthy name who carried me as well through without
them as with them. My people thought themselves at no loss,
and had more peace in my own mind, as their conversation
was rather nauseous and stumbling than edifying on such
occasions; and though the weather was dark and skies lowering, yet it pleased God so to bind up the clouds that we had

little or no rain all the time that gave the least disturbance
to the people going or coming, or during the sermons etc.
And the Providence of God was the more remarkable that
the roof of the Church was very open and crazy. Soli Deo
Gloria. A young probationer was present who gave me no
assistance, and told me I would kill myself with so much
work, having preached six times and served seven tables. I
replied that, in this event, I would die in a good cause.

September 5. Providence afforded as fine a day as heart
could wish for taking

[2 *lines at bottom of page cut away.*]

*   *   *   *   *

August 9th. My wife showed me a large bone forked at
both ends taken forcibly from a young quea's [quey's] mouth
by a woman nigh the hill, to whom the creature came of its
own accord as if on purpose to seek relief, and the same
woman had saved its life the winter before by helping it out
of a mire, when otherwise it would have perished. Doth God
take care for oxen and queas? Doubtless he does, as here.

October 2nd. I went out to catechise the parish, which was
sooner than ever, on account the crop was sooner got in than
usual. In my way to Bigton (the most remote place from
the Manse) my horse fell down on his nose, which made me
tumble over his head, and my foot being entangled in the
stirrup my heel was crushed by the fall, which yet I felt not
till night, when my wife rubbed it strongly, before the fire,
with rum, and e'en then couldn't set it to the ground without great pain, yet next morning felt none. About 8 days
[afterwards] going out to examine again, my horse stumbled,
and the saddle wanting a [crupper?] threw me again over his
head, and, falling upon my side on hard ground, I felt the
bruise so uneasy that I could scarce ride, sit, or speak with
ease for several days; which yet I concealed from my wife, least
she should take it too much to heart, and hoping, by rubbing
the place affected with a little rum frequently, the pain might
gradually abate; and by applying a softning plaster for severall
weeks, it went off, by the blessing of God, and was effectually
cured.

In November I obtained a life-rent tack of Sumburgh's ten marks land in Skelberry, which lies Rigg and Rendal,[1] (as called) with my glebelands, and which I was constrained to take at 3rd more rent than usual, on account of troublesome neighbours who were become so rude and mischievous, by themselves and wicked children, that I could scarcely get a hen chicken keeped for them, through envy, covetousness, and illnature, and this I did without view of profit, but to live in peace.

December 3rd. 'Twixt four and five in the morning being awake I perceived about 8 flashes of lightning, accompanied mostly with loud peals of thunder which, blessed be His worthy name, did no execution : but nothing is like to awaken this stupid and secure generation.

In January, a large ship, load with masts from Russia for **1776** Liverpool, was driven by a violent gale of wind upon Nesting parish. 'Tis said about 27 men were all drowned, while two boys were saved on the wreck : and, not far from said place, another ship which accompanied the former, and had spent her sails, yet got into a creek, cast anchor, and was saved from wreck.

Jany. 21st. Being keeped back from the north parish for two Sabbaths successively, by reason of stormy weather, this day I ventured thither ; and as the frost was such, and snow so deep that I could not go on horseback, I travelled in boots all the way, and returned at night ; but next day found my leggs so stiff that I could not walk without pain and halting, which continued some days ; but the same weather lengthened to next Sabbath, 28th do. I was enabled to walk and lecture in the Ness Kirk—praise to the Lord ; and though I neglect no opportunity for promoting the people's spiritual good, yet understand there are too many unreasonable and ungrateful wretches among them, that reflect on me for not performing what's above my strength. If such have the form, 'tis all they

---

[1] *Rigg-and-rendal*, or *rig-a-rendal* : the ancient system of *run-rig*, common in Shetland, and in many outlying places in Scotland and Ireland, until comparatively recently.

want; and too common with the generality through the whole countrey, 'who have only a name to live' etc., while the 'blind lead the blind, and both tumble into the ditch.' All sorts seem to be in a deep sleep. May the Lord Himself awaken them in mercy.

February. About the beginning of this month a rudder and mast were driven ashore by a gale of easterly wind below the Manse, supposed to come from a Dutch vessel that had foundered at sea, an anker of Hollands gin being found at same time.

In May, the Custom House yacht came to the countrey, and carried off a smuggling vessel with a considerable quantity of gin, tea, silks etc. But these manifold losses never damps the ardor of these Dutch Merchants. Their motto is—Nothing venture nothing have.

The rebellion which kindled in our American Colonies about a year ago at length broke out into a flame in June last, when 1400 were slain 'tis said on both sides, and still goes on.[1] The Disposer of all events knows what will be the issue. They say they will rather die sword in hand than submit to Slavery, which such a good King and Government never intended, but only wanted they should pay their equal proportion of taxes with fellow-subjects, and therefore may justly meet with that slavery they so groundlessly dreaded. In midst of this awful judgment we read that some of their ringleaders are marrying and giving in marriage. O the woful security and stupidity of mankind. Luxury and wickedness occasion of all.

June 14th. 'Twixt six and seven in the morning, while in bed, we were a little startled with a loud clap of thunder, which was repeated with lightnings for some time after, which is usual here only during the winter season, when it broke into the house of one in this parish who was reputed a thief; and though he and wife etc. narrowly escaped, when it suddenly went from the fireside where they were sitting and broke up some chests in the other end of the house, damaged their cloathes and killed severals of their cattle in the byre, yet he was so stupid and

---

[1] This apparently alludes to the battle of Bunker's Hill, June 17, 1775.

insensible of a preserving Providence that his only concern was by an application to the Kirk session for money to make up his loss, though contrary to his wife's inclinations. The lightning broke also into other parishes, as in Bressay, Wharff[1] etc. and did some damage; yet neither word nor rod serves to awaken this secure generation.

Said month George Tocher, a Merchant from Aberdeen, came to establish a correspondence for traffick with this countrey, and carried along a box of an hundred copies of the Catholic Church to sell in the north.[2]

August 25th. The Sacrament of the Lord's Supper was dispensed at Ness Kirk before a crowded auditory, but alas! little visible good effects appear.

At same time we had accounts that General Carleton had beat the rebel Americans from Quebeck, killed their General Montgomery, and about 600 were slain and taken prisoners, and driven them out of the Province. 31,000 forces are sent over, which may occasion a vast expense of blood and treasure. A Government ship came here to recruit men.

In October 14, I set out for examination of the north parish, where gross ignorance and wickedness abound, notwithstanding all the pains taken on them, which shews that nothing will effectually polish the rugged nature of man except divine grace. In the beginning of this month, I had accounts of the death of my nephew, William Farquhar, Captain of a stout Jamaica Merchant ship, who had his scull fractured by a fall from an horse in Jamaica, and proved his death etc.

In November, we had accounts of a vessel that went from this countrey, Captain Bunthorn from Leith Commander, having on board Mr. Mcpherson a Merchant with wife and two children; also Mr. Lyons[3] a Merchant in Lerwick, who left behind a wife and eleven children; that she was wrecked on the coast of Bremen, and all on board perished. Soon after in December a large Danish ship and two Dutch vessels were

---

[1] Wharff: the parish of Quarff (Old Northern *Hvarf*).

[2] This carefulness about the book was a prelude to Tocher's designs upon the minister's daughter, as will afterwards appear.

[3] Matthias Lyons, a well-known shopkeeper, or 'Merchant,' of the time.

wrecked on this isle, the same night that one Captain Lesslie from this parish was on the coast on his return from Hamburgh, yet wonderfully preserved and came safe into harbour after a violent gale of easterly wind, whereby some commissions for family necessaries came safe to hand; and I desire to bless and thank a good and gracious God, that I never lost any of my commissions, though have often been cheated by rogues, and never found but one honest man among these tarrs and merchants.

This month I had a letter from the Sheriff enclosing the King's proclamation for a day of Fasting and Prayer the 12th Dec. on account of the Rebellion of our Colonists in North America. But as the Parish could not be advertised so as to keep that day, the Thursday following was observed in this parish. I preached from Isaiah 58 and 6th. The day was stormy, yet a good many attended; and Sabbath I preached again on same text. During the application, a young man before the pulpit broke out with a strong cry as if he had been stabbed at the heart, which set the people a-staring; but know not if attended with any saving effects; and O! that it might prove a prelude to God's shooting his arrows into the hearts of his enemies, and making them cry out— 'What shall I do to be saved?' etc.

I understood that Sumburgh and William Bruce, brother of Symbister, being in the North Parish, had sent through the people there to fast on the day appointed by the King before the people in Dunrossness had notice of it. What they meant by this step I know not; but it seemed to flow from the enmity of the old serpent's seed, who must be always nibling at what belongs not to them, though they get nothing but broken heads for their pains.

Two battles have been fought with the rebels this season, one in Long Island, where 3300 of them were killed and seven thousand more near New York. Montgomery, one of their Generals, was slain at Quebeck siege, with 600 men, and 'tis said General Washington, another of them, had lost an arm in last battle nigh the city of New York. Thus, first and last, about 12,000 and upwards are slain already, besides some 1000 of King's troops.

January. The 65th of my age and 34th of my ministry.   **1777**
May I be enabled by grace to spend precious time better than
ever, and to hold out and on to the end, faithful to death,
though Israel be not gathered ; yet it is the desire of my soul
to gain souls to Christ ; nor would I wish to live any longer
here than to promote his glory on earth etc. I can't but reflect
with pleasure and wonder on the all wise providence of a gracious
God to his poor people, as many times I have experienced ;
even in what seemed at first against me I found afterwards
was working for my good, not only temporal, but spiritual
and eternal. When two tennants of Symbister's wanted land
in tack from me, he used both threatenings and promises, and
thereby got them prevailed on to stay on his lands, but soon
after another tenant falling in arrears to him, was turned
off and engaged in my service, at a very proper season, when
the man who laboured my glebe failed and gave it up ; and
'tis likewise remarkable that two tennants more providentially cast up, who seem all preferable to the former, and to
answer my purpose better. And as I determined to leave
this affair to the conduct of an all wise Providence was not
disappointed, as I have often been when left to my own
conduct.

In June, a son of Mr. James Spence in Mid Yell, while
attending the school at Sumburgh,[1] went off alone, though only
about 7 or 8 years old, and climbing the rocks in Sumburgh
Head for bird's nests and slipping his hold, tumbled into
the sea below, and couldn't be found, carried off it seemed
by the tide ; and as this fell out on the Sabbath day might
serve for warning both to young and old, especially to that
family, where little regard is paid to the Sabbath or Gospel
ordinances.

In the end of October last, after my return from catechising
the North Parish I was seized with a vehement itching in my
neck and thighs, occasioned by a hot watery humour in the

---

[1] The unfortunate boy had probably the benefit of a tutor resident at
Sumburgh. There is little likelihood of a ' school' having been there.

D

blood, which was very disagreeable and uneasy, and continued
for eight months, resembling Paul's thorn in the flesh, in
which sense I took it as designed by a good and gracious
Father in Christ Jesus, to teach humility, to guard against
spiritual pride, to wean from the flesh, and put me in mind
of mortality, when this vile body shall soon be a prey to
vermin and be crumbled into dust. It pleased God to remove
this trouble as suddenly as it was brought on, by means of
a purging, being much subject to a constipation, through a
natural heat of the body.

Mr. Mitchell, minister at Tingwall, having told in the
Presbytery that Mr. James Finlayson, minister at Sandsting,
had cried out in his congregation at a Sacrament occasion
—Away with that false doctrine of original sin, Messieurs
Mair, Minister at Bressay, and Sands, Minister at Lerwick,
were present, and heard the same; and when I threatened a
prosecution, Mr. Mair said he would join me, and yet when
I petitioned the Presbytery at this June meeting, to call
him to their barr, these three denied they heard such expression, and Mr. Sands said he cried only—Away with all false
teachers—which greatly surprised me to find any, especially
men of their character, so double and deceitful, so great a
scandal and disgrace to their function, that I would be loath
to admit people of such dispositions to a Sacrament or to the
office of a lay elder. As there were none present save these
three and the Clerk, they seemed to have all connived together to prevent a rebuke, which was all I intended at present,
to guard against the spreading of such infectious doctrine;
which emboldened the criminal to turn the chase, and threaten
to prosecute me as a slanderer, which did no way intimi-
date me; for had he made such an attempt, I should
not only have insisted for these corrupt clergy being put
on oath, but many of the most sensible in Tingwall parish
etc.

In July, the people being apprised that the Government
had sent over a tender, with a demand of an hundred men
for their service, they fled from their houses and betook themselves to their hills and skulking places, which made me take
notice of this on the Sabbath from the pulpit, saying they made

great haste in running away for fear of the Pressgang,[1] who did not want to hang them or put them in prison, but only to serve their King and Countrey in the suppression of Rebells in America, who had risen up against their lawful superiors without any just grounds, and might be better employed for a year or two than at home; for when the rebellion was over, they might return again with their pockets full of money; and O! that they were as eager in fleeing from the wrath of a Sin avenging God, to the blood of sprinkling for pardon and cleansing etc.

August 31st. The Sacrament of the Lord's Supper was celebrated as usual about this time as most convenient for the parish. There were between 500 and 600 communicants at seven tables; each table holds about 80. People attend well, but alas with little life, or heat in the affections through great restraint of the Spirit's operations.

In September we were alarmed with American privateers[2] being on the coast, and had taken two Greenlanders etc. The inhabitants of Lerwick were afraid of their coming into Bressay Sound and burning their town. A large three-masted vessel from Archangel came into Quendal bay, Sabbath morning, the 21st, in darkness, and fired several guns not knowing where they were, and threw anchor, but no boats could board her by reason of the height of wind and sea; she run a risk of being wrecked. She was bound for London.

October 7th. The rainy season keeped the corns long green, and 'tis rare to find a dry day from morning to night; and while severals are talking of their hay being rotten and useless, and we dreaded the loss of ours, it was taken in this day in pretty good plight beyond expectation, praise to His

---

[1] Many Shetlanders were seized by the pressgang at this time, and up to near the close of the French wars, in the early years of the century. Many stories are told of escapes from pursuit, and of the hiding-places used.

[2] Privateers: private ships, armed with *lettres de marque*, were at this time recognised in the European and American wars, and made great havoc among merchant shipping. Several Shetlanders, it has been stated, attained to eminence in this questionable line of glory, but the facts have never been sufficiently authenticated.

worthy name, for all his undeserved favours. The bear [bere] is all cut down, and upwards of 15 thrave[1] of oats, when few have come that length, the heavens still lowering and threatening: but O how is mercy mixed with judgment when all was in danger of being lost.

October 13th. The hay stack gathered heat through the carelessness of a servant who had thrown in wet hay mixed with the dry, and occasioned a vehement smoak, which obliged me to cause pull it down forthwith, and put it again in small screws,[2] which, to great astonishment, recovered in four days' time, and was re-stacked upon the 18th day, the driest and best day we have got this harvest, as severals observed; the corns cutt down and mostly taken in, wherefore I intend to go out to catechising work in the parish upon the 20th inst.

November 20th. My daughter Nell, the eldest, was married at Culleaster,[3] by the minister of Lerwick, to George Tocher, Merchant in Aberdeen, contrary to my inclinations. He came here under a pretence of settling a correspondence for traffick with this countrey, June 1776. It appeared they had then been mutually engaged, and were carrying on a secret correspondence by letters, and she had the impudence to desire him to come over at this dangerous season to be joined to her in marriage; and no means essayed could dissuade them from it, which made me passive in the affair, as there seemed to be a hand of Providence in it; and though he could afford her no settlement for life, yet as he appears to be a Sincere Christian I was afraid she might do worse. ~~She was too forward in drawing up with young men~~ [*erased, but legible*]. The late storms have brought several wrecks on this parish.

December 5th. The second packet sailed with the married couple as passengers; they had fine weather. Captain Robinson, a smuggler from Gottenburgh, sold quantities of tea; but the

---

[1] *Thrave* : Old Northern *Threfi*, 24 sheaves.

[2] In the native tongue *Skru* is the term for a stack, or rick, of corn or hay. Icelandic, or Old Northern, *Skruf*, the same. The word occurs as early as in the *Edda*.

[3] Culleaster, in the parish of Sandwick. The marriage did not take place in her father's house, but at a place five to seven miles distant.

Custom Officers were afraid to board him. He went from Levenwick to Walls. Received accounts of the arrival of a vessel from Hamburgh with whom our Commission for house necessaries were sent, notwithstanding of being endangered by a storm and privateers; and desire to bless a kind Providence, that I never yet lost anything in this way. An awful Providence befell a daughter of Symburgh's by an old stupid man thrusting a knife in her eye, that is like to deprive her of the sight of it, which put Sumburgh into such a rage that he stabbed the man in the breast with a knife, but not mortally.

January 1st. Our days are as an handbreadth and years are **1778** as nothing before thee. Man at his best estate is altogether Vanity etc. O! to be helped to improve precious time and talents better than ever, that when the last period of life comes I may be enabled, through grace, to give up my accounts with joy and not with grief. And O! that God would be pleased to smile upon my poor labours and endeavours, that I may see or hear of the travail of Christ's soul in the conversion of poor sinners to God, which my very heart is set upon, and nothing in time would afford greater joy.

Jan. 24. Three men in Cunningsburgh with Sumburgh's clerk and a boy in crossing Clift Sound [1] were so infatuated as to come upon a point that lay out a little from the shore at Sandsere,[2] and a lump of sea arising overset the boat and all were drowned. On Sabbath, the day following, a boy came into the Church during sermon, and called out several men to take up their corpses then driven ashore—'tis said they had been drunk. A little before, a Scotch vessel from Riga loaden with flax and lint-seed was stranded at Cunningsburgh, but the crew were saved.

---

[1] Cliftsound : the sea on the east side of the Clifts of Cunningsburgh. Cliftsound proper is on the west side of the country, between Cunningsburgh and Burra Isle.

[2] Sandsere, or Sands Ayre : the *beach* at *Sand* (Icelandic, *Sands Eyrr*).

In Feb. several vessels came from the south with meal and potatoes very seasonably for supply of Lerwick and the countrey, that were in great straits. The King's proclamation for a General Fast to be keeped on Feb. 26 was read from the Pulpit Sabbath preceding, for averting God's wrath and imploring his blessing on our arms for subduing the American Rebells who had taken General Burgoyn and some 1000ˢ of our men prisoners of war.[1]

In March, the nation was in a great fermentation and unanimous in order to prosecute the war with vigour by raising men and money. City and Counties vied with one another for suppressing the rebellion. In April, we were alarmed with war from France, and numbers were raised in this countrey for sea and land service, who went more readily because of the dearth, the victual being at 3s. 6d. per lispund, and sin the cause of all.

In April my wife was suddenly seized with a violent asthma that threatened a dissolution, which obliged me to run an express for the doctor, and my sister to Lerwick. When my sister came, she was suddenly seized with a stitch etc. that threatened death. So uncertain are all things here. Life and death depend entirely on his sovereign will and pleasure. By the divine blessing on the use of means, they both recovered, when Mrs. Hunter of Lunna that was younger & stronger was suddenly cut off.

In May though 'tis said upwards of 6000 bolls of victual were come (It took as much more to supply the countrey, and cost 8000 Libs. Ster.) to the countrey, yet still needed more, though it rose higher in the price.[2] In Fair Isle they had none till a boat was sent to Lerwick, and

---

[1] The battle of Saratoga, on 17th October 1777, in which General Burgoyne was compelled to capitulate, with the loss of his whole army, 5000 muskets, and a large train of artillery.

[2] The scarcity in the Islands, and consequent suffering, seem at this time to have been really great. On the 6th of August 'the lamentable state of the poor in this year of great Dearth and Scarcity' was taken into the 'serious consideration' of the Kirk-session of Dunrossness, who did their utmost to mitigate the distress.

before it came to the isle one man was found dead for want, (or rather some other disease—*interlined*). Wickedness abounded there also; 'tis said Brough[1] the proprietor brought in a strumpet who set him up against the best people of the isle, for discountenancing their wickedness, which prompted him to give them warnings for removal:—the Sabbath was profaned, the Kirk fallen. Shall I not visit for these things etc. The whole creation groans. Horses, cattle etc. were dying fast through the countrey through scarcity and badness of the fodder. I suffered in the common calamity—two horse beasts and 9 cattle, and two of these milch cows near calving; yet, blessed be His great name who mixes mercy with judgment, they were soon supplied by purchase of three cows and two pretty young staggs.[2]

In August, we had accounts of a running naval fight of one of our squadrons under Admiral Keppel with a French squadron off Brest[3]—is of little consequence, though we got the better of them. Commissioners sent to the Congress in America with proposals of peace—Re Infecta. Severe claps of thunder, with strong flashes of lightnings, were here in the nighttime.

October. We had a sett of fine weather, which ripened the corn well, and all was got in safe, and in good condition beyond expectation, for a severe storm of wind that blasted some and threatened the whole preceded the harvest; but the Lord was pleased to mix mercy with judgment and disappointed our fears; otherwise [we] had been in a worse situation than last season, and numbers in the Countrey would probably have perished by famine. O! that men would praise the Lord for His goodness etc.

November. The packet brings accounts that the war with

---

[1] Stewart of Brough in Orkney, then proprietor of the Fair Isle. On the death of the last of that family, the island was purchased, in 1866, by the present Mr. Bruce of Sumburgh.
[2] Stagg, or Staig, a young horse.
[3] This was the unfortunate engagement of the 12th of July, which led to the trial of Admiral Keppel, in which, however, he was acquitted.

France and America goes on, and 20,000 Russians and 20 sail of the line of battle are expected in the Downs by the end of January from Russia to assist Gt. Brittain.

N.B. A fine young horse of the Norway breed had perished in a marsh, had it not been discovered in the daytime, and seasonably rescued, and the mercy was more remarkable as none I had fitted my wife so well for riding. A Danish ship from Iceland wrecked on Whalsey isle; the cargo of tallow, hides etc. was lost, but the crew saved. I was called to assist at the Sacrament of the Lord's Supper in September at Lerwick, and one Miss Eliz. Grierson, one of the most accomplished and virtuous young ladies in the countrey, was a communicant there. Her wedding was soon after fixed, preparations made for it, and about the same time she was suddenly cutt off, and the provisions served for the funeral—an awful warning to those of her sex whose daft heads are soon laid in the dust.

1779   In Jan. and Feb. All the principal cities and corporations of Scotland finding a Bill had taken place in England and Irland with little or no opposition, and an Act of Parliament passed for the repeal of the penal statutes against Papists, whereby they are put on an equal footing with Protestants for purchasing land and educating of youth, which may endanger the nation's liberties and priviledges sacred and civil ; therefore harmoniously concurred in opposing to the utmost of their power any such Act being passed in Parliament in reference to Scotland, which is a token for good. The Americans are said to be 60 millions ster. in debt, and are so mad as to make over their lands and trade to France ; the Virginias to send 20,000 hoggsheads Tobacco at $6\frac{1}{4}^{d}$, rather than submitt to Brittain, though 'tis said several provinces are repenting of their folly, and that the Carolinas and Georgia are willing to be reconciled to the mother countrey ; however the war with them and France is like to go on with more vigour than ever, and time will discover the event. The will of the Lord be done. Sin is the cause of all mischief. The King's proclamation for a fast, February 9th, will avail little, unless there is true repentance evidenced by thorough reformation of heart and life among all ranks, whereof little appears etc. We had accounts in March that the Popish Bill was thrown out and quashed.

July 2nd. I repaired to the Fair Isle, where I preached two Sabbath days successively, joined two pairs in marriage, baptized 5 children, and rebuked two couples for ante-nuptial fornication, publickly, and several others for Sabbath profanation, for which reason I read from the pulpit the present King George the 3rd's proclamation against profanity and immorality. God had blasted their crops for the two preceding years, yet did they not return to Him. Severals of the best Christians in the Isle had left it, and therefore had not freedom to celebrate the Sacrament of the Lord's Supper among them as formerly I was wont to do. I found a considerable decrease of the number of inhabitants: four families were ruined, their houses lying desolate, and three of the heads thereof were drowned carrying into the isle supplys for their families. I returned July 14th and found my family in their ordinary—praise to His worthy name who also afforded good weather for passage; though in my return under the isle, a blast of wind filled the boat's sail, whereby the mast was like to give way, and made one cry out of returning back; yet, having bound an oar to the place affected, they ventured forward, and it pleased a good God to grant fair and easy weather all the way to our designed landingplace. Soli Deo Gloria.

In Septr. 3 or 4 large ships were seen off Bressay Sound, which had two sloops in tow, which they had taken in their way from Leith to Lerwick, which put the inhabitants of Lerwick in a great consternation. They were said to be one of 50, another of 40, and a 3rd of 30 guns. One of these sloops broke loose in a storm of wind, and came into Bressay Sound, having two Americans and two Frenchmen on board, which a cutter's crew who was then in Bressay Sound enlisting men here for the service of Government, seized, as also the crew of an American merchantman loaded with tobacco and Loggwood, who had stranded on the island of Burray during the storm foresaid. We had the finest crops here ever known, and got in mostly by the 20th of this month. Thus Providence mixes mercy with judgment.

As the Spainyards joined with France in the war, they appeared, 'tis said, before Portsmouth, with 100 sail of their combined fleet, 60 whereof were of the line of battle. But upon Sir Charles Hardy's appearing with one of our squadrons of 30 sail of the line, they fled speedily off for the coast of France, where Admiral Keppel had a skirmish with the Brest fleet, but as he did not renew the fight, was tried but honourably acquitted, as the French veered off, and fled into their harbours.[1]

Sir William How [Howe] was blamed for not prosecuting the war with vigour against the rebellious Colonies in N. America, and General Clinton got the command there.

One Paul Jones,[2] son to a gardiner of the Earl of Galloway's,[3] a wicked desperado, whom the American Congress entrusted with the command of the above 4 ships of war, took two of our small ships of war, and carried them into Holland, which the states refused to deliver up and was like to breed war in Holland. The combined fleets threatened Brittain or Irland with an invasion, but they are prepared to receive them, and are still augmenting our fleets. But may we never trust to the arm of flesh. Gibraltar is besieged, and the Spaniards repulsed. The French have taken Grenada and St. Vincent, West India isles, and used our people badly, which may be retaliated upon themselves.

The Popish ruffians in Irland, called the ' White Boys '[4]

---

[1] There seems to be some confusion between this story and the action under Admiral Keppel in the previous year, 1778, already referred to.

[2] John Paul Jones. Born at Arbigland, in the Stewartry of Kirkcudbright, on 6th July 1747. He went to sea, and, settling in Virginia, embraced the cause of the Colonies, and got the command of a brig of 18 guns, with which he visited the coasts of Scotland, and performed some bold exploits. In 1779 he received the command of a small squadron of French ships, under American colours, which caused consternation on the British coasts. Mill here corroborates the story that he appeared off the east coast of Shetland, but was driven off by a gale, as on the memorable occasion of his visit this same year, 1779, to the Firth of Forth.

[3] This should be the Earl of Selkirk, not Galloway.

[4] White Boys : an illegal association of Irish peasants, originally organised in the county of Tipperary, early in the reign of George III. Professing to aim at the redress of grievances, they committed many cruel outrages, until the movement was suppressed, only, however, to reappear in other forms. They wore white shirts in their expeditions, which, like those of their successors, the ' Moonlighters ' of the present day, were usually by night.

being cloathed with a white jacket, have frequent insurrections.
A Popish Priest at their head offered £5 Ster. for the head of
a Protestant, which obliged the Protestants to raise themselves
into Judgment Companies, to the number about 50,000, seized
on the villanous Priest to be tried for life, and killed several
of these Banditti.[1]

Jan. Though the French trade is mostly ruined by our   **1780**
privateers, and there has been frequent skirmishes by sea, and
also by land in America, yet no decisive action. The war continues, the nation is burdened with taxes and Publick Debt
still increasing to 200 mill. ster.

A large Danish ship from Irland, bound for Christian Sand,
stranded on Vehementrie,[2] a small isle on the west part of this
countrey, was plundered by the country people of Linen, Butter
etc. for which they were imprisoned at Lerwick etc.[3]

In March we received accounts that the Irish had obtained
a free trade to the West Indies and Africa.[4] Count Lestrange
the French Admiral made an attack upon Savannah in Georgia,
joined with General Lincoln and 3000 of the rebells ; but was
repulsed and wounded with the loss, 'tis said, of 2000 men,
chiefly owing, under Providence, to the timeous succour of
Colonel Maitland,[5] (grandchild of James, Earl of Seafield, last
Chancellor of Scotland) with 800 men to the garrison commanded by General Prevost. A strong Spanish fort at Hon-
duras Bay was stormed and taken by Capt. Dalrymple. 'Tis
said affairs wear a better aspect for government in America etc.

---

[1] This is wild rumour rather than sober history.

[2] Vementry, parish of Aithsting, west side of Shetland.

[3] As is well known, a wrecked ship was by some regarded as a gift of Providence. The prayer, not that a ship should be wrecked, but that, if a wreck
should take place, the Almighty would be pleased to send it to the poor isle
of ——, if not verified as an actual and literal address to Deity, is yet entirely
in the spirit and feeling prevalent for long in these islands, as in other remote
districts.

[4] This was prior to the Act of Union, while there were still restrictions on
Irish trade.

[5] This is the Colonel Maitland whose great-grandson lately succeeded to the
Earldom of Lauderdale, on the death of his remote kinsman the late Earl of
Lauderdale, who was killed by lightning in 1884.

than they have done since the commencement of Hostilities. A general fast, by publick authority, was observed through Brittain in February last, when I preached upon text Matthew xii. and 25th—' A kingdom divided against itself is brought to desolation,' which may Heaven in mercy prevent. to our nation, though our sins deserve it.

Sir George Rodney, with 18 ships of war, attacked 11 ships of the line commanded by Don Juan de Langara near the Spanish coast, Jan. 16, took five of 72 guns, sunk one and another took fire, and blew up with powder.[1]

July 16. I received the best news I have heard of a long time, that my youngest daughter Bell was under deep convictions of Sin, both original and actual, and as attended with several hainous aggravations.   May the Lord of his infinite mercy for Christ Jesus his sake, bring this law work to a happy issue in his good time, that she may glorify His great name in time and through Eternity, Amen.   I was afraid that these convictions would wear off, which alas, seems to be the case, as no good effects yet appear.

In Oct.   A Russian frigate was wrecked on an Holm [2] nigh Whalsey, and 'tis said that of 180 souls on board, only 5 were saved, who were sent off for Hamburgh.   'Tis said also that the Spanish Colonies have rebelled against that government and set up a King of their own.

In Aug.   The Sacrament of the Lord's Supper was celebrated at Sandwick.   I had the promise of an assistant, who was suddenly seized with a violent cold and hoarseness that he fail'd, but blessed be His worthy name who enabled me notwithstanding to go through with the work, preaching all the day, and serving seven tables.   A few days after, I was called to assist in the same work at Lerwick, and in October catechised Sandwick Parish.

In Nov. we had accounts that the French had landed 6000 men in New England to assist the rebells, and that they proposed

---

[1] This defeat of Langara's fleet, off Cape St. Vincent, was one of the most gallant of Admiral Rodney's exploits.

[2] *Holm* : a small outlying islet.

to send over 20,000 more with a view to regain Canada, and
that Brittain was sending over 10,000 men to oppose their
designs. Lord Cornwallis gained a complete victory over a
rebel army commanded by General Gates of 7000, though he
had only about 1700 men, took all their cannon, baggage, and
many prisoners.

The President of the Congress was taken on his way to
Holland for obtaining a loan of £600,000 Ster. Said Mr.
Laurens wanted to be treated as an Ambassador from the
American States, but was sent to the Tower, where Lord
George Gordon, brother to the Duke of Gordon,[1] is also confined for heading a mob at London, who wanted to have the
acts against Popery repon'd, and had insulted the members of
Parliament in both houses, and done great mischief, by burning houses and Popish Chappels to the value, 'tis said, of a
million sterling, prompted thereto, as supposed, by the emissaries of France, as severals who were shot in the squabble were
found to be Papists with French gold in their pockets. Many
of the ringleaders were executed, both of men and women.

About the latter end of 1779 we had accounts that two of
my wife's sisters' Husbands, Messieurs Bowie and Polson, were
called off the stage. As Mr. Bowie was a man of a Christian
and publick spirit, and managed my little affairs at Edinburgh,
I was at a loss where to find such a trusty person to succeed
him ; but blessed be His worthy name who soon directed to
one of the same name, Ralph Bowie Esq. a gentleman of an
excellent character, a writer in Edinburgh, and equally qualified, who undertook that business, my first wife's portion being
in dependence, by the final settlement of Bailie Thompson's
affairs, and £200 ster. my wife's present portion, settled on
H. Ford's estate, who had given way, also in danger.

As the Society for propagating Christian Knowledge
threatened to deprive my parish of both their schools, unless a
legal School was established according to law, and had actually
scored them out of the yearly scheme sent to Presbytery, if I

---

[1] Lord George Gordon. Born in 1750. Son of Cosmo George, Duke of
Gordon. The great riots here referred to led to his Lordship's arrest, but he was
acquitted of the charge of treason. He was afterwards committed to Newgate
on other charges, and died there in 1793.

had not timeously sent up two young men to be examined by
them in order to continue them in said station, which they
were pleased to do, notwithstanding my Chief Heritors were
very refractory, though they had been often importuned to set
about this business; and when I obtained their consent, and
was desired to draw up an obligation to this effect, they
boggled at subscribing the same, because I proposed they
should pay the one half, and the people the other; and though
I told them the people would rather pay the whole than the
Parish should be wholly deprived of Schools, being only one
penny ster. upon a mark of land, yet are still so unreasonable
as to stand out.

'Tis said the Americans begin to see their error. General
Henhold has forsaken them, and is raising two regiments for
Government service, and that the French are blocked up in
Rhod Island by Admiral Arbuthnot.

1781   January. O! to be running the Christian race heavenward,
as time passeth. The face of publick affairs still wears a gloomy
aspect. 'Tis said (New Gazette) that the next campaign in
America is like to be the most bloody that has yet been since
the rebellion there commenced, as the French, our inveterate
enemies, are threatning to pour in many thousands of their
troops there for assistance. One Trumble, son to the rebell
Governor of Connecticut province, was found in London, carrying on a secret correspondence with the rebells, in conjunction
with one Tyler, and another called Temple, the worst of the
three, who pretended to be a refugee from the Congress, and
had been employed and rewarded by the Government while he
was acting underhand against the same. Trumble is closely
confined; the other two made their escape, but narrow search
is making for them.

In Feb. by an armed cutter that came to Bressay Sound, we
heard accounts that Brittain proclaimed war against Holland
Dec. 22nd, and had taken 700 of their merchant ships since;
and that Jamaica and most of the Caribbec Islands had their
sugar canes etc. destroyed by a Hurricane, an earthquake
following thereon, with many thousands of lives and ships lost;

yet may truly be said of this blind, secure, and sottish generation 'For all this ye have not returned to me, saith the Lord.
Therefore his anger is not turned away, but his hand is stretched
out still.'

In March a fast was keep'd here on account of the War, by
the King's proclamation, as it had been in Scotland, Feb. 22nd,
and was very proper likewise on account of a pestilential fever
that carried off severals, men and women, young and old,
through the whole ministry, and still continues. O! that the
Lord would pour out a spirit of prayer and supplication,
repentance and reformation of heart and life, that he may be
pleased in mercy to return and restore peace and health to our
land etc. Lord George Gordon was tried, before the Court of
King's Bench last month, for high treason, as heading the
mob foresaid, but was honourably acquitted by a jury and
dismissed.

270 soldiers etc. of the Earl of Sutherland's regiment were
sent to Lerwick by Government,[1] under the command of a
Major, 3 Captains, 4 lieutenants and 7 Ensigns, with 12 guns,
for erecting batteries etc. to keep off the Dutch etc. Eustatia
Isle in West India is taken by Admiral Rodney, with 150 ships,
and 2½ millions of money.

April. A Greenlander took a stout French Privateer, and
brought her into Bressay Sound. Another of the same kind
was taken off Fair Isle by one of our frigates. The French
were so scurvy as to strip the Fair Isle people of the caps on
their heads and other things in the boat. They were brought
to Bressay Sound, and swimming ashore in the nighttime, got
in boats to a sloop in the bay, and while they were cutting the
cable in order to go off with her, the master awaking alarmed
the guard, which prevented their escape. The soldiers are
making a broad road above Lerwick for an easy communication
'twixt the north and south batteries.

---

[1] This is perhaps the only authentic statement in existence of the military
equipment of the Lerwick garrison at this time. The fort, originally erected,
it is said, during the Commonwealth, was repaired and completed at this time,
and named Fort Charlotte after the Queen of the reigning sovereign, George III.

June 11th. A Squadron of warships is cruizing on this coast for the Dutch East or West India ships. Such a long-continued drought without any rain, was not seen here in the memory of man. 'Tis judgment like.

July. Three of the Dutch E. India ships being informed of their danger on this coast by a French Privateer off the Western Isles, changed their course and stood for Norway, whereof the Berwick, of 74 guns etc. having notice, went for that coast. The Packet was taken in her way to Leith, and ransomed, 'tis said, for 500 Libs. Ster. and that one of our frigates took that Privateer of 20 guns after an obstinate fight of several hours on the Orkney coast, and carried her into Kirkwall Roads.

Sep. 19. Received accounts of the Berwick Ship of war foresaid. In an engagement with some Dutch war ships, who were conveying a fleet for the West Indies, [she] had lost 70 men and as many wounded. Mr. Farquhar, my sister's husband, being pilot on this coast, had left her some weeks before, and where he had gone for high wages and good entertainment, there he got his death-stroke, being seized with the jaundice owing to bad water, which soon cutt him off, and this day I am called to attend his funerals at Lerwick.

In said engagement, Aug. 5th, Admiral Parker, with 7 war ships, engaged the Dutch Admiral Zoutmann with a superior number, qrof 'tis said 4 were sunk and the remainder, with the merchant ships, obliged to return home and our war ships were so shattered that they went for England to be repaired; yet both claimed the victory etc.[1]

Dec. There's no prospect of peace—rather fresh preparations for continuing the war. 'Tis said 30 millions ster. are to be raised for the ensuing year's expenses for sending more ships and men against the French, Spaniards, and rebells in America. Yet the nation in general seems to remain secure and senseless under all frowning dispensations of Providence.

---

[1] This was the desperate engagement off the Dogger-bank. After a cannonade of 3½ hours both fleets lay like logs in the water, unable to prolong the fight or do mutual injury. The Dutch bore away to the Texel, losing one of their largest ships, which sank.

May the Lord awaken all ranks in mercy to a deep sense of sin and guilt, with their fearful aggravations, and stir up many to sigh and cry for the abominations of the land, that He may repent of the evils we deserve, return again to us with his wonted favour and leave a blessing behind Him etc.

Jan. One of the hairy Comets, so called, appeared here after **1782** sunset, about the bigness of Venus, on the 22nd of last month, sending forth sprays of light from its disk ; and next night it appeared as bigg as Jupiter. Afterwards seemed less to the 8th of Jany. when it appeared as bigg as Jupiter again, more high and westward, and then disappeared by cloudy weather.

Jan. 13. An English 3 masted vessel load with timber, 'tis said, was stranded said night, nigh St. Ringand's Isle, and none saved of 15 but the mate and 3 more sailors, by a warp. The wreck drove to Burray. Upon the 20th and 21st said comet appeared again more large and bright than formerly. The vessel foresaid came from Dantsick and belonged to Liverpool ; and though the mate called Seabroke would speak to none till on his knees he prayed to God openlie giving God thanks for so signal a deliverance, yet soon forgot it, and gave himself to his bottle etc. and the Captain, 'tis said, perished drunk. Though a fast was enjoyned by Government to be keeped through the Kingdom on the 7th of Feb. yet alas little reformation of heart or life appears. Luxery and sensuality, plays and comedies, are hotly pursued, and hence ensues numerous sales of lands, houses, and bankrupcies. The Island of Eustatia retaken, through the security of Governor Colonel Cockburn, by the Marquis de Bowville, Governor of Martinica, tho' they had in the garrison 677 men with 60 cannon.

General Cornwallis, with 3000 men, taken prisoners by the French and Americans,[1] and no appearance of peace with God or man.

---

[1] This disastrous capitulation occurred at Yorktown, where 7000 men were surrendered, in the month of October 1781, after a three weeks' investment. It was the decisive engagement, and virtually terminated hostilities. Negotiations for peace followed, and the independence of the American Colonies was acknowledged in 1783.

E

In March the Comet foresaid appeared more westerly and declined gradually towards the horizon, and after 3 months' continuance or thereby it disappeared. Such another is said to have appeared in Nov. 1555, called the fiery Besome, for 3 months, and a strange fire descending, as from Heaven, upon the Border, and consumed a deal of corns on each side the Tweed, but most in England, and that warrs ensued etc.

In May, we had accounts of a hot engagement 'twixt Admirals Rodney, Hood and Drake, with the French fleet in the West Indies, commanded by Count de Grass,[1] with about 40 ships of war on each side, which lasted from morning to sunset, about 11½ hours, when 5 line of battle ships of the enemy were taken and one sunk, among which was the Admiral and his ship of 110 guns. In the East Indies, Admiral Hughs took Ceylon, their chief fortress, from the Dutch, and two East India ships, loaden with spiceries from Batavia, and valued at 400,000 £ Ster. and the King of Candy offered to joyn the English for expelling the Dutch out of Ceylon. 'Tis said also that Admiral How[2] was in quest of a Dutch squadron in the North Seas, who were cruising off this coast to protect their East India ships in their returning.

In the beginning of June, the Hairy Comet above mentioned appeared again after sunset, about a due south.

About the end of said month the Packet brought accounts that Admiral Rodney had taken and destroyed 11 sail of the line, and had two French Admirals his prisoners and killed 15,000 of their men ; also that he had retaken St Kitts, with a fleet of ships, arms, ammunition etc. ready to land there, with men of war, their convoys. 'Tis said General Clinton has come over with proposals of peace, and the Congress want to have their Government put on the same footing with Irland, by having a Lord Lieutenant and Parliament.

---

[1] Engagement with De Grasse. Rodney is said to have had thirty-six ships of the line, De Grasse forty-four. De Grasse's ship was believed to be the largest that had ever been built in Europe.

[2] Admiral How: Richard Earl Howe. He died in 1799, after very distinguished service.

There's a strange distemper called Influenza[1] rages through Brittain, in the same manner as it did in the east countries of Russia, Denmark etc. though as yet has not proved so mortal. People are variously affected with it, with swelled faces, sore throats, breasts and stomachs, dizzy heads, coughs, violent pains and feverishness; for remedy is prescribed a decoction of 2 oz. lint-seed, 2 do. of Liquorish-stick bruised and boiled over a slow fire in a pint water to half do. then strained and mixed with 4 oz. powdered suggar candy, also some lemon juice, brandy or rum; take frequently a spoonfull thereoff etc.

July 12. I received the sad news of my sister Elizabeth's sudden death. My father left 8 of us, on a kind and gracious God, who provided well for us all and his relict also. The eldest son James died soon after birth, before my father. There were two sons and two daughters elder than I, and two sons and two daughters younger. Another James and Laurence died, the one in the East, the other in the West Indies; my elder brother Andrew died at London in the service of government; Isabel at Edinburgh a young woman, Margt. my eldest sister at Lerwick, and now Mrs. Farquhar,[2] who was about a year younger than myself, who now alone remain alive of all my father's family; and may I be daily preparing for my unchangeable state, and be ready at my Lord and Master's call and command to enter those eternal mansions of Bliss prepared for them that love and long for his appearance etc. 'Tis said Admiral Rodney has taken 6 Spanish men of war.

Octr. 20. This day keeped back from Publick worship at Sandwick by stormy wind and snow that covered the ground while a great part of the corns through the Parish are not cut down, and thereby hindered from going out to catechising

---

[1] Influenza: *Catarrhus*, epidemic catarrh. This disease, new to the Diarist, has been known and described since the days of Hippocrates. Sydenham, in 1675, enlarged upon it. The influenza of the years 1781 and 1782, here referred to, was said by some to have originated in China, travelling through Asia into Europe, and thence to America.

[2] Mrs. Farquhar, widow of a pilot of that name in Lerwick. The name still lingers in a small property, Glenfarquhar.

work, and longer than usual. 'Tis said that while the 'Royal George,' one of our first rates, was carcening at Portsmouth, a sudden gale overset her, whereby 1200 persons were drowned, and among these Admiral Kempenfield[1]; yet, alas, these awful Providences have little effect upon this blind, secure, and hardened generation. The Sutherland Fencibles at Lerwick were succeeded by a like number of Gordons. Among the Sutherland soldiers I found one James McKay, a Sergeant, who communicated at the Sacrament here in Aug. last, a serious and judicious christian; and blessed be a gracious God, who still keeps up a remnant e'en among the worst and in the worst of times.

1783   January. I am now arrived to my three score and ten etc. O to be always ready to give up my soul into the hands of the faithful God through Christ Jesus, the blessed Redeemer etc. The war goes on with France, Spain, Holland and America, and little hopes appear as yet of peace. The united forces of France and Spain made a furious attack in Oct. last on the Garrison of Gibraltar by sea and land, but were baffled in the attempt by Governor Elliot, a Scotsman, by firing hot bullets on ten of their men of war containing 212 brass guns of 26 Libs ball, whereby they were totally destroyed, and our people saved 'twixt 300 and 400 of their men and let them go home, and though their combined fleet consisted about 50 ships of the line, and Admiral How had only about 36, yet shifted a close engagement and at last fled for Cadiz.[2]

In Feb. we had accounts of peace made up at Paris, Jan.

---

[1] This calamity occurred on 29th August 1782. The ill-fated ship, 108 guns, was the principal vessel of Lord Howe's fleet. About 1100, including 300 women and children, who were on board at the time, went down. About 900, including the Admiral, Kempenfeldt, perished.i

[2] The gallant defence of Gibraltar, by General Sir George Augustus Elliot, Lord Heathfield, one of the most brilliant events in British history. The besiegers opened fire on 13th September 1782, from 400 pieces of cannon, with the disastrous result to them well known. Upwards of 2000 men are said to have been lost by the enemy.

20th, whereby independency was yielded to the States of 13 provinces in America and trade settled with them etc. France gets Tobago in the West Indies and Pondicherry in the East Indies. Spain gets back East and West Florida (This is contradicted), and retains Minorca. The Dutch accedes to the peace, 'tis said, while our luxcry and gross sins of all kinds have cost us an hundred millions stcr. with the loss supposed of an 100,000 lives. 'Tis observable that the crop in 1781 was plentiful in grain, which the people abused by gluttony and drunkenness, but the fodder scarce, whereby many of the cattle died; and the crop 1782 was plentiful in fodder, but lean and scarce of corn, whereby these belly gods are pinched. The meal in Lerwick at 6s 6d. stcr. per lispund.[1]

In July we went for the south, and was some days at Dunbar; all the way saw a rich crop on the ground. They had harvest begun the first of August. Stayed about 19 days and returned to Lerwick Aug. 14th in safety. Soli Deo Gloria. 10,000£ worth of meal was allotted for the Highlands and Islands. 500 Bolls was sent to Orkney, and as much for Zetland, whereof 75 came to this parish; yet still in want.[2] The season rainy and threatening. Turks and Russians are at war. France and England, jealous of one another, are busily building men of war, which threatens a sudden rupture.

In the beginning of Sept. the hairy Comet that appeared last year in the south and west appeared now after sunset in the East. 54 bolls more came from Government for the poor, whereof upwards of 30 lispds. were allotted for this Parish, and 9 bolls sold to pay the freight were deduced from the 54 sent for the whole countrey.

In Oct. there was sent by the Barrons of Exchequer 350 bolls meal for this countrey, and as much to follow, to be sold at 26 pence per lispband to the poor for keeping down the price of meal. Catechising work was finished in the

---

[1] *Lispund*: 18 lbs. Scots measure.
[2] A portion of the Minute-Book of the Kirk-session, embracing a period of about three years, 1782 to 1785, is lost; consequently no corroboration of the circumstances of destitution here referred to is there to be found on record.

end of this month. Though the Irish were put on the same
footing with Great Brittain as to trade, and having 40,000
men raised as Volunteers, and making further demands on
Government, threatens a civil war with them, unless timeously
adjusted. In our passage south, had foggy weather most
of the way, for 6 days, and when opposite to Stonehaven
or thereby, we discovered a large ball of fire, which run
swiftly along the dark clouds in a straight line and gilded
the same like a gold colour till it spent itself and evanished,
which gilding still continued, even when these clouds formed
into a crooked figure. 'Tis also remarkable that one night
while employed in catechising work through the parish, and
being detained at Sumburgh till afternoon's tea was over,
and turning very dark, when I came to the most rugged piece
of the way, about an half mile from the manse, a sudden
light sprung up among the horse's feet,[1] which made me
look about to see if it proceeded from any lights in the
heavens, but finding none, and all the rest of the ground
dark around me, astonished me the more at such a kind dis-
pensation of Providence, to whom be the praise!

This year several strange phenomenons appeared. The
island of Formosa, about 30 leagues from China, was laid
under water by a sudden rising of sea billows, and continued
so for 8 hours, and nothing yet to be seen but the tops of
mountains, whereby 'tis said that 3 cities 20 villages and above
40,000 inhabitants perished.[2]

2dly. A new island near Iceland rose from the bottom
of the ocean, and some people from a Danish vessel went and
took possession of it in their King's name.[3] It was covered
with marle having many crannies running through it filled
with pumice stone, supposed to be thrown out by the

---

[1] Probably fire flashing from the horse's foot striking a stone.
[2] There must be something of the mythical element in this incident as
recorded; but it is the case that in May 1782 an earthquake, attended with a
tremendous hurricane and swell of the sea, threatened for twelve hours
destruction in the island.
[3] It was denominated Nyöe, or the New Island, but the more remarkable
feature connected with it was that before a year had passed the island for ever
disappeared. So says Henderson, writing in 1818.

different Volcanoes of the island, at the time it was first formed.

3rd. A globe of fire, August 19th, was seen both at London and Edinburgh, about 20 times larger in appearance than the moon, travelling from the south, towards the North East, and bursting suddenly from a dark cloud, having a tail resembling that of a Comet, about an hundred yards from the tops of the houses. Its immense size and prodigious brightness terrified the spectators.

4th. Next day, 'tis said, a farmer travelling late from Edinburgh, fell in company with a venerable old man, at the back of Salisbury Craggs, who had long grey hairs and a staff in his hand. The farmer asking him if he had seen the meteor that flew over Edinburgh: Alas! replied he, shaking his head, his eyes sparkling with fire and a radiance glowing from his countenance, 'That ball of fire has passed over more cities and countries than this, and people knew not the danger; and more signs, and strange presages and revolutions would follow, and awful thunders, swellings etc. would swallow up whole islands and cities'; and then, stretching out his right hand toward Edinburgh, said, 'none was more ripe for destruction, and that for contempt of Gospel light, which soon would be removed, and they would be abandoned to whoredoms and all manner of wickedness. Let the guilty tremble, for their destructions draws nigh, but let the chosen watch and pray that they may escape these judgments,' and then suddenly evanished, with a sharp noise, resembling that of a whip struck in the air. Whereupon the farmer fell into a trance, and sleeped on the grass all night, when he saw several awful prodigies, as of inundations, and cities confused and destroyed, as Sodom etc.[1]

In Dec. a sloop arrived with 350 Bolls more for the

---

[1] There does not appear to be any very satisfactory contemporary confirmation of this apparition, which is somewhat suggestive of the Wandering Jew of mediæval story. It also reminds one of the Gibbites, a sect of worthies who, in the year 1681, withdrew to a safe and convenient distance on the Pentland Hills to view the 'bloody sinful city Edinburgh' burnt with brimstone from heaven, as they expected.

countrey at 26 pence per lispd., which serves to keep prices low for benefit of the poor, as the crop was bad, and many straitened for corn and fother; yet weather fresh mostly till now that frost and snow cover the ground.

1784   Jan. This year began with a strong blow of easterly wind, which set people in a great stir for preserving their houses and boats, but, alas, discovered little concern or anxiety for the salvation of their souls. O! that men were wise, that they understood this, and might constantly remember their latter end, with an eye to a future reckoning, that precious time, talents, and the season of grace might be improved to better purpose.

Feb. 23rd. This day I enter on my 73rd year; and O! to be helped by divine grace so to number the remaining days of my pilgrimage as to fill them up with duty, and to have the lamp of my heart well trimmed and burning with love to Christ Jesus, and that I may [be] ready at his call, having a desire to depart and be for ever with the Lord. For 4 Sabbaths past I have been keeped at home from the North Kirk through frost and deep snow, which speaks aloud to improve the season while it lasts. But though people and beasts are greatly straitened for want of food, yet alas! the generality are so fearfully blinded and hardened that they consider not the works of the Lord etc. and continue stupid and senseless under word and rod. May the Lord awaken their drowsy souls in mercy.

In April several ships arrived with meal etc. for supply of the countrey, but as 'tis upwards of a crown per lispd. and the people mostly want money to purchase, will prove small relief to them; and if it pleased the Lord to open the mouth of the sea would be more beneficial. The world is mostly in peace at present, which is seldom the case. But our Government [is] in a fluctuating condition, the Ministry often changed; all striving for posts and pensions, and who shall be uppermost, but never think of the reckoning here-after. They pretend Patriotism when only acted from selfish

principles and motives. Though my eldest daughter got
25£ Ster. at Edin. when she came to meet with me, having
two of her children with her for relief in her present straits,
whereof she was forewarned, and now found to sad experience,
yet [I] had letters lately signifying their family was in danger
of perishing for want, if not seasonably supplied. Whereupon I ordered 60£ Ster. more as her portion by her mother,
or, in lieu of that, to give them £15 Ster. per annum for 5
years to come for family support. They have a boy and girl
dead and two boys alive.

In May the Lord was pleased to send refreshing rains
and dews, which made the grass and corn spring; and proved
a great mean of preserving beasts' lives, many whereof, not
only cattle but sheep and horses, died for lack of fodder. Sir
Thomas Dundas sent 300 bolls meal for supply of his tennants.[1]

In June such numbers came to the Manse crying they
were starving, and many widows etc. had young children at
home in like condtion; and when my wife told me she was
mostly out of meal for their supply, I commissioned for 4
lispds. meal from Lerwick at 5s. 8d. ster. to give them, yet are
not satisfied with meat and drink, and a little meal, unless they
get money also; but no concern for food that does not perish.

The dews and rain make corn and grass to grow, but
little product as yet from the sea, which keeps the poor in
great straits, and most families are such. O! that a failure of
the streams might prove a mean to lead them to the fountain
of all mercies for soul and body.

In July two vessels of 80 tuns burden was sent from
London valued at 1600£ ster. with 500 quarters of Bear and
40 tuns of biscuit for supply of the poor tennants gratis by
order of Government in consequence of an application made
to Parliament by the Commissioners of Supply; at same time
a proclamation from the King for observing the 26th of said

---

[1] Sir Thomas Dundas of Kerse, second Baronet, who in 1794 was raised to
the peerage as Lord Dundas. His son Lawrence, second Baron, was created
Earl of Zetland in 1838. The family since 1766 have possessed what remains of
the ancient earldom of Orkney and lordship of Shetland.

month, as a day of thanksgiving for the peace after 7 years destructive war with France, Spain, Holland, and the revolted provinces of America. Soli Deo Gloria. And O! what mercy in granting also a set of fine warm weather, both for sea and land, after such threatening aspects. O! that men would praise the Lord for his undeserved mercy and goodness to ungrateful sinners.

August 24th. I was informed a whale about 40 feet long came into Gulberwick in the parish of Lerwick.

During the month of September, very little corn was shorn, the people in straits;—had some potatoes—little meat in the oats; but in the beginning of October it pleased the Lord to send several weeks of fine warm weather, which both filled and ripened the corns, and though threatened in the end with frost and snow, yet soon broke up, and a kind Providence gave some fair days for cutting down most of the crop.

In Dec. victual came to the countrey, whereof there will be great need for supply, and much more in other parishes than in this, where it is tolerably good. Accounts came at same time of a war likely to break out betwixt the German Emperor and the Dutch, who stopped one of his ships from passing down the Scheld to the sea from Antwerp, intending, ('tis said) thereby to trade with the E. Indies, whereof the Dutch were jealous, as ruining to their trade there etc.

Do. A ship from Hull in England brought in plenty of Bread and Potatoes etc. and vessels from Leith, who sold potatoes at 7d. per lispd. O! that men would praise the Lord for his undeserved goodness.

Frost and snow came suddenly on, whereby I was detained two Sabbaths successively from the north Parish, and when the same broke up, I got through with difficulty, and preached the 3rd Sabbath. O what cold and hunger the horses and sheep suffer for the sins of men! The whole world groans under the curse still—waiting for the adoption, e'en the manifestation of the sons of God, at the sound of the last trumpet, when all will be restored to their original rectitude and purity, and death, with the curse, cast into hellfire.

Frost and snow came suddenly on again in the end of December, a bright star appeared, about the bigness of Jupiter, in the southwest, having sprays of light issuing therefrom, like an hairy comet; and another lesser about the bigness of Venus, having the same appearance of a hairy Comet, was seen some months before, and now appeared in the south, culminating above the foresaid star, and not far from it.[1]

January 1785 years.

In Feb. the foresaid stars mounted high, and in so much that the lesser appeared no bigger than one of the fix'd stars and soon evanished.

Item. A vessel arrived from the south, with 100 bolls meal for supply of the poor, and more is expected, to be distributed by the clergy. The same was sent by charitable people in York, Newcastle, Hull, Bristol, Leeds, Wigan etc. in England; which so ashamed the people in Scotland that severals at Edinr. etc. determined to send supplies also. In April a vessel came from Newcastle with Barley and 100 bolls meal. 192 lispds. Barley was allotted for this ministry. Another ship with meal is expected from Frazersburgh for relief of the poor families etc. and is now arrived with 500 bolls meal and 200 bolls Bear. Here may be seen how mercy is mixed with judgment, in sending such large supplies to the poor wicked wretches of this country, though few see anything of the Divine Hand in it, and little sense of gratitude either to God or man.

In the month of August, a large hairy Comet appeared in the East. Nothing remarkable, for some months past, of publick transactions.

In Sept. the corns keep green by rains, but seem to fill the better thereby. The 3rd week of this month began harvest, but ended not until the first week of November mostly; and then when some hill towns[2] had a good deal corns on the ground to shear, a great storm of snow lighted on, which over-

---

[1] The astronomical records of the period are confirmatory, generally, of the appearances noted from time to time by Mill.

[2] *Hill towns*: i.e. *túns* (farms, or cultivated townships) in exposed or hill districts.

spread the same, whereby much was lost, and I was, through the badness of weather, keeped two Sabbaths from my nearest Kirk; and through excessive rains, most of the corns lay unskrewed.[1] Yet O! how stupid and senseless are the generality under these judgments. A French man called Lunardi fled over the Firth of Forth in a Balloon, and lighted in Ceres parish, not far from Cupar in Fife; and O! how much are the thoughtless multitude set on these and like foolish vanities to the neglect of the one thing needful. Afterwards, 'tis said, when soaring upwards in the foresaid machine, he was driven by the wind down the Firth of Forth, and tumbled down into the sea near the little Isle of May, where he had perished had not a boat been near who saved him and his machine.[2]

1786   Jan. A large Danish East India ship, bound for Tranquebar, was wrecked on Helleness point,[3] a ridge of rocks. 38 were suddenly drowned, among whom was the Governor of said fort; the captain and 2 women, and only 13 common men saved. A large quantity of money and merchants' goods etc. lost, and a man and woman in Cunningsburgh lost while grasping at the wrecks. Though they discovered land before day, yet were so infatuated as not to attempt getting off till a little before she struck, and then were so mad and sottish as to get themselves drunk and bind themselves with ropes to the windlass etc.; hence the Governor's body appearing erect above the water, were obliged to cutt the same by the leggs before they could get it off for Burial.

---

[1] *Unskrewed*: not put up in ricks or stacks.

[2] The ascents of Lunardi, quite a novel spectacle at the time, caused great excitement in Edinburgh. The first took place on 5th October 1785, from the grounds of George Heriot's Hospital, in view of, as it was calculated, 80,000 spectators, all business in the city being suspended. The excursion, over about forty miles of sea and ten of land, occupied about an hour and a half. He came dangerously near to the sea at Inchkeith, was carried across to North Berwick, and then backwards and northwards to Fife, descending a mile east from the village of Ceres, where he was received with the acclamations of a multitude.

[3] Helleness, on the east side of the parish of Cunningsburgh.

I was keeped four Sabbaths from North Parish by reason of very stormy weather etc. and two Sabbaths more after.

Feb. 23rd.   That day I'm arrived to the 74th year of my age.   O ! that I may always be in a posture of readiness to depart hence, when my dear Lord and Master shall call me home to himself etc.

Feb. 19.   'Tis said that the King of Sweden being at Naples, and expressing a desire to see the experiment of an air Balloon, the Court then ordered an immense globe of 150 feet diameter and 200 high, gilt and bearing on the top an enormous crown sparkling with imitated precious stones of various colours, having a building annex'd of beautiful architecture of the Dorick order, made of pumice stone, and surrounded by a terrace or gallery, railed in with orange and lemon trees and having an Orchestra of 8 capital Performers in musick, which rising at noon in a perpendicular ascent disappeared 27 minutes after for 2 hours, and 'twixt 3 and 4 afternoon lighted down a mile distance from the place of ascent, 12 Italian miles high, having likewise 7 persons of rank, nobles and gentlemen, besides two more to guide the machine by its inflammable air with which it was filled etc.

Frederick 2nd, King of Prussia, died.   Born 1712, aged 74 —my age the same.

Said month, had a letter from Peterhead giving accounts that George Tocher died at New Bythe the 29th of December and had left my eldest daughter Nell a poor destitute widow, with a son seven years old called John—the other two sons and a daughter, all younger, were dead some time before. A loud call to die daily to sin etc. and make ready for departing hence.

In March found the victual much fallen in price through a good crop through Brittain.   But the Kingdom groaning under heavy taxes and 300 millions of debt, an exorbitant sum, the interest whereof might support a war.   Yet little sense of Divine judgment are found among any rank.

In May, we had great rains, followed with a great drought the most of June.   But towards the end of said month a kind Providence sent a plenteous rain again to water the parched ground. O! that men would praise the Lord for rich mercies to the unworthy and unthankful race of mankind.

In the beginning of July, the rains continued, and 1st of August, 15 sail of men of war were on this coast, supposed to be French, but 'tis said Russians exercising their men. They asked some people that went to them if they were not afraid. They answered, as it was in time of peace, and as they were poor fishermen, they feared no harm. As they were supposed to be on some secret plot upon our settlements in the East Indies, our Statesmen were alarmed, and sent out a squadron in pursuit of them. In said moneth our hay came short of the usual quantity, by reason of the drought in May, and much spoiled by the rain when cutt down; and great mercy it is not worse; for had not the Lord in mercy sent a fine dry breeze of wind in the end of September, and recovered it when in great danger of being quite rotten and lost, whereby horses etc. were in danger of being lost for want of it. The day it was brought in threatened rain, yet the same was wonderfully restrained till all was over, and then broke out. Praise to the kind author of all mercies, but through carelessness of servants afterwards, took heat and were oblidg'd to pull the stack down and created a deal of trouble.

October 19th. The last of the corns was cutt down here. These 5 years past Providence has been contending with the countrey by bad seasons and poor crops, yet poor blind sinners are generally more hardened than reformed, while iniquity abounds as much if not more than ever.

In Dec. a sloop from Glasgow going for Irland was driven on Fair Isle by a strong west wind. A pilot from thence brought them for Quendal Bay, but could not get in. They ankord without [outside of] a Holm. The crew left the vessel; she was driven thence on Foula, and wrecked there.

1787   Jan. A sloop belonging to Lerwick coming from Leith was overset nigh this countrey; all the men washed overboard, a boy remained. Amazing Providence! the vessel recovered, and a sea cast two men alive upon the deck, and two more were drowned. They were driven to Bergen in Norway, and returned safe to Lerwick in February 4. English sailors came passengers, who belonged to a Greenland ship which had been frozen up at Greenland to the month of December. When the ice broke up, they escaped and came to Norway, and after some months, had nothing to live on, 'tis said, but Whale blubber, while another Danish vessel in the same condemnation lost most of their men by said food.

The winter has been so mild, and so little frost and snow, that the spring[1] in the ground was as forward in March as it used to be in May; and O! what mercy it was, since otherwise the horses would have been in danger of losing [*i.e.* being lost], through the badness of the hay.

In April, were 30 Greenland ships in Bressay Sound, and a man of war to keep these rough people in aw and order, least when drunk and mad with gin they should set the town of Lerwick on fire.

In June I went to attend the Presbytery in Lerwick with a firm resolution to extract the Decreet of Presbtry for a new Church at Dunrossness, and send south for obtaining and executing a charge of Horning against my Heritors, but was unwilling to proceed to extremities; and therefore Mr. Scott,[2] our Sheriff, was prevailed on to accompany me to Sumburgh, my principal heritor, who had most of his estate in the parish; whereby he was, by a kind Providence, who has the hearts of all men, and turns them as the rivers of water, nay, even the worst of men, as he pleases; and at last I was agreeably surprised to find him ready to comply with all just and reasonable measures, beyond expectation, after he had long refused, and had shifted this and other matters, by granting 10£ ster. to give the undertaker to begin the work, and his written obligation to grant whatever sums were demanded for carrying on and completing the work of building a new Church according to his proportion, and also to pay 7£ Scots yearly for a Pund mortified to 4 poor widows, and pay in all arrears

---

[1] *i.e.* growth.
[2] Walter Scott of Scotshall, then owner of a small estate in Dunrossness.

due.[1] Our accounts were also settled, and the ballance of Stipend due pay'd down. At the same time got a Charter from the Chancery on a house in Lerwick for which I had granted 40£ ster. and got all the right on the same in possession ; when one Heddel, a Custom House officer, had in a subtle fraudulent manner, seized on the house on a pretended right from the heir, and thereby supposed he would cutt off my claim, and deprive me of all, though my design was to grant the benefit of this and my father's houses there for behoof of two poor nieces that had nothing and would do little for their own support, and that during their whole lives. Soli Deo Gloria. About 80 of the Dutch fleet, with a convoyer came in, an agreeable sight to the people of this countrey. The white fishers come into Quendal Bay in the months of April and May; the people traffick with them. They brought gin, and sold at an easy rate,[2] and we have the prospect of getting house necessaries in like manner by commission, which was risen very high, and were for most part cheated by imposing rogues when brought from the Mercat. The corns, 'tis said, looked poorly through the countrey, and the Lord seems to continue his controversy with this unclean land. A deep sleep seems to have fallen on this generation. The Sacrament of the Lord's Supper was intimated the beginning of July to be given at the usual time, last Sabbath of August. O ! for the down-pouring of His Spirit etc. The Church of Dunrossness being in a ruinous condition, was oblidged to give the Sacrament at Sandwick.

The General Assembly in 1786 having proposed a new form of process before Church Judicatories, and sent to the several Presbyteries to know their sentiments of it, I made my remarks on three articles, vizt.—1mo That Kirk Sessions shall give a written warrant to their officer and two witnesses to every delinquent, with the executing thereof also in write ; which

---

[1] The ' Pund of the Brecks,' adjacent to Voe in Dunrossness, mortified by the widow of the Rev. James Forbes, A.M., minister of the parish from 1662 to 1682. See before, anno 1756.

[2] Buying gin from Dutchmen—with apparent approval of the minister. Elsewhere heavy anathemas are found against the demoralising effects of smuggling.

was a piece not only of needless trouble but a charge the Poor's funds could not bear. 2do.—That ante-nuptial fornicators should be dismissed with a rebuke before the Kirk Session ; was partial dealing, seeing the crime was the same as in ordinary fornicators, and attended with this aggravation that, instead of seeking God's blessing upon the ordinance of marriage they had in view, they rushed together like brute beasts, and I had more charity for young people that had no such prospect. 3tio. That when a man was charged by a woman with Criminal Conversation, that his denial should be sufficient, without purging himself of the guilt by oath—all which seemed very senseless and absurd. I wrote our Procurator accordingly to lay these reasons before last Assembly, and was glade to understand by a member thereof that the new form was rejected, as they reckoned the old form of process much preferable.

Sad experience teaches how much the Ministers of the Church of Scotland are degenerate and fallen from the strictness of former times, owing mostly to worldly minded men creeping in yearly by forced settlements; for which reason, in the year 1785, a Society at Edinburgh made an attempt to get the Patronage Act rescinded, and said year sent me over here a bundle of printed papers with proposal and Pamphlets written on the subject, in order to scatter the same among our clergy and gentry, for obtaining their Concurrence ; but found they were so immersed in the world and the flesh that, Gallio like, they cared for none of these things. However I wrote out reasons and arguments at full length showing the absurdity of obtruding men on Parishes, that it was not only contrary to Christian liberty, but of dangerous consequence to the souls of all concerned ; and likewise the advantages attending a contrary course ; which the whole members of our Kirk Session approved of, and it was signed and sent as from them. But when it came before the General Assembly the Patrons had got such a majority of friends there that the design was dropped.

Here the clergy are generally so lax in principle and practice that when I spoke of privy Censures they opposed the same. They have laid aside examinations of their youth and

F

Communicants, and admit scandalous persons to Sacraments, and joined with rogues against me, not only in protecting an erroneous member, one Finlayson, formerly mentioned, who soon left the countrey, in expectation of a great legacy left by a brother of his wife's, wherein he was disappointed, but having procured a settlement in the Presbytery of Biggar of 50£ Ster. per annum, was soon reduced to such straits, through luxcry, that he was oblidged to apply for collections to the support of a numerous family of children. Nay, they joined also against me in defence not only of a fornicator, but an incestuous person, who were obstinate in this Parish.

'Tis said that many of our Greenland ships are lost among the ice—12 at least. 'Tis a wonder of mercy that so many of these curs'd ruffians are preserved. 'Tis said in Holland the people are split in two factions, one part for the Stadtholder, and the other against him, which rose so high that from words they came to blows, and several hundreds have perished in the skirmish.[1]

Aug. 26th. The Sacrament of the Lord's Supper was celebrated at Sandwick. The auditory was crowded, yet the work was decently carried on. I preached on Thursday and Saturday on Isaiah 64 and 6, and on Sab. on Rev. 3rd and 20. Mr Inches, minister at Nesting, preached Sunday afternoon— 1 Peter 1 and 3, on Christ's resurrection, and Munday John 5 and 22, on the General Judgment: 4 Libs. Ster. was collected on Sabbath, and the whole amounted to more than usual, and is the more surprising that the Parish is so much reduced by failure of crops for 5 years past, whereby the number of the poor on the lists have risen to an 100. However it pleased God, who oft mixes mercy with judgment, to grant a good crop this year, the best at least that we have had for 6 years past,

---

[1] Political commotion in Holland. This ended in Belgium being overrun by the French, when the Stadtholder, William v., and his family escaped to England, in a fishing-boat, from Scheveningen. The Batavian Republic was then proclaimed. It in turn fell when Louis Buonaparte was appointed king, in 1806. On the downfall of Napoleon the kingdom of the Netherlands was formed, and it, in 1830, was again divided into the two kingdoms of Holland and Belgium as now existing.

and all brought into the cornyard in safety about the middle of October. 'Tis said the King of Prussia, who succeeded his uncle, has garrisoned Rotterdam with 10,000 and laid siege to Amsterdam with 50,000 men in favours of the Stadtholder, his brother-in-law.

Jan. An Hundred years ago, viz, in 1688, my Mother was born, and died 1772, aged 84. The foresaid year was remarkable also for the Revolution of Government in Great Brittain, and proved so great a blessing to the nation; as the year 1588 was likewise, by providential blasting of the Spanish Armada. The Sheriff this month sent me a paper, called a Memorial, signed by himself, three of my principal Heritors, with those of Lerwick and Bressay, for joining Bressay to Lerwick as one parish, and, taking part of Lerwick and Cunningsburgh from Sandwick Parish, to make another parish with Burray and Wharff etc. pretending the promoting of piety thereby, and desiring me to sign the same paper. But I was so far from putting my name to such a scheme as appeared to be calculated for the worldly ease and advantage of the present incumbents of Bressay and Lerwick, and selfish designs in the Lairds: nay, being fully persuaded it would rather prove detrimental to the interests of religion and Christian Knowledge, I assured them I would oppose the design to the utmost of [my] power.[1] They proposed, at same time, to have only one church to serve for this Parish and Sandwick, and the same to be built at Troswick. This design was baffled.

In Jan. I had accounts from Edinburgh of a great mortality there; that the death of Dundas of Arniston, President of the Court of Session, had made such a vacance that could hardly be supplied with such a well qualified judge.

My dear wife has continued in a valetudinary state for

1788

---

[1] This scheme had at any rate the merit of geographical propinquity to commend it. The union of the islands of Bressay and Burra on the east and west sides of the country, with Quarff on the mainland, intervening, has always proved an inconvenient ministry, and chapels of ease at Burra and Quarff (*quoad sacra*) became ultimately indispensable.

upwards of six months past, occasioned by a severe cold, which brought down the Uvula or Pape so call'd, and opened the joinings of the head, which brought on at same time a great deafness, which most of all discouraged her, and made her weep bitterly, when she could not hear prayers and reading, which grieved me greatly and in tender sympathy made me extend my voice to such degree in both respects that I was afraid it would render me incapable of publick service. All remedies that could be procured have been tried. We desire patiently to submitt, and wait the Lord's good time for perfecting her recovery, and that the troubles of the body may work for promoting the spiritual good and benefit of the soul. She complained also of stitches at her breast, and a sciatica pain in her thigh. But blessed be His great name who soon removed all these grievances, though the body is still weak.

In March we had accounts that a Dutch Greenlander had wrecked on a rock at some distance from Whalsey, and several men being discovered by a glass from said rock, the Captain and mate with 5 more were saved by a boat sent off to them. The rest of the crew, about 50, perished before.

In April, we had accounts that the German Emperor and Katherine Zarina of Russia were at war with the Turks, and that the Imperialists had laid siege to Belgrade, a garrison'd town on the frontier of Turkey in Europe. In this parish two young men were lost in bad weather, and the other fishing boats with difficulty got ashore, and three young men in Irland[1] were lost in one boat by rashness.

In May, Great Brittain entered a strict alliance with Holland for mutual defence; Holland to furnish six thousand troops and 12 men of War, and Great Brittain nigh double, when either is attacked by enemies, and a like alliance with the Prussians. 'Tis said the Russians had killed 20,000 Tartars who were employed by the G. Turk.

May 18. My dear wife was enabled to ride to Church. Soli Deo Gloria.

---

[1] *Irland*: i.e. *Eyrrland*, in Dunrossness.

Do. [May]. 'Tis said the Governours and Directors of the British Fisheries have purchased about 4000 acres of land in the Isle of Mull at Tobermory, and at Ullapool nigh Loch Broom in West of Ross-shire, for establishing a fishery in these places, though 130 miles distant from each other, and erecting work houses for materials necessary to carry on the same ; with Inns for the accomodation of Coopers and tradesmen needful etc. which, by report of people, if they succeed in the design, may raise two considerable towns.[1]

In July, 'tis said the King of Sweden wanted to have the province of Livonia restored to him by the Zarina of Russia, the refusal of which demand had made a rupture, which brought on a naval engagement in the Baltick Sea, and that the Swedes had beaten the Russian fleet. But in the Black Sea the Russians beat the Turks in a naval engagement.

In Septr. Octr. etc. we had fine weather, and the best crop we have had for 7 years past. But the people were publickly warned to beware of abusing it to God's dishonour, as they had done in 1781, by fidling and Ranting, gluttony, Drunkeness, and all unclean abominations, the usual concomitants thereof, and thereby provoke a just and holy God to send sore judgements on the land, by famine and a plague, to sweep such obstinate vermin off the earth into the pit of destruction. The General Assembly having appointed a day of thanksgiving on the 5th of Novr. in memory of the Glorious Revolution in 1688, after 28 years of most dreadful persecution under Charles 2d and James 2nd and their abettors, a cursed malignant crew as ever was anywhere, I took the occasion on said day, from text Exodus 13 and 3, to put the Congregation also in mind of the marvellous interposition of Providence in blasting the Spanish Armada, which they called Invincible, and confident to make a full conquest of our happy isle, and thereby reduce the Kingdom again to Popery, Arbitrary Power and Slavery ; and also of the gunpowder plot which [was] laid by Jesuit villains for the same mischievous end, and to thank a good

---

[1] These schemes of the British Fisheries Society were only partially successful. Ullapool, in particular, is a decayed place.

God, also, for the good crop etc., all which seems to make little impression on the generality, who are as obstinately bent on their evil courses as ever.

Beef is risen so high by sending vast quantities off the countrey, and when a little before harvest I knew of no marts,[1] a kind Providence furnisheed [me] with two of my own, and sent a fat cow to the door, which cost 3 Libs Sterling. Soli Deo Gloria.

1789   Jan. Every year produces remarkable changes—one race of creatures swept off the stage by the rapid flux of time, and others coming on. Lord teach us so to number days, months, and years as to apply our hearts to Heavenly Wisdom, and make ready for an unchangeable state. We had an account of the King's death, more regreted by all ranks and professions than any King of G. Brittain before him, though his royal progenitors were all noted for good princes. But this report was false, and we had sure accounts in March of his being restored by a gracious God to health of body, and soundness of mind. Said month I was greatly surprised when two Nottar Publicks came to the Manse and shewed me an extract from the Sheriff court at Edinburgh that Robt. Thompson, my Precentor, was imprisoned in the Tolbooth there for forging a latter Will in favours of his wife and children by one James Millar, who died at their house at Sumburgh, after he had been two years there, and had acted as a friend by paying Tack duty for them, and taking as good care of their affairs as if done for himself, which made all the Parish believe that his true name was Willm Sinclair, real brother to Ann Sinclair his wife, and that he had changed his name because of a harsh master of a ship he had been bound as an apprentice to when a boy (as Robt Thompson assured me) which made him run from him in America, and, finding a ship bound for Glasgow, had gone there, where he continued till he came in a fishing vessel which was wrecked in this countrey. As none could imagine that they would continue such a

---

[1] *Marts* : fattened cows or oxen for winter provision (killed and salted).

story designedly, and thereby run the risk of forfeiting life, reputation, the loss of the soul, and ruin his poor family of six small children and two aged parents, he got a Testimonial according to the above report, in order to recover the legacy left them. But upon his landing at Leith he was seized and imprisoned at the instance of one Daniel Millar, the true brother of the foresaid James Millar, as appeared from sufficient documents produced from Kilmarnock, where they were both born. Therefore though by letter he made solemn protestations to me and daring appeals to Heaven of his innocency, and his wife brought several servants to prove that James Millar foresaid had called her his sister upon his death-bed, I was determined to have no further concern in the matter, and set them all off Re infecta.[1] So true is what the Prophet Jerem. says, that the heart is deceitful and desperately wicked when men are prompted to go such length through worldly straits and avarice etc. The North Parish was examined said month.

In April a printed Proclamation came to hand for observing the 23rd of said month as a day of thanksgiving for restoration of the King's health. But as the day was elapsed before the Publication could be made from the Pulpits of both Parishes I was obliged to defer the thanksgiving day to May 13th ensuing. In spring we had fine weather for labouring the ground —praise to the Kind Author. Before I set about Examination work in the north Parish, I was much surprised to find that Robt Hunter of Lunna had prevailed with John Bruce of Simbester and Andrew Grierson of Quendal, in March last, to patch up the old Ness Kirk, after same had been twice condemned, and another spot of ground agreed upon having a better foundation, and more central for the Parishioners, notwithstanding a Presbyterial Decreet had passed, and all the heritors had bound themselves upon stamped paper to pay

---

[1] This is one of the very rare cases of crime from the district. The story of a mysterious stranger, Millar, at Sumburgh would almost lead to the surmise that his case, doubtless known at the time to Walter Scott, the young advocate at Edinburgh, might have suggested to the subsequent 'Great Unknown' the character of the gloomy and mysterious Basil Mertoun of *The Pirate*, who likewise came to reside at ('Jarlshof') Sumburgh.

in to the undertaker[1] their respective proportions of the sum
of 300£ Ster. and the work to be set about after Whitsunday
1789; and all under pretence that Sumburgh having died in
the end of 1788 under a burden of debt, so much money
would bear hard upon the heir. But I was of the mind
that it was much more eligible in all respects, even for their
worldly interests, to build the new Church as designed, than
to risk a new roof and windows upon an insufficient and
slippery foundation. They agreed to this measure at last
for the new church.

The Packet comes now here from Aberdeen, which is a
loss both to Government as well as the countrey and can't
hold out long.

It is affirmed that one Dr. Katterfelts, who has travelled
through Great Brittain, and exhibits the solar system in
miniature by a solar microscope, has obtained a gold medal
from the Board of Admirality worth 20 guineas for making
a piece of iron or steel or compass needle point to the east
and west poles only, having all the powrs of the Loadstone,
and, being put on the centre of a watch glass, answers the
same purpose as the needle; and that, by means of three
letters wrote to the Queen and Prince of Wales respecting
the King's distemper, whereby his health was restored, he
expects to have a sallary settled on him, and for various useful
discoveries. The convicts are, now, in great numbers, sent
from Great Brittain to New Holland, called by us New Wales,
an island reckoned as large as all Europe, to a place called
Botany Bay; but as they could not find plenty of good water
there, they removed about a dozen miles thence to a place
called Jackson's Bay, where they get excellent water in abundance, and a better and more convenient place for settling,
where they cleared the ground, and sowed wheat, ry, and
Barley, which thrives well, but 'tis said that peas and beans
did not answer so well with the soil. They found a creature
there shaped like a hare, with short fore-legs, the hind legs
much longer, as big as a sheep, called Kangouras,[2] and eats
like mutton. The inhabitants were naked savages of a copper

---

[1] That is, the contractor.   [2] Kangaroos.

colour, running through the woods, as in America, when it was discovered. They have one Philips for their Governor, and finding proper earth for making bricks, had built an elegant house of the same for him, and have formed a city of several streets, but their houses are little hutts, made of wood branches etc. As the large cattle etc. they carried with them died mostly by the way, they purpose now to have their breed of horses from this countrey, and their cattle etc. from Scotland and Wales, as more fitting and hardy, though one would imagine that as the countrey lies in the East Indies, 'twixt 10 and 34 degrees latitude south, the climate would be very favourable and warm there. 'Tis full of woods. New Caledonia found by Cook is an Isle resembling Zealand in the same ocean. The crop was got mostly in, the beginning of October, and promises well.

In Decemr. we had accounts of the President of the Session's death, Mr Millar of Glenlea,[1] and that Islay Campbel[2] had succeeded ; that the late President's son, Arniston,[3] was placed in his room as King's Advocate, and Mr Robert Blair[4] as Sollicitor in his room ; that Ladhon, the Emperor's General, has taken Belgrade, and thereby paved the way to besiege Constantinople ; that the Austrian Netherlands had raised 40,000 men for shaking off the Austrian yoke they had so long groaned under ; that the Swedes and Russians were still at war, which threatened to involve the other Potentates of Europe, and that all France was in a flame ; that they had erected an Assembly of the States, so called, by whom the King, queen, and all the royal family were in a manner imprisoned and confined to the Palace, having the military on their side ; that they had divided France into 80 Provinces or Shires, and proposed to have 700 members for an House of Commons, aiming thereby to have the same constitution, form of Government, Laws, and Priviledges as in Great Brittain, and

---

[1] Sir Thomas Miller of Barskimming and Glenlee ; died Sept. 27, 1789.
[2] Afterwards Sir Ilay Campbell of Succoth, Bart.
[3] Robert Dundas of Arniston. Was only thirty-one years of age when at this time appointed Lord Advocate.
[4] Robert Blair of Avontoun, afterwards Lord President.

that the King should have only the executive part of the
Government. The extreme fervour among the people, through
a great scarcity of bread, seems to have given rise to this
revolution etc. 'Tis likewise said that the American states had
established Popery among them by setting up one Carlton,[1]
as Bishop of Baltimore in Maryland and chief of all the other
Bishops, Priests etc.

On the first day of the New Year, N. S. a very strange
Providence occurred when the whole roof [of] my stable fell
down suddenly upon 7 of my horses,[2] about 11 of the clock at
night, which alarmed the people round about, so that they
came quickly to the rescue of the horses, otherwise they had
been all stifled, or crushed to death ; and, what is most remarkable, they were not the worse, though 'tis said one was found
lying above another.

1790   Jan. The face of affairs in Europe bears a gloomy aspect.
The Turk continues obstinate, and won't yield to terms of
peace with Germans or Russians. The French General Assembly
have obtained those points which they call the Bulwarks of
the State, viz. the free election of members for Parliament,
Trials by Jury, and Liberty of the Press. They have collected
upwards of 15,764£ ster. to erect a new fabrick for the College
at Edinr.[3] qroff they had great need, to which the Earl of

---

[1] This was John Carroll, cousin of Charles Carroll of Carrollton, who was
possessed of large estates and influence in Maryland, on behalf of which State he
signed the Declaration of Independence in 1776. John Carroll was consecrated
the first Bishop of Baltimore in 1790, and in 1808 was made Archbishop with
four episcopal sees as suffragans. The granddaughters of Charles became
respectively the Marchioness of Wellesley, the Duchess of Leeds, and Lady
Stafford.

[2] It will be understood that this stud of ' horses' consisted only of Shetland
ponies.

[3] The foundation-stone of the new University buildings, South Bridge, was
laid with great ceremony on Nov. 16, 1789, by Lord Napier, Grand Master
Mason of Scotland, lineal descendant of Napier of Merchiston, the inventor of
Logarithms. Orcadians and Shetlanders will not readily forget the important
part which Robert Reid, Bishop of Orkney and Shetland, had in the original
foundation of the University more than two hundred years before this time. In
1558 he bequeathed to the city of Edinburgh 8000 merks for the purpose.

Hopton and Faculty of Advocates contributed 500 guineas each.

Flanders joined with Brabant have shaken off the imperial yoke, and expect that the principality of Liege will unite with them in one commonwealth.

The winter has been so green that vegetables of divers kinds flourished, and the spring has prov'd very favorable. But fish, butter etc. that had risen high, are now fallen low in price. In May we had accounts that the Emperor Joseph of Germany was dead, and succeeded by his brother the Duke of Tuscany; that the Spaniards had taken severals of our men of war, and merchant ships, which occasioned a hot press to man our fleet. A million ster. was voted for charges, and a squadron of 16 capital ships sent forth on a secret expedition, for which they will probably pay, before they can have peace, 'tis said, 3½ millions ster. In June 2nd day, I was called upon to see the foundation for a new Church marked out,[1] which Mr Grierson of Quendal was for postponing till next summer. But the two principal heritors, Symbister and Sumburgh, ordered the undertaker to go on with the work, though oft hindered by frequent rains, for so it seemed good in the Lord's sight.

In March last, one Mr Crighton came here from London, and carried off a considerable quantity of oar of different kinds, one whereof is found to be an excellent, large and rich mine of Iron in Fetwel hill, and the other a copper mine near Sand Lodge in Sandwick parish. Mr Crighton returned in August for getting people to work the same, who carried off a deal of the ore in October and put the same in a sloop belonging to the Company, built of copper, and all went with her to London, whence they designed to return in the Spring, with more hands for working these mines. Mr Crighton forsaid gives accounts of a lead mine in Whalsey and of a coal mine in Unst, and another of the same kind in Fetlar isles.[2]

---

[1] The present parish church, on the ' ground ' of Brew.
[2] Iron mine at Fitfell Head (*Fitfuglahöfdi*, Sea-fowl Head). This mineral prospecting, started by an Englishman, Crighton, a century ago, was resumed in the same quarter about twenty years since, but, not proving remunerative, the

The crop was mostly got [in] in October, and is better filled than was expected, considering the rainy season; and my hay was in great danger of being lost through perverseness of the Grieve's people, who would not leave shearing when the neighbours got in their hay, whereby mine remained in the fields, when others had got in their corns; and had not a Kind Providence sent two days, very seasonably, of dry weather, the whole was in danger of being irrecoverably lost, yet the third part at least is thought to have been lost by Beastly wind and rain, through neglect; and what was remarkable, that though the morning threatened rain, it was restrained, till the remaining hay was got in, safe and in good plight, at last.

In September I got a printed letter, with a great number of queries to be answered, respecting this parish, which I effected in a few weeks, tending not only to give a particular view of what was most remarkable in the parish, but a general idea of the whole countrey, and was sent in October to Sir John Sinclair of Ulbster.[1]

In October I had a printed pamphlet sent me drawn up by a Committee of the Highland Society, for Improvement of British Wool, signifying that, in former times, English wool, that was esteemed the best in the world, was of late so far degenerate as to [cause the country to] pay 600,000£ ster. annually for Spanish wool, and as the finest wool was now found in the North and West Isles of Scotland, the Society foresaid have laid down rules for bettering the breed of wool, and for this end are to give premiums for so many of the breed who have the finest wool, which are to be kept separately by

---

working was discontinued. Copper-mining near Sand Lodge, begun in the same way in 1790, and discontinued, formed the rather chimerical basis of a joint-stock speculation launched as the Sumburgh Mining Co., Limited, in 1879, which terminated with disastrous results for those concerned in it, few of whom were natives. Of lead in Whalsey, and coal in Fetlar and Unst, the Editor has no knowledge; but chromate of iron, discovered in 1817, has proved a valuable product in the latter island.

[1] Account of the Parish of Dunrossness. This valuable contribution to topographical information appears in vol. vii. of the old *Statistical Account of Scotland*, published by Sir John Sinclair in 1791-99, and reprinted in the Appendix to the present volume.

themselves to prevent adulteration.[1] About 20 or 30 ewes and rams of fine wooled sheep are sent south for Islay, as a new plantation, to Shawfield Campbell, the proprietor of said Isle.

Novr. 23rd. In the evening were frequent flashes of lightning with claps of thunder. Soon after I had more than an half year's newspapers sent from Edinr. representing the state of Europe etc. as follows.[2]

Jan. This month was very stormy, and 'tis to be feared **1791** may occasion manifold shipwrecks at sea.

After Feb. 24th I entered into my eightieth year. Some, but few, attain to fourscore years, and they are said to be but labour and sorry. But O! what a wonder of mercy it is that I am still as capable to discharge all parts of my ministry as ever—praise to His great name. May I be helped to hold on, and be faithful in discharge of this important trust e'en to the death. Amen.

The Gasettes of Novr. bears that Spain, after long offsets and delays, had at last agreed to our terms. But as our navy of 413 ships of war are keepd still in readiness, 'tis still uncertain whether peace or war ensue. The Emperor of Germany has made peace with the Turks, as Sweden has done with Russia. France is still in an unsettled state, as also the Austrian Netherlands.

The Emperor and Austrian Netherlands have agreed.

The King of France made his escape from Paris, though a strong guard and watch was set on him by the General Assembly, but was discovered and seized with his queen etc. before he got out of his dominions; and being brought back was imprisoned more straitly than before; nay, 'tis said, they

---

[1] A pamphlet was issued this year by the Society, entitled 'Report of the Committee of the Highland Society of Scotland on Shetland Wool, with an Appendix containing papers drawn up by Sir John Sinclair and Dr. Anderson.' Edin. 1790.

[2] The author has forgotten, or been unable to overtake, his promised narrative of European affairs, digested from his. six months' supply of newspapers! The text is immediately resumed with the entry of January 1791.

had deposed him altogether, and committed his son, of 8 or 10 years old, to such Tutors and Governors as would instruct him in the principles of Government he should prosecute when of age.

The Highland Society has procured sheep not only from Spain but from Thibet in Africa [*sic*], Colchis in Asia, and from the East Indies, for improvement of the breed. Sir John Sinclair sent me 5 different sorts of wool, a little of each dressed. But our Zetland wool bears the vogue of all the world for the finest wool, whereof I sent some pounds to Sir John forsaid, as President of the Society. I got from him the 1st volume of his History of Scotland.[1]

1792   January. In the end of December 3 boats went to sea, in a fine morning, where they used to fish for ling in summer; but a sudden storm of wind and snow arising, they all perished, whereby 8 heads of families and a boy were seen no more; yet these awful judgements, like a nine days' wonder, are soon forgotten, and the thoughtless multitude drives still on in their career of Sin and folly—Nay, though no less than 8 or 9 fishing boats were lost in the north part of the country, and about 50 heads of families thereby perished, in June last, while employed in fishing. Some time after this disaster, Sir Thomas Dundas, accompanied by the Duke of Gordon, arrived in Bressay Sound, in quest of Mines, but met with a disappointment, and after some men from the Anglesay Company had wrought for copper in this Parish, and had carried off a quantity of the oar, they found it would not answer the Charges; and thus, after great expectations were raised, came all to nothing; and such have been, and always will be, the fate of those who set their hearts on this empty and perishing

---

[1] Sir John's *Statistical Account of Scotland* is evidently here referred to.

Note.—The omission here of all reference to the new parish church, which was completed this year (1791), is singular. From the Minutes of the Kirk-session it appears that on July 11, 1790, the minister preached 'at a Tent adjoining the Wall of the new Church building,' and on August 22 he conducted the service ' within the Walls completed.'

world. Europe is in peace, but how long is uncertain. The French Assembly have completed their code of laws, and their king agreed and sworn to maintain their new constitution, whether sincere or feigned is suspected and doubted. In America they have made such quantities of sugar of the maple tree, in the United States, that equals, 'tis said, nay, exceeds the sugars made of the cane, etc.

Prince Frederick Duke of York is married to the King of Prussia's eldest daughter, Frederica Charlotte etc.

Lord Cornwallis being sent to the East Indies with an army to carry on war against Tippoo Saib, a formidable tyrant who threatened not only to swallow up his neighbour princes, but to ruin the possessions of the E. India Company upon that Peninsula, adjoining the Mogul dominions that has the coast of Malabar on the West, and the coast of Coromandal on the East side, and brings to the Company above three millions sterling per an. 'Tis said General Cornwallis had taken severals of his strongest Forts, and was preparing to lay siege to his great metropolis Seringapatam, where he expected to obtain 20 millions sterling for compensating the charges of the war.

Leopold, Emperor of Germany, died suddenly, 'tis supposed by poison. He succeeded his brother Joseph not long ago, and had threatened France with an invasion. He has left a numerous family, and is succeeded by his eldest son Francis.

The taxes are taken off from servant maids, carts etc. that were burdensome on the lower classes of people.

There seems to be a general application to Parliament for abolishing the cruel and barbarous Slave trade to Africa etc.

The victual is at 50 pence per lispd., which bears hard on the poor. Providence has given a fine season for the labouring in March and April, after the great fall of snow that lighted suddenly on in the beginning of March and cutt off many sheep and horses, and also put a stop to my Catechising work of the Parish after it was begun.

Yet the summer proved better ; nay, had here more favourable clear and dry weather during the summer than in England, and south part of Scotland, where they were trysted with excessive rains lightnings and thunder, which did a deal of damage to Gardens, cornfields etc. The crop here was likewise better, and sooner cut down than there. Soli Deo Gloria. When Lord Cornwallis was ready to take Seringapatam by storm, it struck the tyrant Tippoo Saib with such terror that he proposed such terms of peace as was accepted by Cornwallis etc. viz. to give one half of his kingdom and 3 millions sterling for expences of war etc.

1793　　　January. Some seditious pamphlets having been published, particularly one mentioned as done by Pain,[1] who fled to France, and was enrolled a member of their General Assembly, whereby the rabble in many places began to assemble and cry out, in the language of France, for Liberty and Equality, as if oppressed by exorbitant Taxes. The King issued a proclamation enjoyning magistrates to search for the instigators of such mobs, and bring them to condign punishment, whereupon manifold addresses from cities and corporations followed, signifying their firm adherence to the present Government, and readiness to · concur in suppressing all seditious writings and insurrections etc. The French Assembly are carrying all before them. They have deposed their King and General [La] Fayett for corresponding with their enemies the Emperor, and King of Prussia, with their emigrant princes ; and confined the King with his family in an old building at Paris called the Temple, enclosing the same with a deep and broad ditch, and guard to watch them narrowly etc. Their Generals Lukner and Demourier have taken Mons etc. in the Austrian Neitherlands and were threatning to lay siege to Brussels, and General Montescue had broke into Savoy, for deposing the King of Sardinia, and bringing his subjects to a like revolution. As there seems to be a divine hand in these Revolutions, may tend to the final destruction of Anti Christ, which the event may declare.—Amen.—Even so come, Lord Jesus, and avenge

---

[1] Thomas Paine, author of *Common Sense* and *The Rights of Man* ; died 1809.

the blood of thy saints shed by the Beast[1] and false Prophet etc.

'Tis said the Pope sent an ambassador to our King for defending him and Church against that impious people the French, after finding that his usual weapons of anathemas, Pardons, and plenary indulgencies to sin, were now ineffectual. The Convention at Paris having found Louis the 16th guilty of Treachery and Treason against the State, condemned him to have his head struck off, which was accordingly done on the 21st January current;[2] and finding that Great Brittain was arming for War, on account of their opening the Scheld contrary to the most solemn treaties guaranteed by them and other powers of Europe, and also had sent their emissaries into Brittain for raising sedition among the people, they had also the assurance to denounce war against us, and make an attack upon Holland; but were defeated by the King of Prussia, in conjunction with some of our troops commanded by the Duke of York;[3] and as all Germany are uniting against them, and they are in great want of money, meal, cloaths, arms and horses, 'tis hard to say what the event may prove.

Lord Mackartney[4] is sent ambassador from the court of Brittain to the Emperor of China, with a great retinue, and presents of the most curious manufactures in arts and sciences, on board the Lion man of war of 60 guns, and another large ship belonging to the East India Company, for obtaining some Isle or place, to settle a factory near that part of the Countrey where the Tea grows, towards the north of China, and thereby avoid the charges of carrying the same so far southward by land to Canton. Interpreters

---

[1] The destruction of the Papacy seems to have been the great central object in relation to which all things were viewed, and to which all events were regarded as tending. The welfare of nations appears, in comparison with this, to have been almost of minor consideration.

[2] Louis XVI. was adjudged to death on the 17th, and executed on the 21st, January 1793, as here stated.

[3] This campaign of the Duke of York was not a brilliant one, as is well known.

[4] George, Earl Macartney. This mission was a highly interesting one; an account of it was published by his secretary, Sir George Staunton.

G

and Artists are sent along to explain the nature of these curious presents.

One Thomas Pain, Secretary to the Congress of America, and who, by publications on Common Sense, and the Rights of Man, had a chief hand in bringing about the revolutions of Government in America and France, in favours of a Commonwealth founded by representatives of the whole nation, attempted the same in Brittain, but in vain. He was forced to fly etc.

This 23rd day of Aprile 1793 concludes the 50th year since my ordination as minister of this Parish.

The French Convention have denounced Demourier, their best General, a Traitor, and set a price on his head etc.

May 29th. The ground was covered with snow, and all greens look blasted, in the morning.

July 11th. Brough[1] sent out his bigg boat for me to Fair Isle, where I spent two weeks, during which time I examined the Charity School, and all the young people of the isle, on the principles of religion—preached twice every Sabbath day—ordained four elders—rebuked and dismissed from discipline two delinquents, and distributed to the poor the money collected on these two Lord's days. 9 children were likewise baptised there.

The united army of Imperialists, Prussians, Hessians and Hannoverians, joined with some 1000ds of British soldiers, with the Duke of York at their head, attacked the French and beat them from Mentz, Condé, Valencian etc. etc. strong forts on the Rhine.

In Gasette May 20th Sir John Sinclair represented to Parliament that in Great Brittain were 67 mills. of acres, 7 qroff were incapable of cultivation, 5 mills. only tilled for grain, 25 mills. for grass and pasture, and 30 mills. remained, which, being cultivated, might maintain 10 mills. of people, besides 5 mills. of Black cattle, and nigh 30 mills. of sheep ; and wool etc. improving would bring 3 mills. money per an., for which end his Majesty being addressed to establish a

---

[1] Stewart of Brough, an Orkneyman, then proprietor of the Fair Isle.

general Board of Agriculture, 15 Lords and as many gentlemen, Scots and English, were appointed etc. The Duke of York in Sept. laid siege to Dunkirk, but was repulsed with loss; and 'tis said the Queen of France is beheaded.[1]

January. 'Tis said the French have recover'd Toulone Harbour, and most of the conquered cities, Ostend, Valencienns etc. in Austrian Flanders, and taken a vast number of prizes by sea; but June 1st were soundly beaten by Admiral How,[2] in a sea engagement, when six of their principal ships of war were taken, and two also sunk, and scarce anything left them in the East or West Indies, except Guadaloupe. Now in September they are endeavouring to retain also . . . .

1794

The Dutch seem to have totally neglected their fishing vessels. The French Privateers captured and sunk several of the herring vessels off this Isle, and destroyed, 'tis said, all the Cod fishers on the coast of Iceland, and left them only one or two ships crowded with men, that came to Bressay Sound, where one of the Dutch frigates were anchor'd for fear of the French. These French privateers captured also some of our Greenland vessels on their return, and having put 16 men on board one of these to convey the ship to Norway, and left only the mate, Bonsk Lyons (who was born in Lerwick) with another man on board, he suddenly confined 8 of the French, who were intoxicate with liquor, below deck, and drove the other 8 men into a boat by the ship's side, with a whale knife, and then cutt the rope and let them go, and brought the ship into Bressay Sound. Another belonging to Whitby in England being sent for Norway in like manner, having only the mate, called Ramsay, the Captain's son with a boy, left on board:—having prepared some soup for dinner, and the foresaid Ramsay having put in a spoon to share in the entertainment, which a proud Frenchman took in such bad part that he threw some of the soup in his face, the British spirit

---

[1] Marie Antoinette. She followed the King, her husband, to the scaffold, on October 16, 1793, in the thirty-eighth year of her age.

[2] Richard, Earl Howe. This was an important and decisive victory.

rose so high that he gave him a sudden blow on the head. This exasperated the French, that while they got up to lay violent hands on him, Ramsay ran speedily to a hatchet on the deck, with which weapon, having killed two of the foremost, he so wounded the rest, that, with the help of the boy, he bound them with ropes, and keeped possession of the vessel for two days till one of our frigates met with him, and brought him and vessel safe to England. 'Tis said one of our frigates fought a whole day two stout French Privateers off the North Isles in Orkney, and made at last prizes of them both.

'Tis said Lord Mackartney has returned from his grand embassy to China Re Infecta. That Tartar Emperor seems to have been jealous of the settlement of foreigners in any part of his dominions.[1]

At June Presbytery, it was found that Sir Thomas Dundas had neglected to present a minister to Unst within the time limited by law, and that this right had devolved to the Presbytery, who presented and settled Mr. Archibald Gray, a young man, upon a popular call, and that unanimous of Heritors, Elders, and heads of families, for which Sir Thos. now Lord Dundas, has given the Presbytery a summons before the Lords of Session, to render the settlement null and void etc.[2]

The French Convention have struck off the heads of Danton, Robespiere, with all their adherents, called the Jacobins, a bloody crew who had the chief hand in the deaths of their King, and his sister, and the Queen etc.

In imitation of the French Convention, two Societies were found out in Great Brittain, the one in London, called the

---

[1] This a hereditary and traditional jealousy, still a powerful principle in the policy of China.

[2] The case came before the Court on 15th May 1795, when their Lordships disallowed the settlement by the Presbytery in virtue of their claim of *jus devolutum*. Mr. Gray, afterwards D.D., accordingly retired, and John Nicolson, A.M., the presentee of Lord Dundas, succeeded to the charge in 1796. Returning north from a visit in Scotland, the vessel was seized by the French, who carried him a prisoner to Bergen in Norway, whence he returned in 1799. He died in 1821.

Corresponding Society, as connected in principle with another in Edinr. called the British Convention. They had their Committees of Secrecy, emergency etc. and a military department. In their houses were found a fount of Types, also Pikes and weapons of war. Two of them, Wat and Downie were prosecuted by the King's Advocate, and are found guilty by a jury already etc.[1]

In October, a young woman called Marian Hendries Daughter in Noss was found to have been guilty of the most atrocious crime ever known in this parish, by bringing forth a child begotten in adultery to one Malcolm Malcolmson, a married man in said village ; also to have murdered the child, and concealed the body in a skeo[2]; which the Kirk Session took a precognition of, and remitted the same to the Sheriff to proceed therein, as law directs.[3]

There was one of the best crops this year that has been for many years bygone, and safely brought in by the middle of this month ; and, besides, I had as fine Turneeps and Potatoes as are produced in Great Brittain, and also as good butter and cheese are made on my glebelands. Soli Deo Gloria.

Tis said the French are nigh the borders of Holland, threatning an invasion of that Republick. In December, a ship loaden with Reyned Tallow[4] from Iceland (she belonged to one John Watt, Merchant in Dundee) broke in a storm nigh to Scatness. The crew perished, and many run there for the wrecks etc. and were enrich'd by reind Tallow etc. etc.

In January, Frost and snow prevailed greatly, not only **1795** through Brittain, but most of Europe, which the French took advantage of to overrun Holland. The Zuyder Sea was

---

[1] Robert Watt, a wine merchant ; David Downie, a goldsmith. Both were sentenced to death. Watt, in his thirty-sixth year, was executed, confessing their treasonable aims ; Downie's punishment was commuted to transportation.

[2] *Skeo* : small open-built house for drying.

[3] The case is fully related in the MS. minutes of the Kirk-session under date November 2, 1794.

[4] *Reynd*, or *rind*, or *rinded* tallow, is tallow melted.

frozen, and about 20 ships of the line of battle, with frigates etc. became a prey to the French; and their General Pichegrue exacted of the States no less than an 100 mills. of Guilders, and set up a Gullotin at the Hague, saying he knew no distinction betwixt republicans and those who were of the party for the Prince of Orange. 'Tis said also that the French had threatened to invade Great Brittain with 600,000 men and Irland with 300,000 more. It was carried by a great majority in Parliament that the war with France should be prosecute with vigour, and our troups recalled from the Continent, as 1,200,000 Libs. Ster. had been given to the King of Prussia and 6 mills. given in loan to the Emperor of Germany, in vain. 200,000£ Ster. also to the King of Sardinia; though this precipitate war had already cost the nation 50 mills. Ster. of money and 50,000 lives.

The Government is now exerting their utmost for setting forth a formidable navy (which they had better done at first); and though this countrey is drained of men already, I had a letter from Sir John Sinclair desiring me to offer 10 guineas to a man who would take on to be a soldier, with other advantages; and that if I could prevail with one to raise 30 or 40 such, upon my recommendation, he would procure a commission for him in the army. The King appointed a Fast to be held through Great Brittain in February, on account of the war with France, which was over before the accounts reached this countrey; therefore the Presbytery appointed the first Thursday of April to be keep'd in this Island.

The moneth of May was very cold, when 'tis said not only sheep and lambs were killed in numbers thereby through the countrey, but also that much cattle perished through lack of fother.

May 9th. The Caledonian Mercury bears that our forces, commanded by the Duke of York, were recalled from the Continent, and that the Emperor and Kings of Prussia, Spain, and Sardinia, had made peace with the French Republick, and none adheres to us but the King of Naples.

In June, further demands were made by Government upon this countrey for men to the Navy, threatening, in defect of the stipulated number, to lay a cess on the island of 25£ Ster. for each man wanting of the number required, being the sum paid by the King to each volunteer, which oblidg'd those of the landed interest to meet at Lerwick to this effect. [*Apparently not completed.*]

I had a summons in July by the Sheriff's officer, at the request of one Mr John Watts, a Merchant in Dundee, to declare upon oath what I knew anent the Tallow Cargo of the ship forsaid, which was wrecked near Scatness in this Parish winter last. The owner, Mr Watts, pay'd me a visit after, and said though the cargo cost him 5000£ Ster. and that 2000£ Ster. worth and upwards were saved and sent off the countrey, yet he believed I did not concern myself with it but by report what I heard etc.

. Dr. Brodum's Botanical Syrop, said to be taken from the most purifying and healing vertues of the vegetable system, effectually cures all scurvies, leprosies, cancers, evils etc. to be had at Baxter's Italian Warehouse, Edinr. in South Bridge, in Bottles of 1£. 2s.—11s. 6d. and 5s. 5d.

· In August. An Embargo is laid upon all the Still pots in Great Brittain to Feb. next, on account of the dearth of victual, which occasioned the mobs rising at Birmigen in England etc. But the price is now falling.

Admirals Cornwallis and Bridport 'tis said had defeated the French in a naval engagement with half the number, and taken several of their war ships. In Septr. Sir Francis Kinloch of Gilmerton, near Haddington, was shot there by his brother Archibald Gordon Kinloch, a Major in the Army, supposed to be beside himself etc.[1]

'Tis said the crafty French from Guadaloup stirred up the negro slaves, with a promise of liberty etc., to murder our people in St Vincents and the Grenada Isles, which was done accordingly etc.

The Prince of Wales being married to his Cousin-German of Brunswick[2] had 125,000 Libs. Ster. settled per ann. besides

---

[1] This tragical occurrence took place only a few days after Sir Francis's succession to the family estates and honours. The 'maniac,' Sir Archibald, succeeded, dying in 1800, when another brother came into possession.

[2] This ill-starred union took place on 8th April 1795.

payment of his debts of 100,000£ Ster. by the house of Commons. The Nation pays for all, etc.

In October, 1st week, the Barley was cut down, and some of the Oats, and as the crop is likely to be deficient in straw, being thin and short, feared want of fother for the cattle, and what is cut down endangered by continued foggs.

The King was attacked by some desperate ruffians, in his going to and return from Parliament. One shot a wind gun with a ball; others threw stones into the coach, and broke the windows, but happily missed the King and two other noblemen in the coach.[1] One David Collins and another called Kidd Wake, a Baxter,[2] are both in custody for trial.

The French having penetrated a good way into Germany were suddenly defeated by the Imperial Generals Clairfit and Wormser, and with great slaughter driven over the Rhine. All methods are taken to lower the price of victual by mixtures of grain etc.

1796   I have now passed four score years and four in this world. May I be always ready to depart hence at God's call and command, and helped to be faithful to death, and all the days of my appointed time I desire to wait till His good time comes, which is always the best time. There is yet no prospect of peace, though the generality both in Brittain and France eagerly desire it. The Dutch seem to be still under bondage to France, and Brittains have taken from them Ceylon and the Cape of Good Hope, and most of the French Suggar Islands are under our dominion, which our Government will be loath to part with, and the French as loath to be without them, and thereby probably the war will be prolonged.

Pichegrue, having entrenched himself with a great army in Germany, Clairfait, the Austrian General, attacked him in his camp, and at same time an army of 26,000 Hungarians,

---

[1] Incidents of this kind were not infrequent at this time and during the Regency.
[2] Baker.

who had travelled through woods, and over steep mountains, attacked the French in the rear, which they were not aware of, and made a dreadful havock, even to 60,000, with prisoners, in all, though now in Septr. they are said to be carrying all before them in Italy etc.

In the month of Aprile, 10th day, Sabbath morning, I was struck suddenly with an apoplexy in the right ventricle of the heart, whereby the power was taken from the body to such degree that with difficulty I could stand, speak, or walk ; yet it pleased the Lord to preserve all my senses and the faculties of the soul, as well as before ; but being as a weaned child, could do nothing for myself or others, only to sit in a chair, or ly in a bed breathing ; and when I could do this without pain, as was usually the case, the same was a singular mercy. I was oft troubled with stitches, and as this is usually owing to a redundancy of blood, I soon got one well skilled in letting of blood, but he was timerous, nor would draw off as much as I desired. But as the stitch continued, I sent for him again, and caused him take as much, which relieved me of the stitches. But my stomach was gone, and nauseated the best meats. My whole body in very short time reduced to a skeleton. But as it pleased the Lord to spare life, I considered it was duty to use the means of recovery, and therefore my good wife got up early, and gave a cup of port wine mixed with the powder of Jesuits' bark. Two hours after I took some coffee, with bread spread with butter and marmalade. At 4 in the afternoon I got for dinner some fat broth mix'd either with some small bitts of fowls, veal or lamb, and also a little barley and raisons, and all strongly tinctured with black pepper, and usually took a drink of beer before I went to bed. Thus I continued every day for the space of nigh two months before I perceived any increase of strength ; nay it was like a journey to walk from the bed to the chimney. But it pleased God on the 6th day of June to make me feel such increase of strength that I was able to walk round the room and go into the garden next day, and take two turns round the walks. Next Sabbath I went about family worship morning and evening, and about 8 days after desired the Precentor to intimate from the Latterin[1] that the people should bring their children for baptism, and also their marriages might be performed without going to any other minister. But I still continue so feeble of body that I could not venture to officiate in Publick for the space of 5 months. But on the 1st Sabbath of Septr. I lectured at the Ness Kirk to a crowded auditory, and on the 3rd Sabbath of Septr. Do. at the Kirk of Sandwick as usual.[2] Soli Deo Gloria.

Septr. 28. From the Herald Chronicle Edinr. from August 13th to Do. 25th. 'tis said the French are carrying all before them in Italy and Germany. They have laid siege to Mantua, and laid Rome itself, with the Pope's territories, under contribution, and that so high that Churches and Monasteries, plate and money, must go for payment of the sum. Nay, Suabia and other places in Germany are oblidg'd not only to pay so many millions in money, besides many 1000ds of horses, oxen, shoes, and quintals of grain, white barley, oats etc.: That they have reached the Danube, and threatened Vienna itself with a siege, in which event, 'tis said, the Empress of Russia proposes to send an army of 60,000 men to protect the Emperor's hereditary dominions. 'Tis likewise said that the British in the East Indies have taken not only Ceylon, Malacca and other Spice islands from the Dutch, but that our people are gathering plants of cinnamon cloves and nutmegs from these islands to propagate these trees in the lands belonging to the British Company at Madras, which will make them sharers at least in the gains of this traffick, e'en tho' the Dutch should afterwards be put in possession of these islands.

The French have brought the King of Spain into alliance and treaty, and obtained his part of Hispaniola, for which they propose to send 25,000 men to conquer Portugal, and add the same to his dominions; and in case of war with G. Brittain, they, as formerly, will assist him with 16 line of Battle ships, and 18,000 men. Nay, the French are endeavour-

---

[1] *Latterin*: The Lettron, or precentor's desk. Probably the same word as the *Lectern*, or reading-desk, of Roman Catholic and Anglican Churches.

[2] The Kirk-session Minutes of 1796 (eight pages) are lost.

ing to make peace with all other that they may employ their whole strength against us. We never had such a formidable armament at sea, no less than 612 ships, whereof near 200 are of the line of Battle, from 50 to 110 guns, and near as many Frigates from 20 to 44 guns, and of war sloops 110 from . . to 18 guns, besides others. There are about an 180 regiments in England of regular troops and fencibles, and about 58 fencible regiments in Scotland. But may we never trust to an arm of Flesh, but in the great Jehovah, in whom is almighty strength. Then we need not fear what the French, or flesh and blood can do.

Two Danes are wrecked on this countrey, one at Whalsey loaden with gin, 'tis said, for North Faro ; the other loaden with fish and oil for Spain wrecked at Unst.

Missionaries ministers are sent to the heathen to preach the gospel where Christ yet has not been heard of etc.

January. As the Lord has been pleased of infinite mercy, **1797** beyond expectation, to restore me to such measure of health and strength [as to be able] to act in publick as formerly, may it be for His glory and the good of souls. There is a good work of God going on in Wales under the ministry of one Mr Charles [1] etc. The Devil stirred up a malignant crew to crush it ; but through the good hand of God it still prospers in spight of hell. And it has pleased God also to stir up in the hearts of ministers and people of all ranks and denominations to have the gospel propagated among the heathen in all parts of the globe, for which end 200 ministers, not only of Presbyterians, but Episcopalians, Anabaptists [2] etc. laying aside all bigotry and blind zeal for parties, met together in one Church at London, and ministers of each kind preached to crowded congregations, for promoting the design. Great collections were made in money for carrying on the design, for

---

[1] This resulted in the formation of the British and Foreign Bible Society in 1804.

[2] *Anabaptists* : the use of the old (reproachful) name for the modern Baptist denomination.

which purpose they purchased an handsome vessel for 5000 Libs. Ster. called the Duff, and sent out 30 excellent ministers with instructions and printed directions; and as the master and crew, with all on board, were of the same Christian spirit, such order and harmony reigned among them that bore a resemblance to heaven on earth.[1] They were bound for Otta-hittee, a large beautiful isle in the South Sea, for which they had taken pains to learn their language, and from thence to pass into other islands that abounds in these parts and speak the same language. Missionaries are also sent into Africa at Sierra Leona, where we have a Company who readily further the design, and set on these blacks at same time to cultivate and improve the countrey. Missionaries are employ'd on the Malabar Coast, East Indies, and also in the West India islands to good purpose.

The Jews, 'tis said, flock to hear the Gospel preached at London, which prognosticates the fulfillment of the promise, Rom. 11th, and that the end of the world draws nigh etc.

In Jany., the French made an attempt to invade Irland, and ankerd in Bantry Bay, expecting many of the natives to join them. But Providence blasted their design by a sudden storm of wind. Severals were captured by our men of war; others sunk, and a Frigate, with 20,000 stand of arms, were taken.[2]

Bouonoparte, the French General in Italy, boasts at his victories of killing and taking prisoners more than 30,000 Germans commanded by General Wormser, among whom are several general officers, 60 cannons and 20 stand of colours; yet Mantua still holds out against him. Archduke Emperor's brother commands on the Rhine, and Jourdan the French. Fort Kiel is taken by the Germans; the Cape of Good Hope is taken from the Dutch; and some of the best wheat and wine to be found in the world has been brought to G.

---

[1] This, which refers to the foundation of the London Missionary Society, was at the beginning, in the high romance, of Foreign Mission enterprise. Dr. William Carey, the celebrated Baptist missionary, had arrived in Bengal in 1793, nearly four years before this time.

[2] This is the story of the invading expedition of General Hoche, which came to Bantry Bay to aid the Irish rebels in 1796.

Brittain. As confidently reported, all the Spice Islands are
become ours by conquest, only Batavia remains, and is to be
soon besieged, and all the Suggar Islands are to be taken from
the French except Guadalupe. A Fast was observed March
9th through Scotland, according to the King's proclamation,
on account of the war with France, as has been done several
times on the same account, yet these proud enemies insulted
our ambassador—a strong evidence that our fastings were
rather superficial and hypocritical, otherwise our enemies had
been humbled, and had rather sent ambassadors desiring
peace with us.

Lignums Antiscorbutick Drops and Brodums Restorative
Nervous Cordial are become famous for cure of such diseases.

By late Gasetts of Feb. and March 'tis said the French
landed 1200 armed men in Pembrokeshire of Wales, whom
the people there would soon have destroyed had they not
timeously submitted to the Lord Lieutenant of the County
and surrendered as Prisoners. They were commanded by an
Englishman, called Wall, who had narrowly escaped execution
for murder, and had fled to France, and will probably meet
with his due reward. 'Tis said all these men were French
Convicts etc. Mantua has surrendered to the French. The
Pope's defeated, his army ruined, himself in danger, and the
rich chapel of Loretto taken by the French etc.

One Shirnding,[1] a Saxon nobleman, Ranger of the Electoral
Forrests, wrote a letter to King George, and an address at
same time to his subjects of Great Brittain, to join with him
etc. for promoting the good design on foot to send missionaries
etc. into such dark places of the earth where the name of a
Saviour has not been known. William Couper, a poor young
lad, and apprentice to a bookbinder at London, though without learning, yet being well acquainted with the Scriptures
of truth, and endowed with a happy talent of speaking from
them, seems to be employed as an instrument under God for

---

[1] Many interesting notices, such as this, recorded by Mill, are not to be
found in books of general history. The name is suggestive of Count Zinzendorf,
founder of the Moravian settlement at Herrnhut, but he died in 1760.

removing the Vail that hitherto has kept Jews from embracing Christ Jesus, the only Saviour of Sinners of all sorts.

In March we had accounts of taking Trinidad, a West India Island of 90 miles long and 60 do. broad, from the Spaniards by Sir Ralph Abercrombie, without losing but one officer. They burned four ships of war themselves to prevent [their] falling into our people's hands, but they captured one of 74 guns notwithstanding etc. Sir John Jervis' squadron took 6 of their greatest ships, from 1300 to 2500 tons and upwards of Burden, and got a complete victory of their fleet in the Mediterranean sea.[1]

In June. The Cities of London and Edinr. have petitioned for a peace with France; and in order to a speedy and honourable peace, to dismiss Mr Pit and the present ministers of State, for relief of the heavy burdens the nation groans under.

A mutiny arose in the Navy respecting their wages etc. as too small, and, when all their demands were granted, they grew more insolent, and still required more, which the King and Parliament would not grant. Enquiry being made of the incendiary, the knave being discovered and dreading the consequences, he fled to his friends in France, who had bribed him, and several of his accomplices are like to pay dear for it. General Abercrombie intended an attack upon the isle of Porto Rico, but found it so strongly fortified as to require 15,000 men, whereas he had only 3000, and was obliged to desist. Having received a letter from the Missionary Society at Edinburgh in Feb. last, signifying that about 30 ministers had proposed to the Directors of the East India Company at London to transport themselves and families for Bengal in order to preach the Gospel among 14 millions of their subjects there who were living in gross Idolatry and paganism: It appears that some malignant officers among the military who had been there had trumpeted up several lies and slanders of a good minister who had been there, insinuating thereby that their people were rather worse than better by his ministry, and thereby had prejudiced the Directors as being

---

[1] This engagement took place on 14th February, off Cape St. Vincent, where four ships were taken.

prejudicial to their worldly interests; therefore desiring I
would write to the Directors at London in favours of these
missionary ministers, and procure as many ministers etc. to
join in the application as possible; in the month of Aprile
last I drew up a petition to the Directors of the East India
Company at London, wherein such arguments were used
from Scripture and reason that if these did not serve to
convince would not fail to confound them; and as names and
authorities without these could avail nothing, I signed these
reasons alone and transmitted the same to the Missionary
Society at Edinr., who it appears did send my letter to the
Directors of the East India Co. in consequence of which I had
in June a letter from Mr. Love, Secretary to the Missionary
Society, signifying that they had elected me one of their
members for this present year 1797.

In July, the newspapers give accounts that severals of
the mutineers on board the fleet were taken on their way to
France, and that Parker, the ringleader, was condemned to
be hanged by a court martial.[1]

The Earl of Oxford represented that he knew 50 Royal
Burghs in England who had not ten houses in them,[2] and
yet were privilidged to send two members to Parliament,
when a village called Mary le Bone,[3] containing 8000 houses,
and paying £80,000 Ster. Taxes had no representative in
Parliament.

N.B. Some of the mutineers on board our men of war
are made examples of, the chief ringleaders hanged on board
these ships, others scourged severely, others imprisoned for a
time; and to prevent such villany for the future, the military
both by sea and land, in regiments and in men of war, have
offered an 100£. Ster. to such as discover such attempts in
time coming.

The Sacrament of the Lord's Supper was celebrated at the
Ness Church, August 27th. There were about 9 tables and

---

[1] Richard Parker was hanged on June 30th.
[2] Old Sarum had no more houses than two, if so many, yet it was the con-
stituency that returned the elder Pitt to Parliament!
[3] The 'village of Mary le Bone'!

upwards of ten guineas collected.[1] Said month the Belligerent Powers agreed to send Ambassadors to Lisle in Flanders, for treating of peace, and Lord Malmsburgh was again sent by our government and three more conjunct with him.

Paul Petrowits, the present Czar of Muscovy, has made a friendly treaty of Commerce with Great Brittain, and with equal privilidges to the subjects of each government.

In Sept. two despots of the French Republick went from Paris to Lisle, and had the assurance to tell Lord Malmsburgh etc. that, unless he agreed that all the Islands Great Brittain had taken from France were restored, and besides an indemnity granted in money for charges of war, no peace was to be expected, and he behoved, without delay, to leave the French territories, which he accordingly did, and in a few days arrived at London etc.

In Septr. two well qualified young men, Messrs. Campel and Henderson, were sent from the Society at Glasgow as missionary ministers to the Foutah countrey in Africa, for assistance of that good man, Mr Clerk, and were kindly received by him, and the Governor, that excellent man Mr. M^cauley[2]—all Scotsmen. Two missionary ministers were sent at same time from the Society at Edinr. for New York, to labour among the Indians in America. Two missionary Baptist Ministers, Messrs. Carey[3] and Thomas, were sent to succeed Mr Swartz, in Bengal, a large field for propagating the Gospel, where, if many such good ministers were employed, might probably, through divine aid, 'tis said, prove the happy instruments of spreading the Gospel light, not only through that country but through Thibet and Boutan,[4] two large kingdoms bordering thereon, nay, even to Tartary etc.

In Nov. we are informed that a sea engagement had taken

---

[1] This was an enormous collection in the circumstances of the place.

[2] Zachary Macaulay, then a merchant at Sierra Leone, and father of Thomas Babington, Lord Macaulay.

[3] The renowned William Carey, alluded to in a previous note. Besides his direct missionary labour, he was the instrument of the translation of the Bible into many of the languages of India. Died 1834.

[4] *Boutan* : Bootan or Bhotan, a territory on the north-east of India.

place, on the coast of Holland, with the Dutch, prompted thereto by the French Directory, under whose Dominion they presently groan. 'Tis said they were equally matched as to ships, guns etc. about 20 men of war on each side, but it pleased God to give our people such a complete victory that they captured 13 of their best ships, destroyed others, and had they not been so nigh their own coast, none had escaped.[1]

In Sept. 'tis very remarkable that a gentleman, Alex Spiers of Elderslie, nominated 5 young men of good characters to the parishioners, Heritors, Elders, etc. of the Parish of Neilston, that after a hearing of each of these young men, assured them he would present the man they should chuse, and accordingly they choosed Mr. William Hood Preacher of the gospel at Tarbolton. Happy would it be for Scotland and all Patrons that his example was followed, and thereby avoid that aggravated sin and guilt they bring on their own souls by intruding ministers into Parishes over the bellies of a reclaiming people.

Admiral Duncan, who commanded in the naval engagement above mentioned is a Scotchman, and his family, 'tis said, resides in Edinr.[2] He had the dignity of a Peer conferred on him by the King, called Lord Viscount Duncan; and the Vice-Admiral Onslow the dignity of a Barron, called Lord Onslow.[3] N.B. 'Tis said where missionaries are sent in Africa, they cutt old people's throats when unable to labour;[4] and in Bengal 50,000 wives are buried alive annually with husbands corpses or in the funeral pile of their husbands. Horrendum dictu.

In January we had very stormy weather, and thereby had cause to fear that much harm has been done to our trade by shipwrecks etc.

1798

---

[1] The great victory of Admiral Duncan, off Camperdown, was gained on the 11th of October. De Winter's ship, with eight others of the line, and two frigates, were captured.

[2] Admiral Duncan's family at this time resided in George Square, No. 5.

[3] Vice-Admiral Onslow. He was, on 30th October 1797, created a *Baronet*, in consideration of his participation, as second in command, in the victory. The Earl of Onslow is the head of the elder branch of the same family.

[4] *i.e.* The natives do.

Feb. 23. I am now fourscore and six years old; and through the tender mercy of a good and gracious God, am still enabled to keep my tours at both Kirks as well as ever. May it be for his glory and the good of souls that I am spared so long; and, with Job, may I be helped to wait with patience all the days of my appointed time on Earth, etc.

The war with France goes on. They threaten to invade Great Brittain with 300,000 men, by putting 10,000 on rafters of wood so formed and fitted with raw hides etc. as to be proof against our bullets, and also with furnaces to heat their own bullets to fire and burn our ships of war, which our people justly regard to be no more than empty puffs. A considerable number of our East India Merchant ships have arrived with cargoes valued at 6 mills. Ster. and two of these loaded, 'tis said, with cinnamon, cloves, nutmegs and pepper, being the most valuable commodities that ever arrived in England. The nation is loaded with Taxes, which makes the French insult us as unable to continue the war. But to shew them the contrary, voluntary subscriptions were opened at London, and 150,000 Libs. Ster. soon raised, whereof the King signed for 20,000 Lib. out of the Privy purse, so called. Whereupon all ranks, out of love to their King and country, through Great Britain, signified their willingness to contribute. Nay, a subscription is willingly given in this country, by all who have money, and I have signed, with others in this Parish, for ten guineas, to be continued yearly while the war lasts.[1]

March 22nd. A Fast was observed on account of war continued in France, and a long printed paper read, as appointed by Commissioners of the General Assembly, setting forth the enemy's designs to ruin us, as they have done to Holland, Venice etc.

It pleased the Lord to afflict my youngest daughter Bell with a severe cold and sore throat, whereby she was brought very low in two weeks' time, and at last ended in death, April 27th, being 42 years old, and it has proved fatal to many

---

[1] Voluntary contributions in aid of Government for prosecuting the war—not usually noticed in historical works.

thro' the parish, of both sexes, young and old. My greatest
concern was for the salvation of her soul, and O! how gladly
and cheerfully would I part with all relations on earth, had I
solid grounds to conclude that they were gone to their everlasting rest; and if otherwise, better they had never been born.

In August, we have accounts that the crops of corns and
Hay is like to suffer much by the long continued drought there
is through all Brittain as well as here; yet the crop here seems
to promise well.

No matterial action has yet occurred in war with the
French, who sent their emissaries into Irland, who stirred up
the wild Irish Papists to Rebellion. But our British army
there having seized their ringleaders, and killed several thousands of these savages, they were soon brought under.[1]

Accompts are received at London from Captn. Wilson of
the ship called the Duff, who went with the missionaries for
Ottahittee in the South Sea. He attempted from Brasile to
get round Cape Horn, the southmost part of America, but met
with such strong gales of southerly winds, whereby he suffered
some damage, and was obligd'd to take a contrary course by the
Cape of Good Hope, and his first landing was at New Zealand,
consisting of two isles as bigg as Great Brittain, containing
about 100,000 inhabitants; thence to Ottahittee, a course of
16,000 miles, in an 100 days. They were joyfully received, and
left about half the number of missionaries there, and a district
or shire allotted them by their King, and that the best of 33
Districts into which the island was divided, and where our
astronomers made their observations on the Transit of Venus
over the sun's disk in 1769. From Ottahittee the Duff sailed
1800 miles to the Friendly Islands, so called, being a cluster of
small isles containing 200,000 souls, and another group of Isles
at some distance from these, called the Society Isles, being all

---

[1] The rebels seized Enniscorthy, sword in hand, and took Wexford, but were
repulsed at Ross. It is said that nearly 20,000 men, commanded by one Harvey,
were met by General Lake at Vinegar Hill, and overthrown with great loss. In
the north of Ireland, also, at Ballynahinch, a body of 7000 were badly beaten,
and though 900 Frenchmen landed at Killala to aid them, they were, after
some success, repulsed, and the rebellion died away.

mostly of the same complexion, language, and friendly disposition. What remained of the missionaries were left there. 'Tis said they had a very gross notion of the Supreme Being ; that He had a wife and children, who were inferior deities, and presided over the starrs, seas and lands etc. They used sacrifices for atonement, and believed in a state of rewards and punishment for good and bad etc.

August 25th. Harvest begins here, and the crop promises well. Some of our frigates have taken about a dozen of Greenlanders belonging to the Dutch, and brought them into Bressay Sound at Lerwick. The Packet set out from thence last month for Aberdeen, and was captured by the way and carried for Norway, where they let the crew go.

August 1st. The newspapers give accounts of a complete victory obtained by Admiral Nielson over the French Squadron from Toulon, at Alexandria in Egypt,[1] tho' they were superior to his squadron in number of ships, guns and men, after landing the French General Buonaparte with an army in Egypt, who went from thence to Grand Cairo, where, 'tis said, he was encountred and defeated by 20,000 Arabs, and himself killed ; while the French Gasettes (to deceive their people) proclaim the contrary. About the same time, a squadron from Brest was sent for Irland to assist the rebells there, having a General on board the Hoch of 74 guns, called Hardi, with 3000 men and arms and an 100 mills. of livers [livres] etc. which were defeated and taken by Admiral Warren[2] with 4 frigates etc. All lenient measures being taken by Government with rebells to submit in vain from their robberies and murders of good subjects, they threaten to extirpate the whole brood of that hellish crew.[3]

1799   Through the tender mercies of a good and gracious God, I am enabled, at the age of 87 years, to keep my tours to the

---

[1] The battle of Aboukir. The French expedition, under Bonaparte, consisted of 300 sail, with 40,000 troops on board.

[2] Admiral Warren : Sir J. B. Warren. The French squadron consisted of one ship of the line and eight frigates.

[3] The author has not much sympathy with the Irish agitators.

north parish without interruption to this month of Feb., when such storms of snow arose that I was keeped from preaching two Sabbaths successively at my nearest church, and great numbers of sheep through the whole parish were smothered in the snow; though, at same time the snow lying so long and wasting gradually away will be of great value to the land.

The war continues with France, and the nation groans under a heavy load of Taxes to support the same.

In reading the account given of Captn Cook's voyages to the Pacifick Ocean for makeing discoveries there and finding out a north eastern passage to the East Indies, which he found impracticable by ice and cold. He was the first who found out the Sandwich Isles, 12 in number, so called from the Earl of Sandwich, first Lord of the Admiralty, who fitted out a ship for him called the Resolution and another for Captain Clerk, who accompanied him. In the largest and most populous of these isles, called Owhyhee, where he lost his life in attempting to recover a pinnace the inhabitants had carried off, there are reckoned 150,000 inhabitants and as many more in the other isles as amount to 400,000 in all—a large field for Christian missionaries.

In May, the Gasettes bear, the war continues. The French are recruiting their navy for attacking Irland. They have fought several battles with the Germans under the command of the Archduke Charles, the Emperor's brother, and have been as oft beaten under their General Jourdan, though they are always victors in their own newspapers. Buonaparte is still warring against the Turks and wild Arabs in Egypt. He met with a signal defeat by Sir Sydney Smith at the siege of a Fort called Acra[1] in the Holy Land. His design of invading Egypt seems to have been with a view to dispossess our East India Company of their territories in Bengal, by sending a number of

---

[1] St. Jean d'Acre. The defence of Acre is one of the most gallant in history. The Mussulman garrison under Hassan Bey, aided by Sir Sidney Smith, with a small body of British troops, repelled Buonaparte in eleven assaults, compelling him to retire with the loss of eight generals, eighty-five officers, and one half of his army.

French officers to stir up their surrounding neighbours to
make war upon them ; and 'tis said their late greatest enemy,
Tippoo Saib,[1] was again threatening to attack their possessions with 100,000 men.

Two ministers from the Missionary Society in Scotland,
viz. Mr. James Haldane and Mr. Wm. Innes[2] came here July
1st, who preached to a crowded congregation at the manse upon
a very short advertisement.   Text, Ecclesiastes 9 and 10,
Whatsoever thy hand findeth thee to do etc.   'Tis remarkable that the scope agreed exactly with the text, Heb. 3 and
7 etc., I was then preaching upon—To-day if ye will hear his
voice harden not your hearts etc.   They fraughted a boat
next day for Lerwick where they preached, and in the opposite
isle of Bressay on the Sabbath day.   From thence they
preached in every parish of the Countrey, each of them for
most part twice every day, distributing very edifying tracts
among the people for religious instruction.   They visited not
only the larger isles of Yell, Unst, and Fetlar, but Foula,
16 miles from Walls, and a smaller isle called Skerries that lies
12 miles from Whalsey—all which they accomplished in four
weeks' time, and preaching gradually on their return to this
parish, where, being providentially stopped a whole week, they
preached every day to a crowded congregation ; the people
gladly leaving their work to hear them.   As their consciences
bore witness that they preached the true spirit of the Gospel,
and though they did not lay down a method, as I commonly
do, to make the people understand and remember what they
hear the better, yet to Brand their Doctrine with the epithet
of loose Harangues is a gross falsehood, for they never lost
sight of their text either in the illustration or application.
Moreover to suppose that such men would undertake such a
vast circuit, and waste their persons and properties with an eye
only to a shadow of vain glory, is ridiculous to suppose.   'Tis

---

[1] Tippoo Saib. His capital, Seringapatam, was this year taken by the
British, and his body was found under a heap of the slain.

[2] Mr. James Alexander Haldane, afterwards minister for many years of the
Tabernacle (Baptist) Congregation, Edinburgh.   Rev. William Innes, afterwards D.D., Baptist minister, Edinburgh.

much more reasonable to conclude that those who bely and slander their characters and conduct, which throw shame and contempt upon false, unfaithful ministers, who neither understand, preach nor practice according to the true spirit of the gospel; who, like the malignant Jews, when they saw the multitude who assembled to hear Paul, were moved with envy, contradicting and Blaspheming; and to publish lies upon the members of such a society of excellent men, whose chief study and endeavours are to promote the glory of the Redeemer, in the eternal salvation of sinners ready to perish for lake of christian knowledge, as 'tis said is done by an act of a late General Assembly, and appointing the same to be read by every minister, which no conscientious man would or can do, without involving himself in a gross absurdity to read falsehoods from the chair of verity.

Aug. 18th. Mr Haldane preached at Ness Kirk, and Mr Innes at Sandwick, and in the evening went off in a six oared boat, and missing Fair Isle, they landed next morning at Sanda in the Orkneys by a favourable Providence, when the wind shifted suddenly to the south for return of the boat next day.[1]

January. Began and continued two weeks blowing a **1800** tempest with snow, whereby many ships are wrecked on rocks of this and other parishes; many lives are lost, and many more, 'tis to be feared, around Great Britain, with the greater loss of souls etc.

Our trade at present employs 10,000 vessels, and 120,000 seamen. Exports valued at 27 mills. ster. Imports at 21 mills. ster. yet the kingdom is burdened with taxes, whereof great sums are given to powers on the Continent for carrying on war against the French; nay, so infatuated are our statesmen as to send armies to attack them there after several fruitless attempts lately at Holland, and Ostend, to the great

[1] The proceedings of this tour are related in *The Lives of Robert Haldane of Airthrey, and of his Brother James Alexander Haldane.* Edin. W. P. Nimmo.

expense of our nation in blood and treasure, which we had no
concern with while masters at sea.

Notwithstanding the most probable methods had been
taken to prevent Mutiny, several hardened wretches had lately
been found guilty of this crime, and condemned to execution
for the same, whereupon Vice-Admiral Waldgrave, President
of the Court, made a speech to the culprits, representing the
heinous nature of their crime, and exhorted them to repentance
in such a serious and forcible manner that no Doctor of
Divinity could have spoken to better purpose.

The French Government has undergone another Revolution by setting up three Consuls, and the Chief one is General
Buonaparte, with a Salary of 20,000 pounds Ster. per an., the
2nd Consul only 6000 Libs. Ster., and the 3rd. also 6000 Ster.
as their Directory and the Legislative members of Convention
are reduced to 300, while the Royalists, by them called
Chouans,[1] are increasing, and several 1000s of Russians are to
be sent to their assistance as reported.

All methods are taken to supply the poor through defi-
ciency of last year's crop in Brittain and Irland.

May. A complete union betwixt Great Brittain and
Irland takes place by the title of the empire of Great Britain
and Ireland, to have one Parliament, but the Irish members
are double to the Scots peers and commoners, as contributing
double of what Scotland does for support of fleets and armies
etc.

The remainder of the French army in Egypt submitted to
the Turks, and had liberty to leave the countrey; yet the war
goes on as formerly.

Emperial Parliament begins Jan. 22, 1801. Malta is taken
from the French, and General Abercromby goes there with
an army, to fall on the French left in Egypt. The yellow
fever rages at Cadiz in Spain, and, as a plague, sweeps off
multitudes. 'Tis said that the present King George, tho' one
of the best Kings that ever was in Great Brittain, is now to
assume the title of King of the United Kingdom of Great

---

[1] *Chouans* : bands of insurgent royalists.

Brittain and Irland, Defender of the Faith, and of the United Church of England and Irland. On earth the Supreme Head, sacred Majesty and supreme head belongs only to the Lord Jesus Christ, to whom all power in heaven and earth is given. Therfore the Giver . . . is equally guilty of blasphemy.

The wars go on with France, who appears to have drawn over Russia and Denmark with Sweden to their assistance.

1801

The necessaries of life continue as scarce and dear as the former year. But 'tis a token for good that the Lord has put into the hearts of all ranks and all parties, both civil and ecclesiastick, such a catholick spirit for promoting pure and undefiled religion through all parts of the world, at home and abroad, and that the Lord is pouring out of his good spirit, both in the Highlands of Scotland, and in Wales etc.

Feb. 23rd. I entered into the 90th year of my age, and may say, with the good Patriarch Isaac, I know not the day of my death, yet desire, with good Job, to wait patiently God's best time etc.

'Tis said a squadron of an 100 ships of war, including Frigats, had sailed for the Baltick to make an attack upon Elsineur, a fortress at the mouth of the Baltick.

April 10th. This day in 1796, being Sabbath, it pleased the Lord suddenly to deprive me of all strength of body, as above narrated; yet blessed be His Great Name, who has still preserved life, while many and some of greatest note for worldly possessions, and younger, have been since cutt off; and that I have lived to find such a spirit stirred up, among all ranks etc., for promoting the Mediator's Kingdom and interests at home and abroad.

A squadron commanded by Admiral Parker destroyed most of the Danish ships of war, but spared Copenhagen.[1] As peace is made with Denmark, will prove a great blessing

---

[1] Copenhagen. Nelson is ignored by the author in this fight. He and Parker were in joint command. The engagement took place in March.

to this countrey,[1] whence we have dales,[2] boats, Bughts[3] etc. they can't be without.

June. Accounts bear that a great victory was gained over the French in Egypt by our army, under the command of two of our best generals, Abercromby and Sir Sidney Smith, who lost their lives in the cause.[4]

Octr. 1st. Peace was made with France, whereupon great rejoicings took place in both Kingdoms. Hence it appears that of all the isles taken etc. they have reserved only Trinidad in the West Indies, the Cape of Good Hope, and the Island of Ceylon in the East Indies, and Malta is restored to the antient Knights of St John. 'Tis well if the peace continue with that restless nation.

It is remarkable, that while I was lecturing upon one of the 15 Psalms of Degrees so called, I was suddenly seized with a sudden slowness in the Circulation of Blood, whereby my sight and strength beginning to fail, I concluded, and sat down, which the people perceiving, and, imagining I was gone, broke out suddenly with the most lamentable outcries, weeping and wailing, and some fell into convulsion fits. The Precentor and one of the Elders came to me, and proposed to sing part of a psalm. But, soon recovering, I stood up and called the congregation to compose themselves, and concluded with prayer etc. as well as ever. It seems to resemble an apoplexy, as I had several times fallen down as dead, but soon recovered. A gentlewoman in the neighbourhood coming next day to enquire how it was with me, I told her a story of that excellent divine, Mr. Andrew Melvine,[5] who took King James 6th by the sleeve, and told him of his ingratitude in persecuting them who were his best friends, and had preserved his life when he was in his swadling clouts from enemies that sought his death and ruin. And when King James threatened to hang him for this, he told him plainly, it would

---

[1] *i.e.* Shetland.   [2] Deals.
[3] *Bughts*: fishing-lines.
[4] This victory at Alexandria was dearly bought by the death of Sir Ralph Abercromby. The author is misinformed as to the fate of Sir Sidney Smith. He lived till 1840, when he died at Paris, aged seventy-six.
[5] Mr. Andrew Melvine : the famous Andrew Melville.

be only in alusion to children playing Shuggy-shew a while and soon to Heaven. He gives an account of the death of Mr. David Black his collegue, who pleasantly resigned his breath at the Lord's Table, which he calls his translation etc.

January 1st. O! the rapid flux of time, which few observe **1802** or know its worth, to improve aright, and thereby prepare for eternity. When one godless crew goes off, another comes on, the generality still resembling the old world, eating and drinking, marrying and giving in marriage etc. Blessed be God, who still reserves a remnant of true Christians who worship him in spirit and in truth, and for whose sake the world is continued till the numbers of Christ's mystical body are fully completed.

February 23rd. Three score and ten was reckoned the standard of man's life in Moses' days, and this day I am arrived at my four score and ten. Lord teach thoughtless mortals so to number their days as to apply their hearts to heavenly wisdom etc.

The Missionary Societies in England and Scotland still go on with their wonted zeal to propagate the Gospel, in its greatest purity, for the conversion of sinners, both at home and abroad, in every quarter of the world, notwithstanding of many interruptions by wars among the savages in Africa and in the South Sea Islands, where three of the missionaries were murdered at Tongatabow,[1] and the means of subsistence, namely Hoggs, yams, and Plantains etc. utterly destroyed by these savages. And tho' only 5 of 30 sent to Ottahitte, the chief Island in these seas remained, yet ten more are sent there to prosecute the design. Many are brought to the saving knowledge of the Lord Jesus Christ at the Cape of Good Hope in Africa, and also in Bengale, where the whole Bible has been translated by Mr Courie[2] into that language, and he has a son called Felix, who preaches to the natives in the same language.

---

[1] The largest of the Friendly Islands.
[2] The Rev. William Carey is doubtless alluded to.

The Bible is also translated into the Chinese language, and Missioners will probably soon be sent from Great Brittain for preaching the Gospel to that populous nation in their own language. The Moravians still persevere to spread the Gospel light in every part of the Globe. A Jew called Fray, lately converted in Germany, came to London and joined with the Missionary Society there, in partaking of the Lord's Supper, and prayed among them, to the admiration of all that heard him. These are the first fruits, and prognosticat the harvest fast approaching when Jews and Gentiles shall be united in one Body, partly fulfilled already. The Pope stripped of all but the name, and the Grand Turk brought very low —and the consummation of all things fast approaching also.

July 14th. The Lord seems to continue his controversy with this countrey[1] by withholding temporal mercies for the abuse of them by gluttony, drunkeness, and whoredoms etc. They have a poor fishing and lean crop; yet mercy is mixed with judgement; some fair days, after much rain, to fill the corns.

In December we are informed by a vessel, which brought provisions from London for the Copper miners of this Parish, that the French had invaded Switzerland with 40,000 men, and that several men of war of French, Dutch, and Spanish had gone up the Mediterranean Sea, and that the Turk were in league with them; and that our Government had sent men of war to protect Malta etc. which if attacked, may probably involve soon into war again with that fickle treacherous nation.

1803   January 1st. I was born 1712 Feb. 23rd which then completes my 91st year. Being licensed to Preach the Gospel 1739, and after, while employed as an assistant for some time to a minister in Buchan, got a call to be minister of this Parish, where I was ordained in April 1743, which will now complete

---

[1] *This countrey*: that is, Shetland.

the 60th year of my ministry among this people of Dunrossness etc. 'Tis only those who are faithful even unto death who obtain the crown of life. So help me, O Lord etc. Unless the countrey is supplied with seed from the North of Scotland, their labouring the land will be in vain, and Orkney shares in the same calamity. . . .

[With this entry, January 1, 1803, the narrative closes. It is not, however, certain that it really ended here. The termination is at the end of a page, with the probability that the subsequent portion is lost. Well worn with years, his ninety-first being nearly completed, he might well have laid down the pen which for more than sixty years he had so cunningly handled, not only in this narrative but in many other writings. But he did not do so. The Kirk-session Records of the parish bear witness to his conscientious earnestness in the discharge of his duties to the very last. For more than two years longer these Records are indited, almost wholly, in his own hand, the last entry being February 3, 1805, twelve days before his death—'No travelling'; the state of the weather ostensibly the cause of his being detained from conducting service in one or other of the churches under his charge. The last sermon recorded is on the 14th of October preceding. On each subsequent Sunday he is 'detained' or 'keept back' by 'bad weather,' or by 'frost and snow,' or it is simply 'no travelling.' But it is not improbable that while reasons were assigned for his absence in this way, the real cause was that his travelling days were o'er and his work accomplished. He died on 15th February 1805.

While the object in the present undertaking is to emphasise the local and general, rather than the personal, interest of Mill's work, readers who have followed the gallant old man's story up to nearly his ninety-second year, will not grudge to have placed before them what is known of him during the closing years thereafter of his life by way of conclusion to the auto-biographic narrative. The following is therefore extracted from the Kirk-session Records.]

1803   [1] April 17. The Minister lectur'd Ps. 144 from v. 9th
April 24. The Minister preach'd. Text Prov. 4 and 23.
May 1, 8 and 15. No sermon at Sandwick—Bad weather.
May 22. The Minister lectur'd at Sandwick.
May 29. The Minister keept from Church by bad weather.
June 5. The Minister lectur'd Ps. 145 to v. 10th.
June 12. The Minister preach'd at Sandwick.
June 19. The Minister lectur'd Ps. 145 ad finem.
June 26. The Minister preach'd. Text ut supra.
July 3. The Minister keep'd from Sandwick, bad weather.
July 10. The Minister lectur'd at Sandwick.
July 17. The Minister lectur'd on Ps. 146.
July 24. The Minister preach'd. Text ut supra.
July 31. The Minister preach'd at Sandwick.
August 7. The Minister lectur'd Ps. 147 ab initio.
August 14. The Minister preach'd. Text ut supra.
August 21. The Minister lectur'd at Sandwick.
August 28. The Minister lectur'd Ps. 147 ad finem.
September 4. Minister preach'd. Text ut supra.
September 11. Minister keep'd from Sandwick etc.
September 18. Minister preach'd at Sandwick.
September 25. The Minister lectur'd Ps. 148th.
October 2. The Minister preach'd. Text ut supra.
October 9, 16, 23, 30. November 6. (Detained from
    Sandwick.)
November 13. Minister preach'd at Ness Kirk.
November 17. Fast Day appointed by Government on
    account of our war with France and a famine by two
    years' bad crops etc. The Minister preach'd Luke 5
    v. 31st.
November 20. The Minister preach'd at Sandwick.
November 27. The Minister lectur'd Ps. 149th.
December 4, 11, 18, 25. (Detention by bad weather etc.)

---

[1] A portion of the Records is lost from 11th March 1802 to April 17th,
1803.   The service, when not mentioned as 'at Sandwick,' is at the parish
church of Dunrossness. Sandwick is several miles distant, then to be reached
only on foot or on horseback.

January 1. Minister lectur'd at Sandwick.

January 8. Minister keep'd from Church by stormy weather.

January 15, 22, 29. February 5, 12. (Detention by weather.)

February 19. The Minister preach'd at Sandwick.

February 26, March 4, 11. (Detention.)

March 18. Minister lectur'd at Sandwick.

March 25. The Minister keep'd from Church by storm etc.

April 1. The Minister lectur'd on Psalm 50th.

> (A case of Church discipline this day. On payment of
> 30/ stg. to the poor, the parties were dismissed
> for one day's appearance and publick rebuke as
> usual.)

April 8, 15. (Detained from Sandwick by weather.)

April 22. The Minister preach'd at Sandwick.

April 29. The Minister lectur'd. Ecclesiastes 1 Chapter
to v. 4th. (A case of discipline again.)

May 6. The Minister preach'd. Text Luke 5 and 31st
(2 cases of discipline).

May 13. The Minister keept from Sandwick.

May 20. The Minister preach'd at Sandwick.

May 27. The Minister lectur'd Eccles. 1st from v. 4th.

June 3. The Minister preach'd. Text Luke 5 and 31st
ut supra.

June 10. No preaching at Sandwick. Bad weather.

June 17. The Minister preached at Sandwick.

June 24. The Minister lectur'd Eccles. 1st from 11 and
12th.

July 1. The Minister preach'd. Text ut supra.

July 8. Minister preach'd at Sandwick.

July 15. The Minister lectur'd, Eccles. ab initio.

July 22. The Minister preach'd. Text Luke 5 and 31.

July 29. Minister preach'd at Sandwick.

August 5. The Minister lectur'd, Ecclesiastes Chapter 2^d
from v. 12th ad finem cap. [Cases of discipline thereafter.]

August 12. The Minister preached. Text Luke 5 and
31st.

August 19. Minister not at Sandwick, bad weather.

1804

August 26. Minister Lectur'd Ps. 2d at Sandwick.
September 2. The Minister Lectur'd Eccles. 3^d chap. to v. 11.
Septr 9. The Min^r Preach'd. Text ut supra.
Septr 16. Min^r keept from Sandwick, bad weather.
Septembr 23. Likewise keept from Do.
Septembr 30. Min^r Preach'd at Sanwick.
October 7th. Min^r Lectur'd Eccles. Ch. 3 from v. 11 ad finem.

> Robert Jamison and Elspet Laurencedaughter were solemnly Exhorted, Rebuk'd, and Dismissed on Repentance and paying 20 shilling Ster. fine.

Octr 14. The Min^r Preach'd. Text ut Supra.
Octr. 21st. Bad weather kept Min^r from Sandwick.
Octr. 28th. Min^r keep'd from Sandwick by Do.
Novembr 4. Min^r detained by bad weather.
Novembr 11th. No travelling to Sandwick.
Novr 18th. Min^r keept back by Do.
Novr 25th. No travelling, frost and snow.
Decembr 2^d. Min^r still Detain'd by Do.
Decembr 9th. No travelling—Bad Weather.
Decembr 16th. Min^r detain'd from Sandwick by Do.
Decembr 23^d. Min^r keep't back by Do.
Decembr 30th. Bad weather for Sandwick.

1805   January 6th. No travelling.
January 13th. [Writing almost invisible, but undoubtedly ' No travelling,' indicating faded eyesight.]
January 20th. No travelling.
Janry 27th.   Do.
February 3^d.   Do.
Febry. 10th.

[*Note.*—The last date 'Febry. 10th' has apparently been penned at the time when he inscribed the preceding entry, in anticipation of what the record might be; but strength failed, and he never resumed the pen. A long entry, of date October 7th, about the distribution of the Government Charity Meal (*see* APPENDIX), is in distinct and vigorous handwriting. All the subsequent entries exhibit unsteadiness of hand and impaired eyesight. As already mentioned, his death occurred on 15th February, but there is no record in the Minutes of his death or burial, and there is no tombstone to commemorate him. The next entry is dated 30th June 1805, and narrates the settlement of the Rev. John Duncan, formerly Assistant at Bressay, Burray and Quarff, as his successor.]

APPENDIX

I.

EXTRACTS FROM THE KIRK-SESSION RECORDS OF THE PARISH OF DUNROSSNESS, 1764-1805.[1]

MORAL DELINQUENCY.

1764, March 20.—John Halcrow and Helen Roeman. Halcrow 'flatly denied,' and 'was willing to give his oath accordingly.' The case came up again on 16th September 1764, when 'the said John Halcrow being again asked by the Moderator if he persisted in his denial of guilt, as he had done before the Presbytery, answered he did, but seemed not so positive as formerly, whereupon the Moderator told him he was desir'd by the Presbytery to tender him the Oath of Purgation, which was read to him, and told him at same time, that if he could swallow that, under a Consciousness of guilt, he would stick at Nothing, and moreover showed him the dangerous Consequences of such a step, and gave a Copy of the Oath to an Elder in the neighbourhood to read it and warn him of his danger, if guilty —to see if he will confess the Crime next Preaching Sabbath.' Next Sunday, September 23, Halcrow appeared before the

---

[1] It has been explained in the Introduction that the records, so far as preserved, begin in the year 1764. It has not been attempted to give anything like a chronological transcript, but merely to present a few examples, under different heads, to show the mode of procedure and the penalties inflicted in cases which were then within the acknowledged jurisdiction of the Session, and to illustrate the conditions of parochial economics, as regards the support of the poor, and the efforts to meet occasions of destitution, etc.

Session and confessed guilt. 'The Minister Rebuk'd him sharply, and exhorted him to a sincere and hearty Repentance. He was summoned apud acta to appear next Preaching Sabbath before the Congregation. Helen Roeman appeared for the first time, in consequence of the Sentence of the Presbytery to stand a full year.'

1765, March 3.—The Minister Lectur'd Rom. 1st ab initio to v. 6. Session met and Constitute by prayer. John Strang, a young man in Virkie, and Janet Cadil, being delated as guilty, being Cited, Compear'd and acknowledg'd guilt together. They were exhorted to a Sincere and hearty Repentance, and summoned apud acta to appear next Lord's Day to make satisfaction for the scandal.

John Harper and Margaret Charlesdaughter appear'd the 3d time before the Congregation, were Rebuk'd and Dismiss'd from Discipline.

1769, Septr. 24.—A case of antenuptial impropriety. Parties denied the charge, 'and were willing to purge themselves by oath. But the Session did not think proper to be rash, and therefore the Moderator desired them to wait of him at his house, and he would shew them first a Copy of the Oath they were to take, and summoned them apud acta to appear before the Session next Sabbath day.'

The case was not however again brought up. Other similar antenuptial offenders confessing, were 'exhorted to a sincere and hearty Repentance, and summoned to appear next preaching Sabbath before the Congregation to be Rebuk'd etc.' A single appearance was usually deemed insufficient 'satisfaction for the Scandal,' as it was termed, and appearances for the third, fourth, up to the ninth, time are frequently found before the parties were dismissed from discipline.

1773, August 1.—Robert Moodie and Ann Sinclair having obeyed the appointment of Presbytery by standing 26 Sabbaths before the Congregation were Rebuk'd for the last time and Dismiss'd from Discipline. Paid 15 shillings ster.

1774, April 10.—Thos Hay and Barbara Stout having made their appearance before the Congregation for an half year were this day Rebuk'd and Dismiss'd from Discipline, having paid in 12 Libs. [*i.e.* about £1 stg.] of fine to the Treasurer.

1776, October 6.—Parties confessed, but ' this being a relapse to the woman, and a trelapse to the man, were appointed to stand an half year as usual in such cases.'

1776, October 27.—Margaret Stout, whose husband had been off the countrey for four years past, and no accounts of him, or from him ; she had drawn up with an unmarried man called George Arcus, and they both applied first to the Session and again to the Presbytery for Marriage, which was denied, whereupon said George had the impudence to tell the Presbytery (tho' they were advis'd to apply to the Commissary and take the Legal steps usual in such cases) that, if they would not allow them marriage, they would cohabit together as man and wife, and accordingly they seem to have done. [In consequence of this cohabitation and its result Margaret was sharply rebuked, as usual, and summoned to appear before the Presbytery at their next meeting at Lerwick. There is no evidence in the Minutes of what ensued from this compearance before the higher Court.]

BLASPHEMY.

1765, September 29.—George Gilbertson appeared before the Session, being summoned for Cursing and Swearing, and it was proved, by two Witnesses, viz. Malcom Smith and Thomas Johnson, that he prayed that God might Damn his Neighbour Peter Halcrow, for which the Session appointed him to stand before the Congregation next Preaching Sabbath and be Rebuk'd and Pay an half crown to the poor as a fine.

1766, February 23.—Elspet Sutherland in Hilwel being summon'd to this Diet for taking the name of God in Vain, and Marg^t Burgher also for Praying the Devil might go down the s^d Elspet's throat,—the same was proved upon both by Jacobina Arcus and Ursula Andrewsdaughter, who declared upon oath, that they heard them say what was laid to their Charge ; Therefore the Session appointed Elspet Sutherland, being of bad fame, and most Criminal, to stand 3 Lord's Days and be Rebuk'd before the Congregation, and Marg^t Burgher to appear also and be Rebuk'd once, and were both summon'd apud acta to appear next Preaching Sabbath. Closed with Prayer.

1767, March 8.—Thomas Fea in Noss was Rebuk'd before the Congregation for Imprecating Damnation upon his Neighbour and taking God's name in Vain, for which the Session appointed him to appear 3 Sabbaths before the Congregation and Dispens'd therefore with his fine, in Regard of his poverty.

1767, Septr. 27.—Marg^t Burleigh in Scatness being delated as Imprecating and praying that evil might befall her Neighbour Christin Meinlan—that God might make her so mad as to be a wonder to all that saw her, and be made so blind as to go on hands and foot and none to pity her, Laur. Lisk and Helen Ridling were Summon'd as Witnesses; and Compeiring denied that she mentioned the name of God, or that the last part of the Charge was true. She was Rebuk'd and Dismiss'd.

1768, July 31.—Peter Jamison in Rerwick being delated as guilty of the same [imprecating damnation, etc.], and being called denied the Same, whereupon Andrew Work and Laurence Sinclair there, being Call'd as Witnesses, purg'd of malice etc. Sworn and Interrogate, the former depones that he heard Peter Jamison forsd. pray Damnation on George Brown for a Villain, and the Latter depones that he heard him Pray that God might Damn him for a Knave or Villain; And the Session observing further that Peter Jamison being Rebuk'd for the same Crime last year, before them, was attended with this aggravation, the Moderator Exhorted to a Sincere Repentance and Summon'd him apud acta to appear before the Congregation next Lord's day and be Rebuk'd for this hainous Crime, paying an half Crown to the poor, which he had the Impudence to refuse, saying again and again he would be obstinate.

1770, October 21.—Barbara Stout gave in a Bill last Session, undertaking to prove that Marg^t Robertsdaughter had prayed that the Devil might burn her and her Peats, giving Robert Moodie and his mother Elizabeth Sutherland for Witnesses, who both Declar'd that they heard Margaret Robertsdaughter utter the very same words, but that the s^d Barbara Stout pray'd at same time that God might Damn her the said Marg^t Robertsdaughter, and that they were willing to give their Oaths accordingly before any Judge Competent— for both which Scandals the Session appointed Marg^t Robertsdaughter to appear two Several Lord's Days and be Rebuk'd before the Congregation, and Barbara Stout to appear first Preaching Sabbath to be Rebuk'd before the Congregation and pay an half Crown of fine as usual in such cases. Closed with prayer.

1778, October 4.—George Halcrow in Bigton Complain'd that Robert Sinclair there had said in presence of George Brown in Rerwick and Hary Sinclair in Irland, that if he had gotten fish-hooks from Margt. Halcrow (who is a poor woman living in Clifts of Cunningsburgh) and that on the Sabbath Day, that he would have got as many fish as he got, as if it had been thro' Witchcraft. As Hary Sinclair, one of the Witnesses, was absent, the Session Delay'd further proceedings till the Witnesses are Examin'd, and therefore the Moderator Summon'd all the parties to attend on the Session for this effect next Preaching Sabbath. [The following Sunday, the 11th, the Minister was absent at the north parish church at Sandwick, but the next Sunday after, the 18th, was a 'preaching Sabbath,' and the case was again called.] After Sermon, the two Witnesses, George Brown and Hary Sinclair above mentioned, being Call'd, Compear'd and Declar'd upon Oath, that Robert Sinclair in Bigton was guilty of what was laid to his Charge by George Halcrow as above, whereby he not only brought up a bad Report upon his Neighbour, but Derogated from the honour of God by ascribing the Catching of fish to the Devil, as if it was in his pow'r to dispose of God's Creatures, which the Session having maturely Consider'd, appointed the said Robert Sinclair to be Rebuk'd publickly before the Congregation next Preaching Sabbath and Summon'd him apud acta accordingly. Clos'd with prayer.

1779, August 8.—Janet Stout, a poor Widow in Maills, was Charg'd as guilty of taking God's holy Name in Vain by praying God to Damn a Dogg in her wrath—which she confess'd before the Session, whereupon the Mod^r Rebuk'd her for her wickedness and folly, Exhorted to a sincere and hearty Repentance, and Summon'd her apud acta to appear the next two Preaching Sabbaths, before the Congregation, to satisfy Discipline for the Scandal. Clos'd with Prayer.

1792, October 14.—Henry Gilbertson in Scatnes being Delated for Imprecating Damnation on Adam Barnson and William Sinclair in Garth, when at sea fishing—these being all Summon'd to this Diet and Compearing,—Henry Gilbertson Confess'd the Imprecation fors^d, but denied that he mentioned the Name of God, and said also that Adam Barnson had prayed that the Devil might break his Leggs, which he did not Deny—for which Crimes being Rebuk'd etc. by the Mod^r, they were both appointed to appear next Lord's Day and be Rebuk'd before the Congregation, and the fors'd Henry Gilbertson to pay an half Crown fine to the poor. Clos'd with Prayer.

1801, October 18.—Barbara Hay in Tolob being delated as guilty of praying that God would send the Devil down her Neighbours' throat, was attested by John Lesslie, an Elder, and confessed: was Rebuk'd before the Congregation and dismissed, paying an half Crown to the poor [£1, 10s. Scots].

SABBATH-BREAKING.

1765, Jany. 27.—Adam Aiken and daughter Ann Aiken being summon'd as guilty of Sabbath Breach, it was prov'd against them by Peter Halcrow and Robt. Marwick, Witnesses, that they Roll'd an half Barrel Tallow from the Banks on the Sabbath Day Evening, which having given Scandal and offence in the Neighbourhood, they were appointed to stand and be Rebuk'd before the Congregation and pay a Shilling of fine—which they refused to do. [Nothing more heard of the case.]

EXCOMMUNICATION.

1767, October 17.—John Nicol was excommunicated according to appointment of the Presbytery, with the greater sentence of Excommunication, after several years' continued obstinacy, refusing to give obedience to discipline, or make satisfaction for the scandal of the heinous crime of adultery committed with Helen Roeman.

1800, June 8.—Similar sentence on a woman for continued obstinacy to discipline.

PAROCHIAL FINANCE.

1765, January 31.—The statement submitted by their Treasurer to the Session this date shows—

Amount collected . .	£28	6	0
Penalties and Mort Cloath .	19	16	0

[About £4 stg.]	£48	2	0	*Scots*
Disbursements [about £1, 2s. stg.]	13	0	0	

Remains, .	£35	2	0	*Scots*

There are on the roll—

9 Extraordinary Poor, receiving £1, 10/ *Scots*, or 2/6ᵈ each.
11 Ordinary   Do.   „   £1, 4/   „   or 2/   „
4 Widows   „   £1, 16/   „   or 3/   „
and 6 other persons receiving trifling allowances.

Robert Omand, Precentor, receives £4 Scots, or say 6/8 stg.
Robert Ollason, Officer,   „   £3   „   or „   5/ stg.
The Treasurer,   „   £2   „   or „   3/6 stg.

At the same time 8s. stg. is allowed towards the expense of burying an Orkneyman.

The next financial statement is submitted in the spring of 1766, and shows—

11 Ordinary Poor, advanced from £1, 4/ to £1, 16/ Scots [=3s. each].

4 Widows, Do. „ £1, 16/ to £2, 8/ Scots [=4s. each].

The Preceptor, Do. „ £4, to £4, 10/ Scots [=7s. 6d.].

The Kirk Officer, £2, 2/ Scots [=3s. 6d.].

The Presbytery Clerk and Officer, £2, 6/8 Scots [=4s.].

For Summonses and 1 quire Paper to the Clerk, 1/2^d Stg.

To William Stove in Garth to buy a Bible 1/10^d Stg.

N.B.—The statement as to the Extraordinary Poor is apparently not given.

A statement is again engrossed on October 2d of the same year, and the next on February 11th, 1767, showing that these statements did not apply to fixed uniform periods, but were submitted periodically as circumstances rendered convenient. According to the statement last referred to, among the fines owing to the Session is one of £2, 8s. Scots (=4s.) by 'Young Quendal,' who is more than once alluded to in the Autobiography, and 'Lady Brew.'

A year elapses till the next statement is brought forward, 18th February 1768, giving 10 Extraordinary and 10 Ordinary paupers, receiving respectively 3s. and 2s. each, besides a number of smaller donations to other persons. But there is again a distribution in October; and another in the month of February 1769, with again the lapse of a year till 22d February 1770, the rates of distribution on each occasion being about the same. In short, there is always a statement submitted in Spring, in the months of February, March, or April, with occasionally a half-yearly statement in Autumn.

The following figures may be quoted from the Accounts submitted on April 13, 1787, a year from the last previous Statement of March 18, 1786:—

RECEIPTS.

					£	s.	d.
On hand at last Distribution	.	.			£9	17	0
Collections £17, 4s. Fines £12		.			29	4	0
Mort cloth money	.	.	.	.	2	14	0
Donation from Oliver Smith		.	.		2	2	0
Poor Seats money as usual		.	.		0	18	0
Mr. Mill's Donation at this time					12	0	0

[£4, 14s. 7d. stg.]   *Scots.*   £56 15 0

DISBURSEMENTS.

					£	s.	d.
5 Extraordinary Poor	@ 12/	[1s. stg.]		=	£3	0	0
4 Widows	.	.	@ 12/	.	.	= 2 8 0	
15 Ordinary Poor .	@ 18/	[1s. 6d. stg.]		=	13	10	0
29 'Present Supplies'	@ 12/	.	.	=	17	8	0
1 Do.	.	@ 5/	.	.	=	0	5	0
To the Clerk	.	.	[10s. stg.]		6	0	0
To the Officer	.	.	[4s. 2d. stg.]		2	10	0
To the Clerk and Officer for paper [1s. stg.]					0	12	0

[£3, 16s. 1d. stg.]   *Scots.*   £45 13 0

The Widows' Fund of the Brakes, the rent
whereof to be paid by Sumburgh for
Crop 1785, £7 *Scots* [=11s. 8d. stg.]

The usual positions of the Extraordinary and Ordinary
Poor are here reversed (perhaps by a clerical error), the Ordinary
receiving the higher sum of 1s. 6d. stg. and the Extraordinary
only 1s. The next year (April 3, 1788) the normal positions
are resumed, the Extraordinary poor being paid at the rate
of £1, 10s. *Scots* each, or 2s. 6d. stg., while the Ordinary receive
£1, 4s. or 2s. stg. only. The allowances were the same up to
the time of the last statement, in Mill's handwriting, of the
disbursements on behalf of the poor, April 9, 1801.

After the appointment of the new minister, the Rev.
John Duncan, ·in 1805, the financial statements are entered
in sterling money. In the account submitted on 21st April

1806, the Poor of the first class, of whom there are 14, receive 2s. 6d. each; the second class, of whom there are 7, receive 1s. 8d. each; and the third class, 20 in number, 1s. 3d. each; with 4 widows on the Mortified Land, receiving 2s. 11d. each (11s. 8d. in all from that source).

The last annual statement in the volume of the Session Records under review was considered on 2d February 1841, a date approaching the time when the new system, under the Poor-Law Act, came into play. The number on the roll was then 50, with allowances, varying according to circumstances, of 1s. 6d., 2s. 6d., 3s., 3s. 6d., 5s., and 6s., the larger sums being usually in cases where husband and wife jointly were the recipients. The sources of income were the same as formerly, viz. Ordinary and Sacramental Collections (£22, 10s. 10d.); use of Mortcloth (6s.), and Rent of Mortified Lands (11s. 8d.).

Fines for irregularities in morals gradually disappear after the commencement of the century, though inquisitions by the Session in cases of such scandal continued for long afterwards, in much the same way as formerly, but in greatly diminished numbers. In the year 1834 a sum of £1, 10s. appears in the accounts for a breach of the Sabbath, by a number of Scatness and Exnaboe men, in taking ashore, at an early hour on the Sabbath morning, some seamen's chests from Davis' Straits whaling vessels apparently just arrived on the coast with crews partly of Shetlanders. This was reckoned 'a very great outrage and annoyance to the well disposed.'

In all these statements of parochial receipts and expenditure the figures refer to the parish of Dunrossness proper, and not to the parishes of Sandwick and Cunningsburgh, which were united with it as one *ministry*, but whose statistics were kept separately in the respective districts.

The sum charged for the expense of a pauper funeral appears to have been, in 1778, 3 shillings. For the use of the mortcloth, 6d. and upwards was charged.

1778, March 5.—The Session being Inform'd that the friends of some poor that are on the Session funds did at their decease carry off several things that belonged to them which might have serv'd for funeral Charges: Therefore the Session did and hereby ordains and appoints the Elders in the Neighbourhood to certify the friends of such poor people that if they [meddle?] in time Coming with any of their effects till their funeral Charges are Cleared off, the Session will not give one farthing for defraying their funeral Charges after this date.

MISCELLANEOUS.

1793, July 7.—The Minister preached at Fair Isle (as Brough,[1] the Proprietor, had sent out his Bigg Boat for him), and where he continued for the space of two Weeks, during which time he examined the Society's School, and all the young people of the Isle upon the questions in the Assemblie's Catechism, Baptized nine Children, ordained four Elders, Rebuk'd and Dismiss'd two Delinquents, Preach'd two Sabbaths before and afternoon, and Distributed what was Collected at that time among the poor of Fairisle.

1798, March 11.—Malcom Halcrow, an Elder, had a son, an extraordinary object of Charity, as a Bone was taken from his Body and Represented to the Session—whereupon they appointed £1, 10 and 6 pennies Scots [2s. 6d. stg.] to be given etc.

[*Same date.*] It was represented to the Session that as all the Necessaries of Life were risen so, and all the Fees of Clerk and Officer were doubled through the Countrey, the Kirk Session unanimously agreed to make for Proclamation of Marriage Bans a shilling Sterling to the Clerk and 6 pence to the Officer, as also 6 pence to the Clerk for each Baptism and 4 pence to the officer in all time Coming thro' the Ministry.

DESTITUTION IN THE ISLANDS—GOVERNMENT AID.[2]

1804, May 17.—Session met and constitute by Prayer. Took into consideration the state of the poor, and their funds

---

[1] Stewart of Brough in Orkney was then the proprietor of the 'Fair Isle.'
[2] The years 1778, 1783, 1784, 1785, and other years, appear to have been times of great scarcity, and large quantities of meal were sent to Shetland, some

for distribution, and finding by the failure of the two last years' Crops[1] that it pleased God to put it in the hearts of our Governors to send two ships of good Burthen loaded with Victual etc. for supply of the poor; yet as the same could go but a little way for supporting such a great number as the Countrey contains,—Therefore as it has pleased a good and gracious God, who mixeth mercy with judgement, to send such seasonable and refreshing weather for nourishing the Seed sown: Therefore the Kirk Session Resolved to expend what money remained in their Treasurer's hands upon the most necessitous of the poor who could neither work nor want, among whom many small Children would be found, whose parents at present were not in a capacity to maintain them: Therefore the Moderator entrusted the Elders to make an impartial enquiry into the state of families under their inspection, and make a faithfull report that the distribution may be ordered accordingly; and for furthering this good design the Minister gave in to the Treasurer of his own Bounty 20/ stg. to be added to the Stock remaining, and the Session is to Consider the different necessities and distribute accordingly. [This is followed by some details relating to the distribution.]

Closed with prayer [in Mill's handwriting].

1804, Oct[r] 7.—Government being Inform'd of the great straits this Countrey was reduced [to] by the Defects of two years Crops successively, was pleased to order frequent supplies, and towards the end of Last Month, a vessel of 150 Tuns, containing 180 Bolls of Barley and Oatmeal mix'd together for supply of the poor, directed for the Collector of the Customs, who met with some of the Principal Heads of Families in Lerwick to consult upon the most proper mode of Distribution and wrote a letter to me accordingly, whereupon having call'd the Elders of this southmost part of the

---

of which came to Dunrossness, as is recorded in the Diary. The Minutes of the Session 1782-1785 are lost, and this Minute is the first which deals so fully with the circumstances of destitution.

[1] The remainder of this long Minute after the word 'crops,' though unquestionably drafted, or dictated, by Mill, is written out in another hand, as being too laborious for the aged penman.

Ministry to meet at Skelberry, I read to them the Collector's
Letter, which was to consider and agree upon the most
[needful?] objects entitled to this Charity, and upon due
Consideration we unanimously agreed to divide them into
Classes, Ordinary and Extraordinary, the Extraordinary such
as Could neither work or want. Other families had such as
Could work a little but could not maintain them, therefore
to get only one part of what the Extraordinary poor got.
Such as could afford a little money might have a Lispund of
the meal fors'd at 2 shillings sterling, upon delivery of the
money to the Clerk and receiving his Note for the same,
according to appointment of the Kirk-Session who were
accountable to Government for the same. And as this Parish
is double in number to the other Parishes, we appointed our
Treasurer to demand a 6th part of the Cargo, and our Clerk
to give an Extract of this Minute to the Precenter and
Clerk of Sandwick etc. that the Elders of Session there might
act according to the same plan of Distribution among the
poor, the which, with Fair isle, are about an equality of
number with this south part, and Consequently have an equal
Claim for one half as their proportion, and the Clerk was
likewise appointed to send an account of what was done to
the Collector of Customs at Lerwick.

Note.—In connection with the destitution in Shetland in the
year 1804, above reported and exemplified in the Kirk-Session
Records, it appears that a formal Petition on the subject was
sent up to Parliament from Shetland, a Report on which was
ordered to be printed on 29th March 1804. The following
is a copy:

REPORT ON THE SHETLAND ISLANDS PETITION.

The Committee to whom the Petition of the Owners
of Lands in the Islands of SHETLAND, for themselves and on Behalf of the Heritors and Inhabitants of the said Islands, was referred :—

Have, pursuant to the Order of the House, examined the
Matter of the said Petition : To prove the Allegations whereof,

MR. JOHN SCOTT, being examined, said, That he is a

Resident in the Island of Valey, about 20 Miles from Lerwick
—he was there during the last Season—that the last Harvest
was very unfavourable owing to bad Weather—that Seed
was imported from Berwick, and some from the North Country
also, but neither answered—that the Population of the
Shetland Islands is from 20 to 22,000—that the Expence of
the Meal and Bear imported last Season amounted to more
than £30,000—that the Harvest of 1802 was a very indifferent
one—that the Fishery affords a great Supply for the Islands,
and the fishery of 1802, as well as that of 1803, was unfavourable—that the Inhabitants live on Oatmeal, Milk, and Fish—
that great quantities of Cattle were sold last year to purchase
Grain, whereby a great quantity of Land was laid waste on
account of the Cattle being so disposed of—that he only
knows of one Life being lost on account of Scarcity, but as
the Season advances the Scarcity will be more alarming—
that Seed will be wanted, and if not sent soon will be
too late to be sown for the Harvest—that the Seed is put
into the ground in April and May — that they have no
Barley, and they sow Bigg[1] in May—that if no Relief is
given many Lives will be lost—that the Relief afforded by
Government which arrived in the middle of January last
saved the lives of many persons—that he Contributed last
year Four years' Income to the Necessities of the Islands,
and that the Contributions of the Islands in general were
not less—that the Supply in 1784 was sent in Money, and
was of great service—that the Distresses now are much
greater than in 1784—the People were then in a better
Condition, having had several good years ; but by the great
Exertions made last year, on account of the Failure of the
Crop and Fishery, the Funds for their Relief are exhausted :
—And the Witness added, That the Seed Potatoes are very
scarce, and that if some were sent it would be of great
service.

This cry of destitution was not silenced by the generous
aid of Government in the year 1804. It seems to have broken
out anew a few years later, as indeed it has done periodically

---

[1] Bere.

since then down to very recent years. In the Estimates and Accounts of Miscellaneous Services, issued from the Treasury Chambers, Whitehall, 21st March 1814, the following entry occurs :—

An Account of the Sum which will be wanted to defray the Charge incurred in April 1813, in the Purchase of Grain and Potatoes, conveyed to the *Shetland* Islands, for the Relief of the distressed Inhabitants there.

One Thousand Nine Hundred and Eighty-seven Pounds Eighteen Shillings and Two Pence :

Clear of Fees, and all other Deductions.

II.

EXTRACTS FROM THE RECORDS OF THE PRESBY-
TERY OF ZETLAND ANENT THE GLEBE
LANDS OF DUNROSSNESS.

At a meeting of the Presbytery of Zetland at Lerwick, 3rd June 1737, on an application by the Rev. William Maxwell, minister of Dunrossness, anent the ruinous state of the kirk at Sandwick and the manse at Skelberry, it was resolved to hold a meeting at the said Manse on the last Wednesday of the month, and another at the kirk at Sandwick on the following day, in order to determine what might be requisite in the circumstances.

The Presbytery met on 29th June accordingly, at Skelberry : present, Mr. William Archbald (minister of Unst) moderator, Messrs. Robert Gray (minister of Nesting), James Grierson (minister of Tingwall), Walter Hugens (minister of Sandsting and Aithsting), Thomas Waldie (minister of Lerwick), William Maxwell (minister of Dunrossness), and James Buchan (minister of Walls and Sandness). The other members absent.

Mr. Maxwell, the minister of the parish, being interrogated whether he was in possession of a glebe as Law requires, answered 'that he was not in possession of any glebe; but, at the same time, he was informed that there were ten merks land in the room of Skelberry which are commonly reckoned the glebe, which he had given the present tenants a legal warning to flit and remove themselves from, notwithstanding of which they still continue their possession ; and at the same time Mr. Maxwell informed the Presbytery that Robert Sinclair of Quendale affirmed that although former ministers had been in possession of foresaid lands yet they had not

possessed them as a glebe, and that he and his predecessors
had paid feu and scatt for said lands.

'The Presbytery, taking the above affair into their consideration, find that Mr. Walter Hugens [the previous minister of the parish, now of Sandsting and Aithsting] had
obtained a Decreet of ejection and removing against Robert
Sinclair of Quendale, from the said lands, before Mr. John
Mitchell of Westshore, Stewart Depute of this Country, in the
year 1722, upon which he had entered into the peaceable possession of the foresaid lands, and that he continued therein
during the whole time of his incumbency in the foresaid united
parishes [Dunrossness, Sandwick, and Cunningsburgh]: Considering also that Mr. Maxwell is entitled by his presentation
to the glebe as possessed by Mr. Hugens, do therefore recommend it to said Mr. Maxwell to pursue a removal against the
present possessors of the said lands before the Stewart or his
Depute, in order to his peaceable possession thereof.'

At the Kirk of Lerwick, June 7th 1739.   After prayer.
Sederunt: Mr. William Archbald, Moderator pro
tempore, Messrs. Robert Gray, James Grierson,
William Maxwell, William Gifford (minister of
Northmavine), and James Williamson (apparently
an elder).

Mr. Maxwell the minister of Dunrossness again presented
a petition in reference to his stipend, in which the following
occurs—

'He [Robert Sinclair of Quendale] also kept violent possession of the ruinous manse, glebe, grass and pertinents thereof,
formerly possessed by the ministers of the said parish past
memory of man, and for which the former incumbent obtained
Decreet of removing against him and Hornings thereon, and
has uplifted three years' land mails and duties of the said glebe,
manse, and pertinents since the petitioner's admission to the
ministry of these parishes, whereby the petitioner has been put
to the trouble, first, of pursuing a removal against the said
Quendale's pretended tenants, occupiers of the glebe, and, after
obtaining decreet against them, to pursue anew, the following
year, a removing against the said Quendale, and for paying

back the three former years' mails which he has uplifted and refuses to pay, denying the petitioner's incontestable right to the said glebe in the process thereanent before the Stewart Court of Zetland.'

In 1740 the question was brought before the General Assembly, on a Petition and Complaint by Maxwell setting forth the ruinous state of the kirk, want of manse, glebe and grass, and non-payment of stipend.

Mr. Mill succeeded Mr. Maxwell in the incumbency of Dunrossness, Sandwick, and Cunningsburgh, in 1743; and, as is abundantly evident in the pages of the Diary, he too was soon under the necessity of taking up the vexed question of the glebe, its extent and boundaries. His views are expressed in the following communication, which is apparently a mandate to Sinclair of Quendale to represent him at a meeting, under orders of the Sheriff-Substitute of Zetland, for the purpose of dividing the Scattald, or Commonty, belonging to certain properties :—

DEAR SIR,—I, Mr. John Mill etc. understanding that the Sheriff-Substitute has appointed a day towards the latter end of this month of May 1753 for choosing 45 m . . . and 15 . . . of the N . . according to Act of Parliament for dividing the Commonty belonging to the lands of Skelberry, Outvoe, and Boddom, and as I'll probably be obliged to repair to Fair Isle before that time, and therefore can't attend that meeting, Hereby Commissions, empowers and warrants you, John Sinclair of Quendal, to act in my name Conform to the following Instructions :—

Impr. That the Commonty from the Mills of Troswick to the green road on the east side of Skelberry, and from said road running in a straight line by the large grey stone which goes above the minister's sink to the stripe which separates Skelberry and Scousburgh punds, be divided into 8 parts, 3 whereof to Quendal in proportion to his lands, and the other 5 equally divided betwixt Sumburgh and the minister in proportion to their 10 merks each. As also that the punds of Foggrafield, Bremer, Symragarth, Dalster, and all that shall be found improved and taken off the said Commonty be likewise divided according to the former proportions, and, as it will be no loss to any concerned, that the minister may, for conveniency sake, have his share of said lands, after valuation, adjacent to the glebe lands.

2do That the Commonty adjoining the dykes of Skelberry immediately and so upwards to the grey stone above mentioned, and reaching from the said green road to the stripe of Scousburgh beyond the minister's sink, together with the whole Room of Skelberry lands, moss, grass, meadows etc. be divided equally conform to the 20 merks land of Skelberry, 2 whereof only belongs to Sumburgh, and therefore he has a right to the 10th part of said moss, muir, and meadows and no more; Quendal 4-10ths. and the minister 5 do. in proportion to each one's property of said lands; and the moss called the minister's sink was never questioned as his property.

3^{tio} As, by consent of parties, there was an excambion already made by honest men chosen in hunc effectu and for conveniency of the minister his manse and yard etc. therefore desires the same may be continued statu quo without division, the rest being planked according to the quality as well quantity may be all distinctly marked according to the nature of each, and the choice of each person's share accordingly may be delayed till the minister return, if the Lord will, as no damage hereby can ensue to either party.

4to That if any step is taken contrary to the above Instructions, and prejudicial to the interest and property of the present incumbent or successors in office, which I should look upon, if designedly made, as a piece of sacrilege, and consequently an attack upon Christianity itself, as whoever detracts from the subsistence of a Gospel minister would root out the Gospel of Christ itself were it in their power, and therefore hereby further enjoins you in my name to protest and take Instruments accordingly, that nothing be done in my absence prejudicial to the just rights of the present minister and his successors in office, and Herein you'll oblige etc. etc.

JOHN MILL.

Three years after the date (1753) of these instructions the question of the settlement of the glebe boundaries seems to have been no further advanced, as appears from the following proceedings before the Presbytery of Zetland in 1756.

At Lerwick, 16th June 1756, Mill gave in to the Presbytery a Representation and Petition, the tenor whereof follows:—

> Unto the Reverend the Moderator and the remanent members of the Presbytery of Zetland, The Representation and Petition of Mr. John Mill, Minister of the Gospel at Dunrossness, Humbly sheweth,

That whereas the Glebe lands belonging to the minister of Dunrossness lie blended with the property lands of other heritors (commonly called Rig and Rendal[1]), and as the town[2] of Skelberry where the Glebe lands of ten merks lie, scatts[3] with Outvoe and Boddam, containing in whole 32 merks land only, whereof 12 merks belong to Quendale's estate, and consequently his share of the pasture, muir and privileges is but as 12 to 32, so that the minister draws nigh a third share, yet true and of verity it is that Robert Sinclair of Quendale did set in tenants upon several places of the said pasture without so much as asking the concurrence of the minister as usual in such cases, whereby five punds[4] (as they are called) are taken off the privileges of Skelberry, viz. two punds adjoining to the dykes of said town eastward, called Colapund or Foggrafield,[5] set at the rate of 14 pound yearly rent Scots; a third pund at Sumragarth, a fourth at Dalsetter, and a fifth at Troswick, each at the rate of Three pounds Scots per annum, in all 23 pounds Scots of yearly rent, according to best information. Moreover, the tenants on Quendale's estate from Laigh Ness, and several from other places, are casting up said pastures every year, insomuch that, by encroachments of punds and

---

[1] *Rig and Rendal*: equivalent to *run-rig*. Apparently the closest approximation to *rendal*, in the northern tongues, is in the Swedish *Ren*, 'unploughed border of a field,' and *Del*, 'share,' 'division.'

[2] *Town*: i.e. *tún* or township, village lands.

[3] *Scatts*: i.e. possesses mutual *Scattald* or Commonty.

[4] *Punds*: parks or enclosures surrounded by stone or turf dyke. Anglo-Saxon *pynd*, to enclose.

[5] *Foggrafield*: Norse *fager*, fair.

delvings, the minister is like to be cut out of his privileges of
moss and muir if a speedy stop is not put to their career.
Besides, John Bruce Stewart of Symbister and Bigton[1] has
lately set up marches of his own accord on the west part of the
town of Skelberry and pastures thereof, taking possession about
the same time of part of the Glebe lands without any proper
legal warrant, and as the confused way of Rig and Rendal is
attended with many great inconveniences as occasioning dis-
putes with neighbours about grass and corns, marring of
improvements, and exposed to continual encroachments
especially in a time of vacancy whereby both land and pasture
may be further wasted, as are actually done already, in a great
measure, especially the pasture where numbers of people claim
the same privileges with the minister, until a division is made,
on all which accounts your petitioner Humbly craves the
Reverend Presbytery would be pleased to gratify him with a
visitation of said land and pasture of Skelberry that the
boundaries thereof may be ascertained according to use and
wont as shall appear to the Reverend Presbytery by honest
Knowing sworn men, and that he may have his just proportion
of said lands and pasture together with the lands taken off
said pasture by past rent due since the same was debted, That
the Presbytery's decreet may pass accordingly, ingrossed in the
Presbytery records in futuram memoriam, and craving the
Lords of Session's authority may be interponed in hunc effectu,
and your petitioner shall ever pray etc. Given at Lerwick
this 16th day June 1756 years by   sic subr. JOHN MILL.

At Skelberry, the 7th day of September 1756 years ; After
    prayer. Sederunt: Mr. Thomas Miller, Moderator,
    pro tempore. Messrs. William Mitchell and Francis
    Gilbert, ministers. The said Mr. Mitchell was
    chosen clerk pro tempore.
    This being the day appointed for the visitation of the
Glebe of Dunrossness, grass, and pertinents, in order to

---

[1] John Bruce, afterwards of Symbister, obtained the estate of Bigton in
Dunrossness, and took the additional surname of Stewart, on his marriage to
Clementina Stewart, heiress of Bigton.

consider encroachments, Mill brought in the following honest
men as evidence of the Bounds of Skelberry etc., to wit,
George Burgess, James Leslie and Gilbert Irvine, tenants in
Clumley, Andrew Harper, Andrew Charleson and John
Shewan, tenants in Skelberry, Alexander Cheyne, tenant in
Lunabister, John Shewan in Troswick, and Robert Marshall
in Dalster, who being proposed to the said John Morrison,
[acting for John Bruce Stewart of Bigton] and he declaring
he had no objections against any of them, were solemnly
sworn. Thereafter Robert Scott of Scotshall, an heritor of said
parish, having come up to the Presbytery, went along with
them, together with John Morrison and the witnesses, to inspect
the Boundaries foresaid, which being done and the Witnesses
severally called into the Presbytery, they deponed as follows :—
    GEORGE BURGESS, aged seventy-six years, married, purged
of malice and partial counsel, solemnly sworn and interrogate
depones as follows: *Primo.* As to the Boundaries of Skelberry
within the old Dykes. That said Dykes run from the mouth
of the Burn called Hogard to the Sandy Slap[1] northward,
and from thence north east, and from thence north west
across the Burn to the house of Durigarth, and then north
east to the Burn again, including all the land lying betwixt
said Dyke and said Burn called old Durigarth. Being
asked whether or not he ever heard or knew of anybody
that ever laboured said ground betwixt said Dyke and Burn
besides the people of Skelberry? answered negatively. Depones
also that the said old Dykes run from the Burn at the Water
Slap eastward, including Reswick and Collapund, to the ruins
of an old house sometime possessed by Charles Williamson,
and from thence to the southward including that piece of
ground commonly called the North Meadow, where it joins
the east Burn, and runs down said Burn to the place called
the hole of Clowell where it crosses said Burn eastward,
and incloses that piece of ground called Voesgarth, and from
thence westward inclosing the south meadow and new pund
until it join the Dyke at the mouth of the Burn Hogard
mentioned above at the north side of the Loch. *Secundo.*

---

[1] *Slap* : a breach in a dyke to admit of persons passing through.

As to the boundaries of the Scattald of Skelberry, Outvoe and Boddam, Depones that they run from the west water Slap along the old mark of the Burn northward through the town of Bremer, and from the upper Dyke of said town at a place a little to the westward of that, where the Burn presently enters, which seems to be the old entry of said Burn, to two Standing Stones in a line to the stone by east the Bleat, as he hears, and from thence eastward to the north Stony Pund to two tuicks[1] on the height by east the Loch of Wadslay[2] to a march stone near the Dyke of John Shewan's pund to another march stone at the old Mill of Troswick within said Pund, and from thence southward and along the old Dykes of Troswick to the Law Dyke, and along said Law Dyke through the town of Dalsetter till you come to the Burn running eastward to the town of Outvoe to the sea immediately to the westward of Keotha's pund, and that the Scattald runs along the Dykes of Outvoe, Boddom, and the old Dykes of Sumragarth to the joining of Brew's Dyke to the westward till it ends at the mouth of the Burn of Hogard. *Tertio.* Being asked if he knew of any punds taken off the above Scattald? answered that John Shewan's pund was taken off, and Robert Marshall's pund, and the potatoe pund of Sumragarth, Andrew Charleson's pund, and John Shewan's pund commonly called Fografield : *Causa scientiæ* petit, that he has lived in the neighbourhood all his days, Declares he cannot write, and that is truth, as he shall answer to God.

Sic subr. Tho. Miller, Modr. p. t.

William Mitchell, P. Clk. p. t.

It is not necessary to continue the depositions of other witnesses, which are much to the same effect. One of them, Robert Marshall, states that he 'laboured Old Durigarth, and brought in the proportion of the crop thereof[3] to the Rev.

---

[1] Apparently a variation of the Shetland term *Toog*, a small hillock with a tuft of grass : a diminutive of Danish *tue*, a hillock (Edmondston).

[2] Now usually spelt *Vatchly*, i.e. *Vats-ly*, the watery place, a very accurate definition.

[3] *Proportion of the crop* : *i.e.* the 'teind sheaves,' etc.

Mr. James Key, the first minister of the place after the Revolution ;[1] that he pays three pounds Scots money for the pund at Dalsetter taken off the Scattald, and that his son pays the like sum for the potatoe pund at Sumragarth also taken off the Scattald foresaid.'

*　　*　　*　　*　　*

The Presbytery having considered the above evidences Find the Bounds of the Town of Skelberry, one half whereof belongs to the minister as his glebe, to be within Dykes ascertained as in the first deposition, and that there have been encroachments made upon the Scattald or freedom of peat muir and pasture etc. within Dykes of Skelberry, Outvoe and Boddom, the third part whereof almost belongs to the minister, by taking in of the punds of Troswick, Dalsetter, Sumragarth, and Fografield, and part of Bremer not yet rentalled, paying £23 12/ Scots money, of which the minister's proportion is as Ten to Thirty-two, but all paid at present to the Factor on Quendale's sequestrated estate, and no part to the minister notwithstanding of his claim to a share thereof. Therefore the Presbytery did and hereby do Humbly beseech the Right Honourable the Lords of Council and Session would be pleased to interpone their authority, not only for the minister of Dunrossness and his successors in office their peaceable possession in time coming of the glebe pasture and peat muir, with their just proportion of the Rents and profits of the punds or outbreaks above mentioned which were taken off from the said Scattald by Robert Sinclair of Quendale and claimed as a part of his estates, But also for redress of what loss Mr. John Mill, the present Incumbent, hath already sustained by the said encroachments on his glebe, pasture and others above mentioned, as accords of the Law, to prevent all such injurious and illegal practices in time coming.

---

[1] James Kay, A.M. Translated from Kirkwall 2nd Charge. Admitted in 1682. He petitioned the General Assembly, with five others, in January 1698, that he might be received into Communion ; and having disclaimed Episcopacy, and stated he never had any hand in the late persecutions, he was received 23rd June following ; died 15th September 1716, in the 36th year of his ministry. —(*Fasti Ecclesiæ Scoticanæ.*

At a meeting of the Presbytery of Zetland, at Lerwick, the 2nd March 1763, a Petition was again presented by Mr. Mill on the subject of these encroachments, no effectual remedy having apparently been provided. He recapitulates the grievances complained of in his Petition of June 1756, and the evidence thereof placed before the Presbytery at the meeting on the spot in September of that year, all as above narrated. He then proceeds :—

This being a part of the Church's patrimony 'tis hoped the Presbytery will please recommend this affair also to the ensuing General Assembly to employ their Procurator and Agent to defend their own property out of the public funds. And as the foresaid Robert Sinclair of Quendale out of pretence of being Vicar,[1] and paying the minister's stipend, withdrew the Vicar days' works[2] payed to the ministers for leading their peats, a privilege which all the ministers of the country are still possessed of, and have been time immemorial. As the Factors appointed by the Lords on the sequestrated estate of Quendale claim three days' works to which the minister has a preferable title 'tis hoped this grievance will be recommended also for redress, and also for having my glebe lands set apart and separate from others, which at present, by a confused mixture of what they call Rig and Rendal, or Run-rig, mars improvements, and occasions much strife and wickedness. . . . . . To put an effectual stop to such encroachments is of the utmost consequence to prevent delapidations for the future and especially in remote parts of the Kingdom, otherwise wicked men may be emboldened to seize them piece meal till they leave the ministers little or nothing. . . . . Given at Lerwick the 2nd day of March 1763 years.

Sic subr. JOHN MILL.

The Presbytery agreed to 'warmly recommend' the Petition to the General Assembly. It is not germane to the purposes of this volume to follow the course of proceedings in this matter before the Assembly. It may only be mentioned

---

[1] *Vicar*: that is, holding Assignation to the Vicarage dues.
[2] *Days' works*: days' labour due by tenants.

that at a meeting of the Presbytery at Lerwick on the 14th
March the following year (1764) a Representation on the subject was again presented by Mill, in which it was stated that
Mr. Buchan, minister at Walls, had been instructed to report
the matter to the Assembly, by whom it had been referred
to the Procurator of the Church to examine and submit his
views to the next Assembly. The complaint goes on to allege
that . . . 'John Bruce Stewart of Symbister and Bigton has
had the assurance since my last Representation to the Presbytery
to send his factor and officer with a considerable number of his
tenants to cut and destroy my peats after they were casten,
and thereafter causing his tenants likewise cut a deep trench,
and build a dyke hard by it upon the privileges of my glebe
that thereby he might appropriate some of the pastures and
moors for behoof of his tenants, against which violent intrusion
and encroachments I entered two protests before Witnesses.'

He therefore craves that the General Assembly should be
urged to institute a process of redress before the Lords of
Session, especially as the estate of Quendale was to be exposed
for sale on the 5th of August ensuing, Robert Sinclair of
Quendale being still living.

The Presbytery, on 13th March 1765, granted commission
to Mill himself to represent the matter to the General
Assembly, which he did, but, as it would appear from the
narrative in the Diary, with little or no practical success.
With this the vexatious question of the encroachments upon
the glebe lands seems to terminate.

III.

ACCOUNT OF THE PARISH OF DUNROSSNESS IN ZETLAND (COUNTY OF ORKNEY—PRESBY-TERY OF ZETLAND) BY THE REVEREND MR. JOHN MILL. 1793.

NAME AND SITUATION.—Dunrossness means the hill of the promontory of Ross.[1] This parish is on the southern extremity of Zetland. It is a peninsula washed by the sea on three sides, and is comparatively the most fertile district in the Zetland Isles. Two other parishes are united with Dunrossness, under the charge of the same minister. These are Sandwick, which means the Sandy-bay; and Cunningsburgh, the same name with Koningsberg, which, in the Norse or Scandinavian language, means Kingsburgh.

SOIL, AIR, AND PRODUCE.—The soil in the arable parts of the parish is various. In some places sandy; in others loam and clay. Considerable tracks are of moss, and consequently of little value. The air is moist in a great degree, but by no means unhealthy. Many of the people live to a great age —some to 100 years and upwards. The hills in this parish are green, and the land for the most part firm. By these circumstances it is rendered more valuable, as well as a more agreeable residence than the black[2] mountains and morasses to the north. The arable grounds are chiefly by the sea shore,

---

[1] It really means the Ness, or promontory, of the *Raust*, a strong tideway well known to mariners.

[2] *Black* : bleak?

and on the margins of the creeks, which on all sides run up into the country. On these grounds barley [1] and oats are raised; large fields of potatoes are also planted, which are of great benefit to this country. Cabbages, turnips, carrots, and other kitchen stuffs, are to be found in the gardens of the Zetlanders, in the same abundance as on the Continent of Scotland. No grass seeds are sown in this parish; but it is remarkable, that on the sandy grounds, when properly protected from cattle, natural crops of clover and ryegrass spring as richly as on the sown fields in other parts of the kingdom. No trees are to be seen in this region, excepting a few shrubby, roan trees, and willows in the more sheltered valleys. The spray of the sea, which is blown over the whole country by the westerly winds, forms a natural obstacle to the success of plantations. The force and duration of the tempests from the west are among the most striking features of a Zetland winter; and if to these are added the thunder and lightening which often occur in that season, it will appear, that the Zetlanders have their share of the inclemency of the heavens, although they have less of frost and snow than the inhabitants of wider Countries.

MINERALS.—There are many mineral springs in this parish, as in other districts of Zetland, which bear the appearance of iron ore. Near the island of Whalsey, which lies to the eastward, mariners have observed, that the Compass reels, and cannot fix as usual to a point, which is believed to be owing to the attraction of iron mines in that place. In the years 1789 and 1790 Zetland was visited by some gentlemen from London, who found on the estate of Quendal a rich iron mine; and in various parts of the islands, the ores of copper, lead, and iron, samples of which were carried to London, particularly of copper, in considerable quantity.[2]

AGRICULTURE, CATTLE, AND SHEEP.—The lands are reckoned by a peculiar measurement, by what are called merks-land. Each merk-land ought to contain 1600 square fathoms. To each one cow is allotted; and the parish contains 2000

---

[1] *Barley*: *i.e.* the native *Bere*.   [2] See Diary, 1790.

of these merk-lands, and consequently as many cows. In
Sandwick and Cunningsburgh, the farmers plough chiefly with
oxen, and at Ness with horses; 4 oxen or 4 horses in a plough,
which go all abreast; but the ground is chiefly laboured
with spades of a light kind; with these, 5 or 6 men and
women will turn over as much land in a day as a Scotch
plough with 8 or 10 oxen. The oxen, with the young cattle,
are about 1000. The parish of Dunrossness, having more
arable, and less pasture ground than the neighbouring parishes,
the number of sheep is, of course, smaller than in the other
districts. It was, however, considerable, till within these few
years; a large English scabbed ram was imported into this
district, which infected the flock to which he was brought,
and the infection has spread among the sheep through the
whole parish, notwithstanding every precaution and effort of
the farmers to prevent it. In consequence of this unhappy cir-
cumstance, the whole number of sheep in the united parishes
of Dunrossness, Sandwick, and Cunningsburgh, does not now
exceed 5000.

BIRDS.—Eagles, hawks, ravens, etc. are so numerous, as
to make havock of the lambs and poultry, insomuch that the
Commissioners of Supply give a Crown for every eagle that is
destroyed. Swans in great numbers resort to this parish in
October and November, and remain about the lochs of Skelberry and Scousburgh during the winter. In the end of
April, or beginning of May, they migrate to Norway, where
their young are hatched. The ember goose, as it is here
called, is a bird larger than the tame goose; has a long
bill, and doleful cry; it seldom leaves the sea—its legs are
so short that it can hardly walk. Of ducks there are various
species, which resort to the lochs above mentioned. Besides
the wild duck, are scale drakes,[1] equal to the wild duck in
size; the points of their bills turn up a little; they are of
a beautiful brown colour, and hatch their young in rabbit-
holes. There is a large species called the stock-duck, and
smaller species called teales and attiles. Sea birds of various

---

[1] *Scale-drake* :   Query, Sheldrake ?

kinds abound, several species of which become white in winter. There are also here in their season, the lapwing, the grey and yellow plover, and the night-rail.

Fish.—The lakes already mentioned produce considerable quantities of trouts of a large size, which resemble grilses, or young salmon, and abundance of large eels. At sea, the fishes most usually caught, are ling, cod, tusk and seth; these last are taken in the tideways, and chiefly at the southern extremity of the parish; few of these are sold in Zetland, either fresh or dry salted; they are sent to Hamburgh or Leith, or where the best markets can be found. For the use of the inhabitants, the fishers take abundance of turbot, skate, small cod, haddocks, whitings, herrings, mackarels, floûnders, etc. particularly in the spring season. The fish, butter, and oil, sent to the Hamburgh market, yield a return to Zetland of wines, spirits, tea, coffee, sugar, tobacco, linen, hooks, lines, etc. The rocks on the coast produce abundance of lobsters, crabs, oysters, etc.

Population.—In the three united parishes, in 1755, the number of families was 451; of souls, according to Dr. Webster's list, 2295, besides the Fair Isle, which had about 200. In 1770, the families, including Fair Isle, were 561; the inhabitants, 2942. In 1790, the families, including Fair Isle, were 570; and the inhabitants 3327. The number of females greatly exceeds the males, as the young men leave the country in numbers every year; being commonly inclined to a sea-faring life, they resort to England and Holland, but chiefly to London, where they serve on board the navy, merchant ships, or Greenlanders. The annual number of marriages depends much on the seasons: In good years they may amount to 30 or upwards; but when the crops fail, will hardly come up to the half of that number.

Church and Poor.—A handsome church, with a pavilion roof,[1] covered with Easdale slate, was built a few years ago at Dunrossness. There is another Church for the districts of

---

[1] The parish church, as it has long stood, has gables carried up to the ridge of the roof.

Sandwick and Cunningsburgh, whither the minister goes to officiate every third Sunday. That Church has a Kirk-Session of its own, and ought to form a separate parochial Charge, if there were funds sufficient for the support of a minister. The united parishes altogether form what is termed a *ministry*; and this ministry is 12 miles in length, and in some places 6 miles broad. The Stipend is 1000 merks Scotch (£55, 11s. 3d. sterling), and 50 merks (£2, 15s. 7½d.) for Communion elements. The whole people are members of the established Church. The presbytery of Zetland is not subject to the jurisdiction of any provincial Synod, but depends immediately on the General Assembly.

The poor are supported by weekly collections, and the fines levied from delinquents; the distribution is made by the Kirk-sessions. The number of poor was small, and some little stock was happily accumulated previous to the year 1782, when a scene of misfortunes opened upon Zetland, which made it necessary to give away both stock and income. For 5 years successively, beginning with 1782, the crops almost wholly failed, and above 100 poor persons came upon the sessions of this ministry. No country in the world can bear a failure of crop better than Zetland, if the sea continues to render its supplies, particularly when the small fry of seth or cole fish fill the bays in their usual abundance; but from 1781 to 1787, the sea, as well as the land, withheld its usual products. These circumstances were attended with a great murrain and mortality among the sheep and cattle. In this situation, the people owed their relief to the bounty of Government. Vessels, loaded with provisions, arrived seasonably from England; and it was understood in this country that the supplies were hastened by the anxious sympathy of our gracious Queen. In the event, no person died of want.

MISCELLANEOUS OBSERVATIONS. Sponges are found upon the shore in great plenty, shaped like a man's hand, and called by the people *Trowis Gloves*.[1] There are no beacons

---

[1] *Trow's Gloves*: *i.e.* gloves of ' Trows '—fairies, mermaids.

L

or lighthouses on the coast.[1] The principal creeks are
Quendal Bay, Grutness, and West Voes, which lie on each
side of Sumburgh Head, separated by a neck of land. In
Lerwick[2] Sound, ships anchor and ride securely, as they do
also in Aithsvoe of Cunningsburgh. On the Fair Isle in this
ministry, the flag ship of the Spanish Armada was wrecked
in 1588; and the Duke of Medina Celi[3] resided for some time
in the house of Quendal.

There are no manufactures here, unless for domestic use,
viz., blankets and coarse cloth, excepting, perhaps, some
stockings, gloves, and garters, sold to the Dutch fishers. A
linen manufacture was attempted here some years ago by the
gentlemen of the country, and a considerable sum of money
was expended, but the adventure came to nothing: For its
failure two reasons may be assigned. The want of a profes-
sional owner, to combine his interest and skill in the manage-
ment; and the choice of the spot, which was inconvenient.
The fittest place for works belonging to this manufacture
would be the Loch of Sound near Lerwick, where there is
a regular resort from all parts.—The prices of provisions are
greatly raised within these 30 or 40 years. A fat ox or cow
was then 30/, now it is £3, 10/ and other provisions in proportion. Butter, from 4/ is now 7/ or 8/ per 30 lb. weight.
The proprietors, in letting their lands, proportion the extent
of farms to the number of persons in a family. Thus two
merks-land is usually let to a man and wife at first; but, as the
family increases, they may have 3 or 4 merks-land. The great
object is to set out as many boats as possible to the fishing,
as, through this medium, the rents are paid. Hence the price
of land on sale in this country is higher in proportion to
the rent than almost anywhere else. The estate of Sumburgh,[4]
to the surprise of the gentlemen of Edinburgh, was bought

---

[1] There is now a lighthouse on Sumburgh Head, erected in 1821.

[2] *Lerwick*: a mistake for Levenwick.

[3] The shipwrecked officer was not the Duke of Medina Sidonia, Commander-
in-Chief of the Armada, but Juan Gomez de Medina, Admiral of a division
consisting of about twenty ships.

[4] The estate of Quendale, sold for behoof of creditors, is meant.

at 52 years purchase: It was a good bargain, not because
the rents were low, but from the mode in which they are paid.
The rents of this country are chiefly paid out of the sea.
The tenants have from their landlords threepence allowed
for a ling, a penny for a cod or tusk, and a half-penny for
a seth (cole fish); and these, when salted and dried, will,
in the Hamburgh market, yield four or five times as much,
besides debentures[1] from Government. Add to this, double
or triple the prime cost for goods brought back and sold to
the people, viz., linen, tobacco, spirits, hooks, lines, etc.—
There are three sorts of boats used in the fishing trade, a
larger and a smaller size of 6-oared boats, and 4-oared boats.
In all, there are about 200 boats through this ministry.
Some brigs have formerly belonged to owners in this district,
the last of which was captured by the French. Of late, a
small sloop that goes upon the fishing, and to different parts
of the country, was built by one Robert Thompson, a native
of Fair Isle, and who was for several years a Schoolmaster
there, under the Society for propagating Christian Knowledge.
He is now a farmer and mariner, an excellent cooper, a
wright and mason, by the force of a mechanical genius, without having ever been an apprentice to any of these professions.
His sloop was built from the keel, and completely rigged and
equipped by himself. One of the principal means of improvement to this country would be good roads, as, at present,
no cart or carriage whatever can be used for the transport
of goods on the soft surface of the country, particularly to
the northward. Two roads are specially needed, viz., from
Lerwick to Scalloway, the two principal towns of Zetland,
the distance is only 4 miles; and from Lerwick through
Tingwall parish to the parish of Delton, and thence to Yell
Sound, through the very heart of the country, which is not
above 12 miles; but in some places, the peat moss is so deep as
to be impassable on horseback. Another great improvement
on the state of this country would be a better division of
the small farms, which are parcelled out in discontiguous
plots and run-rigg, termed here *rigg* and *rendal*; even the

---

[1] *Debentures* : *i.e.* bounties.

inconsiderable merk-lands, lying scattered in several patches, intermixed with patches possessed by other people. This unaccountable arrangement produces endless quarrels and vexations among neighbours, on account of trespasses which must unavoidably occur almost daily while the fields remain thus interwoven.

IV.

LIST OF PARISH MINISTERS OF DUNROSSNESS, SANDWICK, AND CUNNINGSBURGH, 1567-1843.

1567. The parish of Dunrossness, with Sandwick and Cunningsburgh, was supplied by JOHN CRAB, Reader, from 1567 till his death in November 1571.

1571. JOHN KINGSONE or KINGSTOUN, entered in November to the united parishes. Stipend xl merks (£2, 12s. 6d.); removed to Sandwick prior to 1574.

1575. MALCOLM SINCLAIR, Reader, was presented to the Vicarage by James VI. 29th December; continued in 1601.

1610. LAURANCE SINCLAIR, Vicar and Titular. He was Reader from 1576 to 1580.

1640. NICOL QUHYTE (or WHYTE), A.M. (University of Edinburgh).

1662. JAMES FORBES, A.M. (University of St. Andrews).

1682. JAMES KAY, A.M. Translated from Kirkwall 2d charge; admitted 1682.

1720. WALTER HUGENS, A.M. (University of Edinburgh). Presented by the Earl of Morton 1717, and ordained in the Kirkyard of Sandwick 4th Aug. 1720. Translated to Sandsting and Aithsting 1733.

1735. WILLIAM MAXWELL, A.M. (Glasgow). Was six years in South Carolina before being presented to the parish. Translated to Rutherglen 1742.

1743. John Mill. Author of the Diary, and of other writings described in this volume. Died 13th February 1805.

1805. John Duncan, native of parish of Cruden, Aberdeen-shire. Drowned in the *Doris* on her passage to Shetland, 22d Feb. 1813.

1813. James Denoon, A.M., from Inverness-shire. Graduate of University of Aberdeen. Translated to the parish of Kingarth in Bute 1822.

1822. Thomas Barclay, A.M. (Aberdeen). Son of the Rev. James Barclay, Unst. Translated to Lerwick 1827; admitted at Peterculter 1843, at Currie 1844, and was finally appointed Principal of the University of Glasgow 1858.

1828. David Thomson. Translated from Walls and Sand-ness. Died 5th Oct. 1841, in the 83d year of his age.

SANDWICK.

1574. John Kingston. Removed from Dunrossness, Fairyle, Braza, and Burra also in Charge, with lxxx. lt. (£6, 13s. 4d.) of stipend.

1580. Adam Mudy. Translated from Walls and Flotta in Orkney, having also the charge of Balista and. Crosskirk of Dunrossness. (This combination of the Crosskirk with Balista, presumably Baliasta in the island of Unst, is not easily explained. The two places are situated at the extreme opposite points of the country, south and north.)

1585. Laurence Sinclare, Reader at Dunrossness, etc., from 1576 to 1580; continued in 1586.

1588. Laurence Young. Exhorter at Rousay, Egilsey, Wyir, and Enhallow in Orkney, from 1574 to 1594; continued in 1591. He appears also as Reader at the Kirk of Westray.

1593. Laurence Sinclare, resumed prior to 1593; continued in 1608.

At this time the church was suppressed, and the parish was united to Dunrossness. It was eventually erected into a Parliamentary church, and declared a *quoad sacra* parish in terms of the Act of Assembly of 25th May 1833.

1830. ALEXANDER STARK, A.M. Ordained in 1808 as minister of the Old Light or Original Burgher Congregation at Falkirk. Presented to this charge and re-ordained 17th Sept. 1830. Joined the Free Church and ceased to be minister of the Church of Scotland in 1843.

CUNNINGSBURGH.

The church here seems to have been suppressed at the Reformation, but it was standing for at least half a century later. Its degradation and falling into ruin are referred to in the INTRODUCTION, under the head of CHURCHES AND CHURCH SITES, ETC.

V

LIST OF CHURCHES AND CHURCH SITES IN DUN-ROSSNESS, SANDWICK, AND CUNNINGSBURGH, WITH THEIR DEDICATIONS.

1. Cross Kirk, Dunrossness—St. Matthew ; replaced by the modern church near Brew.
2. The 'North Kirk,' Sandwick—St. Magnus.
3. Church of the Fair Isle—dedication unknown.

The following sites of ancient churches :—

4. Cunningsburgh, at Mealsair—St. Colme, or St. Paul (?).
5. St. Ninian's Isle—St. Ninian.
6. Ireland (*i.e.* Eyrr-land)—dedication unknown.
7. Levenwick—St. Levan ?
8. Clumlie—St. Columba ?

The evidences for the dedications assigned to the above Churches are explained in the INTRODUCTION.

Churches or Chapels recently erected :—

9. Dunrossness—Baptist.
10.   Do.   —Methodist (2).
11.   Do.   —Free Church of Scotland.
12. Sandwick—Congregational.
13.   Do. —Methodist (2).
14. Cunningsburgh—Free Church of Scotland.
15. Fair Isle—Methodist.

VI.

ECCLESIASTICAL REVENUES OF DUNROSSNESS, SANDWICK, AND CUNNINGSBURGH, 1571-1888.

1571.

From the *Register of Ministers and thair Stipends sen the yeir of God*, 1567.[1]

Dunrosness, Cannisburgh, Sandwik and Fair Isle—being Johne Crab reidar xx lī.[2] deid November 1571,—in his rowme Johnn Kingsone minister. xl merkis[3] sen November 1571.

1574.

From the Register of Ministers and Readers in the *Book of the Assignation of Stipends* (1574).

Sandwick, Dunrosness, Fair Yle, Braza, Burra — Johne Kingstoun, minister £80 [Scots]. ——— (vacant) reidare at Dunrosness, Cunnesbourg, and Fair Yle, £13, 6s. 8d. [Scots].

1576.

From the *Buik of Assignationis of the Ministeris and Reidaris Stipendis* (1576).

Dunrosnes	Malcolm Sinclair his stipend the
Sandwick	haill Vicarage of Dunrosnes, quhair-
Cunisburgh.	into he is newlie providit extending
	to 80ī. he payand the reidare at
	thir Kirkis.
Croce Kirk	Laurance Sinclair reidare at thir
Fair Isle	Kirkis his Stipend xx lī. to be pait be
	the new providit Vicar.

---

[1] Printed in the Miscellany of the Wodrow Society, vol. i. Edinburgh : 1844.
[2] The *pound* Scots was of varying value, decreasing latterly to 1s. 8d. stg.
[3] The *merk* Scots has usually the value assigned to it of 1s. 1½d. stg. In the *Fasti Ecclesiæ Scoticanæ* this 40 merks stipend is set down as £2, 12s. 6d. stg.

To the 'Commissionaire of Zetland,' *inter alia*, is assigned at this time—

The thrid of the Croce Stouke of Dunrosnes, vj ħ. xiij ş. iiij đ. and furthe of the bischopis umbothis of Zetland the rest, and for payment thereof vj barrellis.

c. 1610.

From *The Just Rentelis of the Benefices callit the Vicarages w^t the Number of the Kirkis pertening thairto as thay have beine of old and as thay are now callit in Prebentis*, by the Rev. James Pitcairne, c. 1610.[1]

St Matthew St Magnus St Colme The Kirk off the Fair Yle	*In primis* the Vicarage of Dunrosnes in Corne teynd nync peise ilk peise calculat to twenty pundis the bowteind[2] communibus annis foure barrell butter the bot [boat] teind fyfe gudlingis w^t halff lamb halff woll the other halff of lamb and woll usurpit and taken up be my Lord Orknay sine titulo bothe heir and frome the rest of the Vicarages within the Cuntrie notwithstanding that the haill woll and lamb perteins to the Vicar properlie. The Vicarage has thrie Kirkis in the maine of the Cuntrie of Zetland and the fourt in the Fairyle. The Vicarage is set be Lawrence Sinclar Vicar and titular thairof to Malcome Sinclar of Quendell for sax scoir pundis. It hes ane manse and glebe.

---

[1] Printed by the Editor in vol. xviii. of the *Proceedings* of the Society of Antiquaries of Scotland, 1884.

[2] *Bowteind* : teind of cattle. The word (Icelandic *bu*) still lingers in the Scottish term *Steelbow*.

1739.

From *List of Parishes in Scotland briefly described*. MS. Advocates' Library, volume 35. 3. 11, bearing a marginal date 1739, but probably of earlier date.

Dunrossness properly so called has a Church called the Cross Kirk 2 miles north from Sumburgh head, and the Min[rs] Gleib is att Skelberry 2 miles north from the Kirk, and 6 miles S.S.W. from Sandwick Kirk. it is ten merk land of Danish extent worth only per annum 44 lib. *Scots*. The Stipend is 800 merks [say £44, 10s. stg.].

1793.

From the Account of the Parish of Dunrossness by the Rev. John Mill, in Sir John Sinclair's *Statistical Account of Scotland*, vol. vii. (1793).

The Stipend is 1000 merks Scotch (£55, 11s. 3d. sterling),[1] and 50 merks (£2, 15s. 7½d.) for Communion elements.

1808.

From the Appendix to the *General View of the Agriculture of the Shetland Islands*, by John Shirreff. Edinburgh, 1814.

The Stipend £120, paid in money by the heritors, in which case they receive the teinds from the tenants.

[Up to this time, and for some time later, the teinds were taken up from the tenants in kind, *e.g.* the tenth sheaf of corn, etc. etc.—*Ed.*]

1841.

From the *New Statistical Account of Scotland*. Parish of Dunrossness, by the Rev. David Thomson.

The Stipend, by decreet of Valuation, is £200, besides a sum for Communion elements; and the Glebe is reckoned

---

[1] This statement of the value of the stipend is confirmed in a letter to the Editor, dated 22d March 1880, from the late Mr. Bruce of Sumburgh, whose grandfather, probably the largest heritor of the parish at the time, paid the largest portion of it.

good, the soil being of excellent quality; it contains 13 acres of arable ground, and 14 or 15 acres of meadow; but the pasture is not valuable.

1888.

From *The Year-Book of the Church of Scotland.*

Stipend £262, with Manse [and Glebe].

VII.

EARL ROGNVALD AND THE DUNROSSNESS MAN.[1]
AN UNPUBLISHED STORY OF THE TWELFTH
CENTURY.

It so happened one day south in the Dunrossness sea[2] in Hjaltland[3] that an old and poor country man (*bóndi*) was waiting long for his boatmen, while all the other boats that were ready rowed off. Then came a man with a white cowl to the old country man, and asked him why he did not row off to the fishing as the other men did. The country man replied that his mates had not come. 'Bondi,' said the man of the cowl, 'would you like me to row with you?' 'That will I,' says the country man, 'but I must have a share for my boat, for I have many children (*bairns*) at home, and I must work for them as much as I can.' So they rowed out in front of Dynraust-head[4] and inside Hundholm.[5] There was a great *stream* of tide where they were, and great whirling eddies; and they were to keep in the eddy, but to fish outside the *raust*.[6]

---

[1] The word in the original Icelandic for the Dunrossness 'man' is *bóndi*, the common term in the Scandinavian north for husbandman, land-cultivator, yeoman, *i.e.* the ordinary *farmer* of the north, who at the same time derived a portion of his sustenance from the sea, as he still does in Iceland, Faroe, and the Scottish Isles. The term lingered in Orkney and Shetland until comparatively recently. In the present translation, 'country man' is used as perhaps the simplest equivalent. The proper place for the story is in the *Orkneyinga Saga*, but it does not appear in the English version of that Saga (Edinburgh, 1873), not having been brought to light at the time of its publication.
[2] Literally *Dynraust*-ness *Voe*.
[3] *Hjaltland*: the old Northern form of *Shetland*.
[4] *Dynraust-head*: *i.e.* Sumburgh Head.
[5] *Hundholm*: *i.e.* Dogholm. The name has disappeared.
[6] The *Raust* of Sumburgh, still so called, a fierce tideway, but a favourite fishing-ground.

The cowl-man sat in the front part of the boat and pulled,[1] and the country man was to fish. The country man bade him take care not to be borne into the *raust*; and he said that he was quite alive to the danger. But the cowl-man did not attend to what he said to him, and did not take care though the country man should come into some danger. So a little after [this] they bore into the *raust*, and the country man was much frightened, and said, 'Miserable was I and unlucky when I took thee to-day to row, for here I must die, and my folk are at home helpless and in poverty if I am lost.' And the country man was so frightened that he wept (*grét*) and feared his end was come. The cowl-man answered, 'Be cheery, man, and don't cry, for we must find our way out of the *raust* as we got into it.' Then the cowl-man rowed out of the *raust*, and the country man was very glad. Then they rowed to the land, and pulled up the boat. And the country man bade the cowl-man to go and part the fish. But the cowl-man bade the country man part it as he liked, and said he would have no more than his third. There were many people come to the shore, both men and women, and a number of poor folk. The cowl-man gave to the poor men all the fish that had fallen to his share that day, and prepared to go on his way. At that place the way was up a cliff, and a number of women were sitting there. As he went up the cliff he slipped his foot, for it was slippery with rain, and fell down the cliff. A woman saw that first, and laughed much at him, and then so did the other folk. And when the cowl-man heard that, said he :—

> The girl mocks my dress,
> And laughs more than becomes a maid.
> I put to sea early this morning;
> Few would know an earl in a fisher's weeds.

Then the cowl-man went his way, and afterwards men became aware that this cowl-man had been Earl Rognvald. And it thereafter became known to many men, that these were great

---

[1] The term in the original is *andœfdi*, most accurately expressed by the identical Shetland word 'andowed' (pulled leisurely about).

tricks of his, creditable before God, and interesting to men. And men knew it for a proverb, as it stood in the stanza, ' Few know an earl in fisher's weeds.'

(Translated from the Old Northern version of the story in *An Icelandic Prose Reader.*   Oxford, 1879.)

VIII.

FEUDS AND BLOODSHED IN DUNROSSNESS IN THE SIXTEENTH CENTURY.

I CAN hear of no Battels fought in this place; only here (as in other places) they have not wanted Feuds, which have occasioned some skirmishes. One in the reign of Queen Mary between Oliver Sinclair of Brow in this parish and Hutchen of the Lews, the occasion whereof was this. William of the Lews having married an Heretrix in this Countrey, Oliver Sinclair being Foud or Governour of the Countrey, feared lest William [Macleod] of ye Lews being a great man should possibly have opposed him; therefore he concluded to make him away, to which he was not a little instigated by his wife. And because he could not avowedly effectuate his murderous design, he resolves at length upon this expedient, that he would go, and, in show of friendship, visit him, which done, under pretext of intimate comradship, he would exchange pages with him. In the meantime he had conduced his page, thus exchanged, to kill him, which he did that same night. In revenge of whose death Hutchen of the Lews, brother to the deceased William, made several inroads into this Countrey; but his people here having advertisment given them by some of the inhabitants of the Fair Isle quhom they had conduced to that purpose, for the first two attempts he prevailed not. But the third time he overtook the Fair Isle boat before she landed, and put the Boatmen to the edge of the Sword. Which done, he landed at Gairth Banks without opposition, and made a great slaughter, especially about Quendale, a quarter of a mile from Brow, where in one morning fell above sixty souls. But Oliver himself fled to Soumburghhead, where being hotly pursued he leapt over, but eventually falling upon a bit of green in the clift of a rock, he escaped without more prejudice but the loss of an eye, and Hutchen is by Queen Mary commanded back.

Not long after this happened another between Henry Sinclair of Sandwick and Henry Dillidasse, occasioned by some little prejudice done in the House of Brow to the servant of Henry Sinclair. In revenge whereof, being instigated by his wife, Henry Sinclair conduced his man to stab Richard Leask, son-in-law to Oliver Sinclair of Brow, which he did as he was entering the door of the Church, and so he died. Henry Dillidasse, son in law to the deceased Richard, being in Orkney at the time, and hearing of the Murder, went over to Caithness, and assembled some of his Friends to revenge his Father in law's death, with whom he came over to Zetland. But Henry Sinclair, with some of his friends and followers, being fled north the length of Laxfoord, he pursued after them, and they not advertised of his arrival were returning southward. So they met upon a Moor between Laxfoord and Lerwick, where at first meeting Henry Dillidasse desired them to surrender the Murderer, on whom he might inflict condign punishment for his crime, promising that upon so doing there should be nothing but peace and friendship betwixt them : which the other refusing to do, they prepared for a skirmish, in which Henry Dillidasse slew the murderer with the shot of a Pistol, and the rest were forced to flight. Henry Sinclair himself narrowly escaped, and one Sinclair of Burra swimmed over to Trondra, near a mile of sea. In this skirmish several fell on both sides.

> (From 'A Description of Dunrossness, by Mr. James Kay, Minister thereof,' part of *A General Description of ye Countrey of Zetland, by M. T. V.*, a manuscript Volume, No. 13. 2. 8, in the Advocates' Library. Kay was minister of the parish from 1682 to 1716.)

M

IX.

MINUTES OF A DISTRICT COURT HELD AT SUM-BURGH IN DUNROSSNESS, ON 5TH, 6TH, AND 7TH AUGUST 1602, BY MR. JOHN DISHINGTON, DEPUTE TO PATRICK, EARL OF ORKNEY AND LORD OF ZETLAND.

The Court of the prochin of Dunrosness haldin be
Mr Jhone Dischingtoun at Soundbrughe the fyve day
of August 1602 the suitis callit the court lawfullie
fenceit the essejs[1] chosin sworne and admittit.

The namis of the essejs.

William Bruce of Simbuster   Malcum in Culbinsgarthe
Jhone Newein of Skowsbrughe   Androw Smithe in Sand
*Hew Halcro   Ollaw [in] Howland
Earik in gord   *Malcum Halcro in Hoiswik
*James in Fladabuster   Magnus in Channerwik
       Magnus [in] Lewanwik in Netherbie
       *Magnus in Troswik
       *William Crewkschankis
       Lowrence Leisk in Scatnes
       Magnus in gord in Hilwall

James Barnetsoun and Adame Cromertie bayth provin in
the foldis[2] buikis[3] to have disobeyit to gang to my lordis wark[4]

---

* The persons marked *, summoned apparently against their will, were adjudged the following day to a fine of ten pounds (Scots) each, for non-compearance.

[1] *Essejs*: *esseys*: assize.

[2] *Fold*: i.e. *Foud*, or *Fowde*. The Great Fowde of Shetland was the chief judge and representative of government in the Islands (Norse *Foged*).

[3] *Buikis*: books.

[4] *My lordis wark*: the building of the Castle of Scalloway, to which they were obliged to repair, without meat, drink, or pay. The castle is now a ruin.

in Scallowy as they wer decernit. Theirfoir ilk ane of them ar decernit to pay for disobedience xl s.

Jhone parkie for disobeying the fold in nocht entering in Adam [of] Browis serwis as he wes commandit, Thairfoir is decernit to pay for disobedience iiij markis, under the paine of poynding.

Airthour Cowpland, Dauid Sinclair and Magnus Fidlair for disobeying the foldis dwme[1] in non payment to him of certaine leispundis[2] of comprysit Corne as thay wer dempt, Thairfoir ilk ane of thame ar decernit to pay ane dwmra[3] under the paine of poynding.

Jhone in Ringesta, Thomas [in] Lophill, Catherein Cumming and Olaw in Lie for breaking the foldis dwme in non releifeing of James Hea [Hay] at the handis of Edame Sinclair of Brow anent certaine comprysit barrell of Corne, as thay wer dempt, Therfoir ilk ane of them ar decernit to pay ane dwmra wnder the paine of poynding.

William Werk and William Lowttit for gripping of the nes of Excanabe[4] by[5] the leif of the awner, ilk persone to pay xl s. for gripstair,[6] wnder the paine of poynding and sicklyk inhibeitis all personis that thay nawayis scheir diffettis[7] therinto fra thes furthe without leif of the awner, ilk persoun to pay x ħ.

Magnus and Alexander Fidleris for breking of the foldis dwme in nonpayment of ther dettis to Jhone Scott as thay were dempt, Therfoir decernis ilk ane of them to pay ane dwmra wnder the paine of poynding.

Jhone Gibsoun and Hendrie Waltersoun for eiting of the girss[8] of Francie Stokis iiij merk land in Excanabe by the foldis dwme is decernit to pay betuix them ane dwmra wnder the paine of poynding.

Ollaw [in] Quendaile has failyeit quittance of non delyverie of his motheris guidis and gere to Lowrence in Garth as he wes

---

[1] *Dwme*: doom.
[2] *Leispund*: a weight containing originally 12, but latterly 18 lbs. Scots measure.
[3] *Dwmra*, or Domera, a fine.
[4] *Nes of Excanabe*: Ness of Exnaboe.
[5] *By*: without.
[6] *Gripstair*: gripping.
[7] *Scheir diffetis*: cut divots.
[8] *Girss*: grass.

dempt Therfoir is decernit to pay j dowmra wnder the paine of poynding.

Jhone Sinclair Officiare in Garth is dempt to quyt[1] his guddis[2] of the citing of his nychtbouris Coirnis and twergordis[3] and that with the laryt aithe[4] and in caise he quyt the haill nichtbouris of Garthe to pay to the King ane dwmra, and to wpmak the skaytht of the girss to the saide Jhone be the sycht of nychtbouris wnder the paine of poynding.

Thomas [in] Lophill for disobedience of the foldis dwme in non payment of certaine dettis restand[5] to Thomas Barnesoun as he wes dempt and therfoir is decernit to pay ane dwmra wnder the paine of poynding.

Airthour in Skelberie is fand to have grippit wrangouslie ane halff of ane rigg of Thomas Blackbeirdis lyand in Skelberrie and therfoir is decernit to pay for gripstair xl s. to the King, and to restoir the halff of the rigg againe to the said Thomas with the haill crope and byrun profettis thairof by the sycht of nychtbouris and siclyk ordainis the haill land in Skelberrie of the King Kirk and Wyell[6] to be pairtit be the fold, and sax honest nychtbouris and ilk awner to be possest with thair awin pairt according to use of nychtbourheid.

It is fund that Magnus in Skerpagarthe and Dauid Lesleis dogis[7] wes fund sleand[8] ane scheip of Malcum of Cobinsgarthe and this by and attour[9] aucht scheip alledgit slain of the said Malcumis of befoir Thairfoir ilk ane of them ar decernit for keiping of unlawfull dogis to pay xl s. and ordainis them to quit ther dogis of the slauchter of the said aucht scheip and theirwith the laryt aithe and falyeing thairof to pay ij merkis and to opmak the skaitht to the awner, be the sicht of nycht-bouris, and in   to slay ther doggis.

Anent the accusation of Thomas Antensoun for the stowcht[10]

---

[1] *Quyt* : acquit.   [2] *Guddis* : goods, *i.e.* cattle.
[3] *Twergordis* : meaning uncertain.
[4] *Laryt aithe* : the oath of the *Lawrightman*, an official appointed in every parish to guard the rights of the people.   [5] *Restand* : remaining due.
[6] *Wyell* : probably *Weall*, i.e. the commonwealth, lay owners.
[7] *Dogis* : dogs.   [8] *Sleand* : slaying.
[9] *By and attour* : besides.   [10] *Stowcht* or *stowtht* : stealth, stealing.

of ane lamb of Nicole in Culzeasetteris quhairof he failyeit
quittance as also the twelter ayt[1] of befoir Compeiris the said
Thomas and passed fra the regour of law and submittit him
selff in the jugis will thairfoir.

Yung Gilbert in Skelberrie for non payment of corne mendis[2]
to Thomas Blackbeird as he wes dempt is decernit to pay ane
dwmra wnder the paine of poynding.

The haill tennentis fra Daill to the schoir syd ar dempt to
quyt them selffis and thair howssis of stowcht of Alexander
Smythis fische and corne stollin fra him this last winter and
that with the laryt aithe failyeing thairof ilk persoun to pay
ii merkis and to wnderly the law therfoir as stowcht.

[*Margin*] All quyte be Sandie Smyth awner of the skeo[3]
vpoun ther greit aithes, except Airthour Cowpland and his
houss.

William Ballentyne hes dwm lawit with Jhone Sinclair
officiare as for himselff and in name and behalff of the rest of
the inhabitantis of the parochin of Dunrosnes within quhat
day thay sall pay ther haill dettis restis and wthir thingis
restand to him the yeir he wes Chalmerlaine of Zeitland quhilk
the juge and the essys fand ressounable and ordanit thame and
ewerie ane of tham to enter ane Compt rakning and payment
with him and quhat beis fund restand to him ather be con-
fessioun or probatioun to mak payment thairof to him within
terme of law, ilk persoun wnder the paine of ane dowmra.

Ollaw [in] Nos, Nicole thair, Magnus in Nos, Magnus yunger
in Nos, Gilbert in Brek, Inggrahame Sinclair in Toun, Thomas
Beirnis yunger, William Beirnstoun, James Beirnstoun, Robert
Linklett, Mareoun Tulloche, Ollaw [in] Quendaile, James in Lud,
Magnus in Gord, Jhone in Gord, Ollaw Sinclair in Gershous,
Thomas Bairnsoun and Rinycan Archebald, for breking the
foldis dwme in nocht bigging up the haifiers[4] dyk with the
gudis thairof as thay wes dempt. Thairfoir ilk ane of them

---

[1] *Twelter ayt*: twelfter oath, *i.e.* the oath of twelve reputable neighbours,
compurgators, testifying to innocence.
[2] *Mendis*: this term seems equivalent to compensation, fine, payment
(amends).
[3] *Skeo*: an open-built hut, or house, for drying.
[4] *Haifiers*: half-ers, *i.e.* joint.

ar decernit to pay thairfoir ane dwmra, and to big vp the dyk
foirsaid within the space of aucht dayis wnder the paine foirsaid. Lowrence [in] Fugtoun for breaking of the foldis dwme
in non payment of the corne mendis to Magnus Grige as he wes
dempt and thairfoir to pay ane dwmra wnder the paine of
poynding.

Anent the accusatioun of James Kintoir in Dunrosnes for
sclander and ewill speiche calling Patrik Kinnaird merchand
ane brokkar and ane fals knawe Compeiris the said James in
jugement and confest that he had ovirseine himselff in his yre
and wraithe aganis the said Patrik in speiking outtragious
werdis aganis him for the quhilk he craivit the said Patrik in
jugement pardoun for his offence, and in the mcintyme gaife
that he knew nathing to him bot guid and honestie nocht the
les the said James for his sclanderous speiche quhilk could
nocht be provin aganis the said Patrik, decernis him to pay iiii
merk to the King and iiii merk to the pairtie and absoluis the
said Patrik of all cryme or penaltie quhilk can be laid to his
cherge thairanent, and ordanis that nane repruife him thairfoir
fra this furthe ilk persoun wnder the paine of xl li.

Proceidis at Soundbrughe the saxt day of August 1602.

Hew Halcro, James in Fladabuster, Malcum Halcro in Hois-
weik, Magnus in Troisweik and William Crewkschanke for non
cuming to the Court this day as thay wer commandit ilk persoun is decernit to pay x li wnder the paine of poynding.

William Vork is tryit to hawe complenit in the foldis Court
upon certaine sclander spoken aganis him be Thomas Main-
soun and now in this Court hes compeirit and denyis the samyn,
quhairbe it appeiris that it is concertit betwix them Thairfoir decernis the said William to pay viii merkis thairfoir to
the King wnder the paine of poynding.

The quhilk day compeirit Dauid Reid and desyrit the juge
and the essyssis testimoniall gife Magnus Flett and Gellis
Keillo wes lawfullie mareit or nocht, and gife Francis Flett
wes laufullie gottin vpoun the said Gelis be the said Magnus
or nocht. Vnto the quhilk the haile essyes anserit that they
knew the saidis persounis to be laufullie mareit and that the

said Francis is thair laufull begotten sone.   Vpoun the quhilk
the said Dauid askit act of Court.

William Wirk and Thomas in Vestano[1] ar decernit to quite
them selffis of trubling[2] of wtheris witht the laryt aithe, and
failyeing thairof to pay ii merkis wnder the paine of poynding.

Marcoun Tulloch is dempt to quyt hir selff of ane peice
pellok[3] seine at the bankis and of the speiking thairof to Mans
Magnussonn and that with the laryt aithe, and failyeing thairof
to pay ii merkis and to wnderlye the law therfoir as stowtht.

Herman Sueman dutche man at Alixfuird[4] for bleiding of
Marcoun ollaws dochter abone the end[5] within hir avin hemefrie[6] is decernit to pay twys xl s. wnder the paine of poynding.

Bessie Lews is dempt to quite hir selff of the bleiding of
Marcoun sinclair abone the end and that with the laryt aithe
and failyeing therof to pay xl s. wnder the paine of poynding.

The quhilk day annent the actioun and clame of ten angel
nobillis[7] persewit be Lowrence tulloche in Skeldberrie in north
mawing[8] aganis Dinneis sueman dutche man of brahame[9] quha
is outreikitt be Zanie Himmel quha wes air[10] to wmquhill Court
mair dutche man Compeiris the said Lowrence and produceit
ane obligatioun maid be the said wmquhill Court mair to
wmquhill Dauid tulloche and his relict vidow Gotherone and
him vpoun the saidis ten angellis in anno 78 yeiris[11] Subscryvit
with the said Court mairis avin hand wretin in Dens[12] compeirit
the said Dinneis and alledgit that he knew nocht thairof nor
yitt is decernit to pay the samyn.   Nochtheles becais the said
Lowrence gave his aithe in Jugement that nayther he nor nane
of his ressaiveit ony pairt of the said summe and that the said
Dwneis is outreikit be the said Zanie quha is air to the said

---

[1] *Vestano* : now known as Vestanore, Cunningsburgh.
[2] *Trubling* : molesting.   [3] *Pellok* : porpoise (?).
[4] Trafficking Dutchmen seem to have been well known in the district.
[5] *Abone the end* : meaning obscure. ' Above the ene ' (eyes) seems a more
natural reading, but the MS. will not permit such a variation.
[6] *Hemefrie* : house, home.
[7] *Angel noble* : a gold coin (10s. sterling).
[8] *North mawing* : the parish of Northmavine.
[9] *Brahame* : Bremen.   [10] *Air* : heir.
[11] 78 *yeiris* : i.e. 1578.   [12] *Dens* : Danish or Norse.

Court Thairfoir the Juge and the essys decernis the said Zanie as air foirsaid and the said Dunncis quhom he hes outrcikit to mak payment thairof to the said Lowrence within xv dayis wnder the paine of poynding Reseruing actioun to the said Duncis to call Garthe himmel for his warrand as law leiwis.

Gilbert sinclair elder in Skeldberric is dempt to quite him self of the bleiding of his yungest brother Gilbert Sinclair abone the end and that with the Laryt aithe and failyeing thairof to pay xl s. wnder the paine of poynding.

The quhilk day Lowrence Sinclair of Gott and Jhone Newen of Scowsbrughe becumis actit cautioneris ilk ane of them for thair avin pairtis for the entrie of Dauid Leslie to compeir befoir my lord and his deputis at Skalloway bankis the secund or thrid dayis of the Lating Court[1] nixtocum To wnderly the law for airt and pairt and furnesar of frances Sinclair eftir the murthour of wmquhill Mathow Sinclair of Nes wnder the paine of j⁰ lib. [*i.e.* 100 pounds]. Lyk as the said Dauid bindis and obleissis him his landis guidis and gere to releife his cautioneris foirsaidis.

The quhilk day William bruce of Simbuster becumis actit cautioun for the entrie of Adame Sinclair of brow To com-peir befoir my Lord and his deputis at Skalloway bankis the secund or thrid dayis of the Lating court nixtocum In maner foirsaid and this for obedience of my Lordis precept execut be Jhone hecfuird wnder the paine of j⁰ lí⁰ Lyk as the said Adame bindis and obleissis him his landis guidis and gere to releife his cautioner foirsaid.

Malcum Sinclair of Quendaile becumis actit cautioner for the entrie of Lowrence Sinclair of Gott according to my Lordis precept lykwyis execut be Jhone hecfuird To the Lating nixt in maner foirsaid wnder the paine of j⁰ lí. and siclyk for the entrie of Androw nicolsoun wnder the paine of xl lí. Lykas the said Lowrence and Androw bindis and obleiss thame ther lands guidis and gere to releife thair cautioner foirsaid.

It is tryit and fund that Thomas grig and Lowrence Sinclair hes trublit and domiraxterit wtheris and thairfoir ilk

---

[1] *Lating Court* : the Lawting Court, the chief Court of Shetland, the shadow of the ancient ALTHING.

ane of them ar decernit to pay ij merkis wnder the paine of poynding.

Jirga bege is dempt to quite hir selff of the bleiding of Annie Williams dochter abone the end and failyeing thairof to pay xl[s] under the paine of poynding.

James Vrowing[1] for bleiding of Jhone Leisk vpoun the cheik to pay iiij merkis wnder the paine of poynding.

Adame Cromertie for gripstair of elspett rettrayis muck[2] and bleiding of hir thairfoir is decernit to pay twys xl[s] under the paine of poynding.

Henrie Jamisoun for bleiding of Jamis Mansoun beneth the end is decernit to pay iiij merkis to the King wnder the paine of poynding.

Giffin vp in dittay that Mairiorie Sinclair the guidwyff of Lie wantit ane gwis[3] and that scho sould have skuildit[4] Lowrence Sinclair of Gottis hous thairfor quhairin the essys takand tryall and finding nather liklines nor probatioun thairinto; Obsoluis the said Lowrence and his hous for ony thing knawin as yitt And ordanis that nane repruife him thairfor fra this furthe ilk persoun wnder the payn of xl li.

William in burrowland is dempt to quyt him selff and his hous of the stowtht of ane pullit gwis fund in his peit stak and that with the laryt aithe and failyeing thairof to pay ij merkis to the King and to underly the law thairfor as stowtht.

[*Margin*] Quite be Malcum halcro and Walter Leisk vpoun thair aithis.

Tryit that earling Jamesoun for bleiding of Mareoun Manis dochter vpoun the hand thairfor is decernit to pay iiij merkis selver under the paine of poynding.

Jonat Airchbald for giffing ane blea[5] to Mareoun tulloche to pay j merk under the paine of poynding.

Jonat Archbald is dempt to quite hir selff with the saxter aithe[6] for the turning of ane siff[7] and riddill for ane pair scheiris[8] quhilk wes tane fra hir guidman and failyeing thairof

---

[1] *Vrowing*: Irving or Irvine.   [2] Seizing of manure.
[3] *Gwis*: goose.   [4] *Skuildit*: suspected, charged.   [5] *Blea*: blow.
[6] *Saxter aithe*: the oath, in testimony of innocence, of six honest neighbours.
[7] *Siff*: sieve.   *Turning the sieve and riddle*: practising sorcery or divination.
[8] *Scheiris*: scissors.

to pay sax merkis and to underley the law thairfoir as Witch-craft.

William and Lowrence Rendaillis ilk ane for trubling bleiding and domiraxtering wtheris ar decernit ilkane of them to pay iiij merkis under the paine of poynding.

Grigerous in Lie and Mareoun patersone ilkane sclanderit wtheris and thairfoir ilkane of them ar decernit to pay iiij merkis to the King and to tak thee mendis in thair avin handis becais thay sclanderit wther alyk wnder the paine of poynding.

Jhone in ringyista for sclandering of Catherein Linklett of harlettrie without ony probatioun and thairfoir decernis him to pay iiij merk to the King wnder the paine of poynding.

Airthour Sinclair of Aithe actis him self for the entrie of Gilbert [in] Futtoun befoir my Lord and his deputis at Skallo-way bankis the thrid or feird[1] dayis of the Lating Court nixtocum, To wnderly the law for the slachter of Jhone Ollawsoun wnder the paine of xl lł.

Hendrie Waltersoun for fyve blea straikis giffin to Annie Androws dochter is decernit to pay v merk selver and for bleiding of hir to pay iiij merkis under the paine of poynding.

Proceidis vpoun the sewnit day of August 1602.

Margret thomson is fund to haive stollin sum fische of herman Sucmanis and thairfoir becaus it is said to be the first falt decernis hir to pay iiij merkis under the pane of poynding.

Ollaw Sutherland and hendrie Sinclair ilkane for trubling wther is decernit to pay iiii merk under the paine of poynding.

Jonat porteous for twa straikis giffin be hir to Mareoun Thomas dochter is decernit to pay ij merkis under the paine of poynding.

It is tryit that Magnus Melling hes trublit Magnus Cowp-land ane frie Cowpastay[2] is decernit to pay xls. under the paine of poynding.

---

[1] *Feird*: fourth.
[2] *Frie Cowpastay*: meaning uncertain.

It is fund that Stewin [1] Lowtit hes bled Alex^r butter vpoun the Sabothe day in thomas sinclairis hows and thairfoir is decernit to pay thrys xl^s wnder the paine of poynding.

James broun for giffing ane straik with his steikit neff[2] to Hendrie Sinclair is decernit to pay j merk silver under the paine of poynding.

Lowrence and Jhone rendailes for the trubling of Jhone Scottis hous is decernit to pay twys xl^s and for calling Jhone Scottis wyff ane harlott is decernit ilk ane to pay iiij merk to the King and iiij merk to the partie.

It is fund that nicole in Culyesetter hes done wrang in bigging ane pwnd[3] vpoun the boundis of Howlland viasetter and cumlawik without leife of Malcum Sinclair and his pairtineris awneris of the grund Thairfoir it is statut that the said nicole nor na wther sall big na pwndis nor keip na pastorage within the saidis boundis without tollerance and licence of the awiner thairof under the paine of xl ℔.

Nicole [in] Culyesetter is dempt to quite himselff of the turning of sieve and the scheiris and that with the saxter aithe and failyeing thairof to pay vj merkis and to wnderly the law thairfoir as witchcraft.

It is statute and ordanit that na peittis fra this furthe salbe cassin[4] within the ness of excanabœ nones[5] and Scatnes without leife of the awneris of the grund ilk persoun wnder the paine of x ℔. als oft as thay salbe fund to contraweine.

It is tryit that Wm Crewkschank bled robert hodge abone the end Thairfoir is decernit to pay xl^s wnder the paine of poynding.

Mareoun thomas dochter is dempt to quite hir selff of the bleiding of Mareoun Mowat beneth the end and that with the laryt aithe And failyeing thairof to pay iiij merkis wnder the paine of poynding.

It is tryit that James broun hes giffin hendrie Waltersoun ane newell[6] and thairfoir is decernit to pay j merk silwer wnder the paine of poynding.

---

[1] *Stewin*: Stephen.   [2] *Steikit neff*: closed fist.
[3] *Pund*: a park enclosed by a dyke.   [4] *Cassin*: cast, *i.e.* cut.
[5] *Nones*: i.e. Noness.   [6] *Newell*: or Nevell, a blow with the fist.

Adame Cromertie and James barnatsoun ar tryit to be commoun pykaris[1] and theifeis of corne timmer heiring peitis claithe and wther thingis qualefeit in dittay againis ather of them in this court besydis sindric wther crymis and poyntis of thift tryit aganis them of befoir quhairof thay failyeit quittance of befoir. Quhilk being considderit be the Juge and the essys ordanis thair haill guidis and gere and landis gife ony be to be escheit and thame selffis to be baneist the contrie to norroway in the first passage at the leist within the space of ane moneth and giwe thay be apprehendit with the walour of ane uiris thift[2] heirefter to be tane and hangit be the crage quhill thay die in exempill of wtheris.

It is tryit that James browne hes callit elspett [in] bw ane theife and ane harlott and thairfoir decernit to pay viij merk to the king and viij merk to the pairtie And becaus the said James gawe his aithe in Jugement that he knew nathing to the said elspett bot guid and honestie Thairfoir obsolwis hir thairof for ony thing knawin as yitt and ordanis that nane repruife hir thairfor fra this furth ilk persoun wnder the paine of xx lib.

The quhilk day Malcum Sinclair of Quendaile becumis actit cautioner for the entrie of W^m fermour befor my lord and his deputis at Skalloway bankis the secund or thrid dayis of the Lating court nixtocum To wnderly the law as airt and pairt and furnesar of frances Sinclair efter the murthour of umquhill Mathow Sinclair wnder the paine of j^c li. lyk as the said W^m bindis and obleisis him his guidis and gere to releife his said cautioner.

The quhilk day William Bruce of Simbuster becumis actit cautioner for the entrie of Garthe Hemlein[3] befoir my Lord and his deputis at Skalloway bankis the secund or thrid dayis of the Lating Court nixtocum To wnderly the law as airt and

---

[1] *Pykaris* : pilferers.
[2] *Ane uiris thift* : a theft of the value of an *ure* (Danish and Norwegian *öre*).
[3] *Geert Hemelingk* : or ' Garthe Hemlein,' as here termed, whose connection with the Earl of Bothwell is mentioned in a footnote in the Introduction.

pairt of the slachter of Mathow Sinclair, under the paine of jᶜ
℔. lyk as the said Garthe bindis and obleissis him to releife his
cautioner forsaid.

(From the original *Records of the Sheriff and Lawting
Courts of Shetland*, in the General Register House,
Edinburgh.)

X.

FEU-CONTRACTS BETWEEN PATRICK, EARL OF ORKNEY, AND WILLIAM BRUCE OF SYMBISTER, OF LANDS IN DUNROSSNESS. 1592-1605.

On 28th March 1592, Earl Patrick by 'Charter and Infeftment of few ferme' set to William Bruce, 'of Symbestar' in the island of Whalsey, the '20 merk land 6 pennies the merk of Soundburgh [Sumburgh] callit Kingis Landis,'[1] and the '4 merk land 6 pennies the merk callit Provestis landis lyand rynrig with the said 20 merk land of Soundburgh,' and also the 20 merk land of Scatnes, with all pertinents, as fully described in that Charter.

In 1604, by a contract between the Earl and Bruce, the parties made an Excambion of lands, the Earl taking possession anew of Sumburgh and others, and Bruce resuming from him the lands of Sandwick, etc., with a proper accounting for the 'ky oxne horss and scheip' stock upon these different lands, etc. etc.

On 11th November 1605, a fresh contract was entered into between the parties, signed at 'the Cannogait' of Edinburgh, whereby the last named agreement of excambion

---

[1] These 'Provestis Landis,' consisting of only 4 merks, lying intermixed ('runrig') with the 20 merks of 'King's land' of Sumburgh, belonged originally to the Provost of the Dom-Kirk, or Cathedral, of Bergen in Norway. Their subsequent transfer to Captain Laurence Middleton, a Shetland proprietor, for 1050 rix-dollars, under distinct provision for redemption, the confirmation of this transaction by King Frederick the Third of Denmark and Norway, by deed of 28th August 1662, still preserved at Sumburgh, and their conveyance by Middleton, on 16th February 1663, to William Bruce of Sumburgh, are fully related by the Editor in the *Proceedings* of the Society of Antiquaries of Scotland, December 8, 1879, vol. xiv. p. 13.

was annulled, and the parties were reinstated as before under
the contract of 1592.

This final contract of 1605 is a lengthy document, but
may be abbreviated, preserving all essentials, and to a large
extent the original spelling, as follows. It is of interest,
local and otherwise.

After a full narrative of the preceding contracts, briefly
referred to above, the deed proceeds :—

'The said nobill Lord gives grants and dispones and
perpetually confirms to the said William Bruce his airis and
assigneis the said 20 merk land of Soundburgh, together
with all ryt titill and kyndnes that he or his foirsaidis hes or
may have to the said four merk land callit the Provestry Landis
lyand rynrig with the said landis of Soundburgh, and the 20
merk land of Scatnes with all pairtis and pertinentis from the
heichest of the hill to the lowest of the eb, reservand alwayis
the ryt and titill of ye houss laitlie biggit be the said nobill
lord upon the ground of the said landis of Soundburgh, on the
south syd of the new hall, togidder with ane yaird adjacent
thairto at the south eist gabill of the said new hall off the
lenth and breid of threscoir futes in everie quarter thairof
with frie ish and entrie thairto, Togidder with the pasturage
of tua ky and tua oxne in the somer seasoun to be pastured
vpoun the said landis of Soundburgh corne and meadow being
exceptit, togidder with the pasturage of 20 wedderis within
the boundrie of the Lobitnes[?] of Scatnes at quhat tyme the
said nobill Lord and his airis sall happen to mak actuall
residence in the foirsaid houss and fortalice of Soundburgh,
and in his absence the said William and his foirsaidis to have
the keping of the said hous and yaird, he and they being an-
swerable to the said nobill lord and his foirsaidis for the
Insycht [inside] plennissings and utheris guidis and geir that
sall be delyverit to the said William at the Earls removing
thairfrom, and William and his forcsaids to be free of all
such pasturage during the absence of the Earl and his foresaids, to be haldin in feu ferme and heritage for yearly payment
of threttene lispund and aucht merk butter with threttene
schillingis twa cuttell wadmell with Scatt and Watle thairof
use and wont, togidder with ye soume of six schillingis four

pennies money forsaid as for the auld few ferme dewtie and augmentatioun usit and wont to be payit for the foirsaid landis in tyme bygane at the termis of payment usit and wont, and also gevand thre suttis at the said nobill earles heid Courtis in Zetland yeirlie in name of few ferme allenarlie as in the first Charter of few ferme But [*i.e.* without] prejudice of the Earl's action and exceptions before specially excepted,[1] the Earl obliging himself to remove himself, his tenantis, servantis, Chamerlane, and speciallie the said Malcolme Sinclair,[2] and all other possessors of the said lands of Sound-burgh, Underhoull,[3] Scatnes, and Provestis landis, with houssis biggingis and pertinentis, and to mak the ground of the said landis voyd and red, and to enter the said William his tennantis and servandis in his name to the possessioun of all and sindrie the said landis betwixt the dait heirof and the 25th day of November nixtocum, and to deliver to him the Cornis that grew upon the ground of Soundburgh this present Crope 1605 yeiris and quhilkis war put in the barnis and barnyairdis thairof without any claime hereafter whatever by the Earl or his foresaids, reservand and exceptand his actioun as said is, Binding him to warrant William's entry against all action of intrusion, spoliation, wrangous intromission etc. and to maintene him and his foresaids in the possession thereof.

It is expressly agreed that the Earl and his successors shall have full right to receive and uplift the haill profeittis and commoditeis of all Orknay fische boittis and Cathnes fysche boittis upon the ground of the said landis of Soundburgh ffor their grund yierlie during the tyme of the fysching to be bigit above the said 　　　 be the saidis fyscheris of Orknay and Cathnes conforme to use and wont, and the said William

---

[1] This refers to a lawsuit between the parties.

[2] Malcolme Sinclair, previously designed 'Vicar of Dunrossness.' This was Malcolm Sinclair of Quendal, who then was in possession of the Vicarage dues of this and other parishes ('Lay Vicar'). See the Discharge to him, by Earl Patrick, of Umboth and other duties, of date 9th June 1609 (Appendix No. XI.).

[3] Underhoull, in the island of Unst, formerly the property of William Sinclair of Underhoull, whose widow, Margaret, daughter of Lord John Stewart, Prior of Coldingham, William Bruce had married.

obliges himself to give them ground-leiff [leave] to that effect, and for uphalding of the said ludgis to cast fuill and devot on the ground of Sumburgh or Scatnes according to use and wont, the Earl and his foresaids in the meantyme causing the said fishers of Orkney and Caithness to keep William's cornis, meadow and grass fra all dystructioun and skaith that may befall thairto be the saidis fyscheris and thare gudis and be accustomit of making of unlawfull gaittis and passages throw the saidis Cornis meddowis and Grass quhilkis war not of use to be maid of befoir, the Earl and the fishers to pretend no right or interest in the lands of Sumburgh by reason of the privilege foresaid, but only to the fishers' lodges. For the quhilk caus the said William Bruce for himself and his heirs and successors renunceis, quitclaimis and dischairgis and ouergives to the said nobill lord the said twa last[1] of land in Sandwick, making the former infeftment cancelled and of none effect, agreeing to warrant the same and to re- move himself and his wyff bairnis familie servandis gudis and geir fra the saidis landis of Sandwick and to enter the noble lord to the possession thereof with haill cornis thairupon so soon as the Earl shall cause William to be entered in pos- session of Sumburgh. And forsamekill as the said William was in use to pay to the said Earl twentie angell nobillis or the sum of aucht [scoir merkis] Scottis money for the landis callit Provestis landis yeirlie before the making of the present Contract [of 1604] by which the Earl dischargcd the said William of the payment of the said 20 angel nobles, not- withstanding William Bruce now binds himself and his fore- saids to pay the same to the Earl, or the said soume of aucht scoir merkis money foresaid for the same and that yeirlie as long as he sall bruick joyse and possess the said landis callit Provestis landis, but if they should happen to be evicted[2] by any person or persons fra the said William he or his foresaids sall be na farder astricted nor oblist in the payment of the said 20 angellis; Reservand allwayis to the

---

[1] A 'last' of land was 18 merks.
[2] This shows the consciousness of an imperfect title at this time (1605) and the apprehension of possible eviction by claimants from Denmark or Norway.

N

Earl and his foresaids the action of nonentrie competent to him aganis Margrat Stewart spous to the said William Bruce and the said William for his entres [interest] of the landis of Uye [Uyea] with the pertinentis as accordis of the law. The parties discharge each other of all actions, quarrels, causes etc. quhatsomever quhilkis ather of thame can propone move or persew for anything preceding the date hereof. For further security they consent to the registration hereof in the buikis of Counsall.

The document is written by a clerk to Mr. James Shirlaw, Wrettar in Edinburgh, of the date above written (11 Nov. 1605), before these Witnesses James Sinclair of Murkell (Murkle in Caithness), Hew Halcro fear of that Ilk (Halcro feuar of Halcro in Orkney), and James Annand, servitor to the Earl. The deed, which is in the Charter-chest at Sumburgh, is a contemporary official extract signed by 'Joannes Skene,' the Lord Clerk Register.

XI.

DISCHARGE, PATRICK, EARL OF ORKNEY, TO MALCOLM SINCLAIR OF QUENDALE. 1609.

We Patrik erle of Orkney lord Zetland be ye tennor heirof
Grantis ws to have ressavit fra Malcolme Sinclair of Quendaill
the sowme of four Angellis as for the pryce of ilk barrell
of Tuelff barrellis buttir and ye soume of thrie Angellis as
for ye pryce of ilk barrell of sex barrellis of oyll as for the
Dewtie of Umbothes[1] of Dunrosness and ye soume of four
Angellis as for ye pryce of ilk barrell of thrie barrellis buttir
and the sowme of thrie angellis as for the pryce of ilk barrell of
thrie barrellis oyle as for the Dewtie of Wallis and the sowme
of tuentie angell nobillis for the Umbothes of Sandsting and
Aythsting and the sowme of sevin angell nobillis for the
Dewties of St. Petires Stowk[2] in fair Iyle addetit and awand
to ws be the said Malcolme Sinclair Conform to ane tak
and assedatioun maid and sett be ws to hym and that of the
Crope and yeir of God j^m vj^c and aucht yeiris [1608] of ye
quhilkis Dewteis respective abone wrettin and pryces therof
respective foirsaid off ye Crope and yeir of God abone specifeit
we hauld ws weill contentit satisfeit and compleitlie payit
and for our heiris executoris and successoris exhoneris quhit-
claimis and simpliciter dischargis the said Malcolme Sinclair
his airis executoris and successoris of the same and all utheris

---

[1] *Umboth duties.* These were the dues belonging to the Bishopric of
Orkney, at that time in the hands of the Earl.
[2] *St. Peter's Stouk.* It is not clear what this precisely was, whether some
small revenue or tithing, or a collecting-box for donations in the name of St.
Peter. Its existence in the Fair Isle is remarkable.

yeiris preceiding the said crope and yeir of God j^m vj^c and aucht yeiris and for the mair securitie thairof we ar content that thir presentis be registrat in ye buikis of Counsall for sure conservatioun ad futuram rei in memoriam Lykeas for registering heirof constitutis Archibald boyd our procuratour to consent to the registratioun heirof In witnes wherof wrettin in Edinburgh be Mr James King nottar we haive subscribit thir presentis with our handis at the burgh of the Cannogait the xvj day of Junij the yeir of God j^m vj^c and nyne yeiris befoir thir Witnessis Michaell balfour of Garth ye said Mr. James King and James Annand our servitor.

ORKNEY.

Michaell balfour Witnes.
James King Witnes.
James Annand Witnes.

Note.—The above deed is transcribed from a contemporary official extract in the possession of the Editor, bearing the signature of Sir John Skene, the Lord Clerk Register.

XII.

DIARY AND BAPTISMAL AND MARRIAGE REGISTER OF THE REV. JOHN HUNTER, EPISCOPAL CLERGYMAN IN SHETLAND. 1734-1745.

THE following are a few examples of entries: see INTRODUCTION.

BAPTISMS.

1734, Novr 30. Robert Bruce of Sumburgh and Alice Dammahoy [Dalmahoy] his spouse had a son baptiz'd called John. God Fathers: Ja. Scott of Gibliston and Robert Sinclair of Scalloway. God Mother, Madam Fraser.

Dec. 7. Ro. Mouatt in Scatness and Barbara Sinclair his spouse hade a son baptiz'd called Robert. God Fathers—Ja. Scot of Gibliston, Rob. Dick of Fracafield, Ro. Sinclair of Scalloway, Ro. Bruce of Sumbrough. God Mother Lady Scalloway etc.

1735, Decr. Robt Dick of Fracafield and Jean Dickson his spouse hade a Daughter baptized called Frances. God Father—Ro. Sinclair of Scalloway. God Mothers Mrs Peggy pitcairn and Mrs Wilson.

1736, April 30. M^r Jo: and Christian Hunters hade a son baptized called Robert. God Fathers: Ja: Scot, And: Dick of Wormidale, Godmother Lady Giblistone.

[The father is the Rev. Mr Hunter, author of the Diary.]

1736, May 19.   James Forbes and Janet Haucrow in Skelberry hade a son baptized called John.   God Fathers And: Forbess his father and John Morison in Bigtoun   God mother Elizabeth Forbess spouse to James Calder.

1737. At Whiteness.   Dec. 29.
Laur: Tulloch and Grisell Watson —— James. G. F. Alexander Sinclair of Brow and Ro: his brother, G. M. Jean Sinclair, sister to Brow.

1738. At Scalloway.   Jany. 20, 17$\frac{37}{38}$.
John Scot of Melbie [formerly designed 'of Valley'] and Elizabeth Mitchell, a son James. G: Fa: James Scott of Gibliston and Alex: Innes, Physician.   G: M: Miss Lillias Scott their sister.

1738. At Scalloway.   Dec. 24.
Gilbert Bairnson and Sweety Sanders daur [*i.e.* Sandersdaughter]—a son—Murdoch.   G: F: Ro. Sinclair of House and And: Dick of Wormidale. G: M: Philad. Damahoy Lady of House.

1743. At St. Barnaby's Chapel.   April 10.   William Stout and Marg: Scot in Tob—daughter—Alice.   G: F: ye parent, G: M: Penelope Jonson.

MARRIAGES.

1741. At Sumbroughgerth [Sumragarth near Boddam, in Dunrossness].   Novr 12.   Mr John Skinner, Chaplain at House and Grissel Hunter lawfull daughter Mr John and Christian Hunter, Min^r.   [The bridegroom was Skinner, the poet, afterwards an episcopal clergyman, and father of Bishop John Skinner, and grandfather of Bishop William Skinner.]

At Skelberry.   Novr 5.
Henry Jameson and Ursula Gilbertsdaughter in Rerewick in the parish of Dunrossness.

HIS PRIVATE ACCOUNTS

1735.

By 1 ox	£10	0	0
By six Geese	1	16	0
By six lispund meal	6	0	0
By six lispund bear	3	12	0
By six bottles wine	4	4	0
July 13, 1736. By Cash	6	0	0
July 20 by Cash	12	12	0
Octr 20 by Cash	3	0	0
By a mart or cow 1736	8	0	0
By six Geese 1736	1	16	0
By Ballance paid in Cash . . .	3	0	0
	£60	0	0

[This, being Scots money, estimated at 1s. 8d. to the £, shows a modest income of £5 stg. per annum. Elsewhere the following items appear, convertible into sterling money in the same ratio :—]

1 lispund Salt	£0	16	0
1 lispund malt	1	0	0
1 anker Butter	8	0	0
1 Sow	1	16	0
½ anker Waters			
4 pints ditto			
2 rolls tobacco			
a stick course linnin			
4¼ ells Scots linnin			
12 ells damask	3	12	0
¼ lb Tea			
2 lib. Bend leather			
½ lb. Hops.			
5 lispund wool	8	0	0
5 pair Stockens [1735]	1	10	0
72 Tusk [fish salted].			
2 pints Brandy			

Jamaica pepper
2 Bottles Brandy [1740]
2 Bottles Rum
2 Bottles Gin
½ mutchkin oyle
½ firkin soap [1736]
2 sugar loaves [1738]
a Hollander Cheese
a new black Wigg
an other white wigg
7 ells stuff
4½ ells black cloath
4 Geese from Marion Hacro in Vadsgirth
    Dec. 16. 1737.
Fracafield—to my encouragement .   .   12 12 0
To cash from [Gilbert Niven of] Scousbrough, 9 0 0

(Per MS. Diary in possession of Mr. Bruce of Sumburgh.)

XIII.

EARLY STATE OF EDUCATION IN DUNROSSNESS, SANDWICK, AND CUNNINGSBURGH.

1. *From Reports of the Society in Scotland for Propagating Christian Knowledge.*

THE SOCIETY'S SCHOOLS AND SCHOOLMASTERS IN THE DISTRICT.

	School.	Master.	Salary.	Boys.	Girls.	Total Scholars.
1774	Bremer	Robert Macpherson	£3	23	16	39
	Fair Isle	Robert Thomson	4	·17	7	24
1775	Bremer	Robert Macpherson	4	23	16	39
	Fair Isle	Robert Thomson	5	18	8	26
1780	Quendale	Robert Thomson	10	24	21	45
	Fair Isle	John Irvine	7	14	5	19
1781	Quendale	Robert Thomson	10	64	12	76
	Fair Isle	John Irvine	7	21	10	31
1786	Ridewick[1]	James Strong	10	[*no statistics of attendance given*].		
	Fair Isle	John Irvine	7	17	13	30
1790	Ridwick[1]	James Strong	10	33	10	43
	Fair Isle	John Irvine	8	20	17	37
1793	Ridwick[1]	James Strong	10	60	14	74
	Fair Isle	John Irvine	8	20	14	34
1810	Brew	William Henry	14	...	...	80
	Cunnings-burgh	Robert Gaudie	15	34	11	45
	Fair Isle	John Irvine	12	23	7	30
1820	Brew	William Henry	14	...	...	...
	Cunnings-burgh	Robert Gaudie	15	...	...	...

---

[1] Ridewick, or Ridwick. There is no place of this name in the parish. The Society's Schools were changed occasionally to different suitable centres, and this may have been Rerwick, on the west side of the parish.

School.	Master.	Salary.	Boys.	Girls.	Total Scholars.
1820 Fair Isle	Andrew Henderson	12	...	...	...
1823 Brew	William Henry[1]	15	...	...	...
Cunningsburgh	Robert Gaudie	15	36	16	52
Fair Isle	James Cheyne	15	...		...
1831 Brew	[not mentioned]				
Cunningsburgh	Robert Gaudie	15	20	50*	70
Fair Isle	James Cheyne	15	50	27	77†
1838 Vatchley	Magnus Manson	15	...	...	...
Cunningsburgh	Robert Gaudie	15	...	...	80
Fair Isle	James Cheyne	15	...	...	70†

In 1848 the name of Mr. John Thomson appears as master at Cunningsburgh, with the same salary—£18—as that of his predecessor, who retired on an allowance; and in 1851 Mr. George Stewart is entered as master at Vatchley (i.e. *Vatz-lie*, 'the watery-place') in Dunrossness, at the same figure.

2. *From Parliamentary Returns from Sheriffs of Counties, Session 1826, vol. xviii.*

QUERIES as to the state of the Establishment for Parochial Education in the several Parishes within the County of Orkney and Zetland, and Answers to the same from Dunrossness, 1825.

1. *Q.* What were the Salary and Emoluments of the Schoolmaster at the earliest period at which they can be

---

[1] William Henry appears in 1829 on the superannuated list, with an allowance of £10, continued to teach at Brew, but not required to report. His name is quoted as late as in 1853.

* The attendance stated here as 20 boys, 50 girls, at Cunningsburgh, seems to be reversed. The boys were always in a large majority, education having been thought to be of but little value for girls.

† This attendance at the Fair Isle is enormous in proportion to the population, which was under 300. There may possibly be a mistake in the figures.

correctly stated, and the Branches of Education taught at the same period?

2. *Q.* What were the Salary and Emoluments of the Schoolmaster between 1780 and 1803, and the Branches of Education taught at the same period?

1. and 2. *A.* Nineteen pounds ten shillings.

3. *Q.* What were his Salary and Emoluments between 1803 and 1824, specifying Salary, School Fees, other Sources of Emolument, size of his House?

3. *A.* Salary £16, 9s. ; payment in lieu of ground £2, 1s. ; fees £1 ; size of house 32 ft. by 12½ ft.

4. *Q.* What were these for the year ending in 1825?

4. *A.* The same as stated in the answer to the preceding query.

5. *Q.* State whether there is at present one or more Schoolmasters established on the legal Provision : if two, Whether there be two Schoolmasters' Dwelling Houses, their size, the proportion of Salary allotted to each, and the Amount of School Fees received by each?

5. *A.* One. (1.)

6. *Q.* What is the present rate of School Fees?

6. *A.* Tenpence per quarter for reading; 1s. 8d. for reading and writing; 2s. 6d. for reading, writing, and arithmetic.

7. *Q.* What is the Average Number of Scholars who attend one or both Schools annually?

7. *A.* Twenty-five. (25.)

8. *Q.* What are the Branches of Education which the present Schoolmaster is qualified to teach, and the Branches actually taught?

8. *A.* Reading, Writing, and Arithmetic are taught. The Schoolmaster is qualified to teach book-keeping and navigation also.

9. *Q.* State whether there be at present any, and what, other Schools in the Parish ; if there be, when established, by whom

maintained, whether Dissenters or others, the Emoluments of the Schoolmasters, the rate of School Fees, Branches of Education taught, and by what number of Children attended ?

9. *A.* There are at present two other Schools in the ministry, supported by the Society in Scotland for propagating Christian Knowledge. The emoluments of the Schoolmasters may be estimated at £16, viz. £15 for Salary and £1 for fees. The rate of School fees is the same as in the parochial School. The average number of children attending the two Society Schools is 70.

10. *Q.* What is the greatest Distance at which Children go daily to School ?

10. *A.* About two miles.

11. *Q.* State whether there be any part of a Parish so distant from a School as to prevent attendance ; if there be, what is the Distance, and what is the Population of such part of the Parish ?

11. *A.* There are three districts in this ministry so distant from all the Schools as to prevent attendance. None of these districts is nearer than three miles to a School, and the Population of each of them is about 300.

12. *Q.* What proportion does the Population of any Towns or Villages in the parish bear to the Population of the whole Parish ?

12. *A.* There are no Towns or Villages in the ministry.

T. BARCLAY, Minister.

[Mr. Barclay was afterwards minister successively of Lerwick and of Currie in Midlothian, and latterly Principal of the University of Glasgow.]

3. In Shireff's *General View of the Agriculture of the Shetland Islands* (Edinburgh, 1814), it is stated that in 1808 there existed in Dunrossness 'two Charity Schools, the number of Scholars, 47 males and 23 females. Each of the Schoolmasters' income is £25. One parochial School, number of

Scholars 20, viz. 13 males, 7 females. The teacher has £25 income.'

4. In the *New Statistical Account of Scotland*, Parish of Dunrossness (1841) the position of educational matters is thus described :—

'This parish is much in want of proper Schools for the education of the rising generation, there being, besides the parochial, only some private ones kept by young men, employed by the parents at their own expense, and that only for a part of the year,—they betaking themselves to the fishing in summer, as what they earn from teaching does not compensate them. The parochial School is stationed in the parish of Sandwick. In Cunningsburgh, there are a School, appointed by the Society for Propagating Christian Knowledge, and a Sabbath evening school. There are few or none of the people who cannot read.'

INDEX

INDEX

O

P

THE END.

Printed by T. and A. CONSTABLE, Printers to Her Majesty,
at the Edinburgh University Press.

Scottish History Society.

THE EXECUTIVE.

President.
THE EARL OF ROSEBERY, LL.D.

Chairman of Council.
DAVID MASSON, LL.D., Professor of English Literature, Edinburgh University.

Council.
Sir ARTHUR MITCHELL, K.C.B., M.D., LL.D.
Rev. GEO. W. SPROTT, D.D.
Rev. A. W. CORNELIUS HALLEN.
W. F. SKENE, D.C.L., LL.D., Historiographer - Royal for Scotland.
Colonel P. DODS.
J. R. FINDLAY, Esq.
GEORGE BURNETT, LL.D., Lyon-King-of-Arms.
J. T. CLARK, Keeper of the Advocates' Library.
THOMAS DICKSON, LL.D., Curator of the Historical Department, Register House.
Right Rev. JOHN DOWDEN, D.D., Bishop of Edinburgh.
J. KIRKPATRICK, LL.B., Professor of History, Edinburgh University.
ÆNEAS J. G. MACKAY, LL.D., Sheriff of Fife.

Corresponding Members of the Council.
OSMUND AIRY, Esq., Birmingham ; Very Rev. J. CUNNINGHAM, D.D., Principal of St. Mary's College, St. Andrews ; Professor GEORGE GRUB, LL.D., Aberdeen ; Rev. W. D. MACRAY, Oxford; Professor A. F. MITCHELL, D.D., St. Andrews ; Professor W. ROBERTSON SMITH, Cambridge ; Professor J. VEITCH, LL.D., Glasgow ; A. H. MILLAR, Esq., Dundee.

Hon. Treasurer.
J. J. REID, B.A., Advocate, Queen's Remembrancer.

Hon. Secretary.
T. G. LAW, Librarian, Signet Library.

RULES.

1. THE object of the Society is the discovery and printing, under selected editorship, of unpublished documents illustrative of the civil, religious, and social history of Scotland. The Society will also undertake, in exceptional cases, to issue translations of printed works of a similar nature, which have not hitherto been accessible in English.

2. The number of Members of the Society shall be limited to 400.

3. The affairs of the Society shall be managed by a Council consisting of a Chairman, Treasurer, Secretary, and twelve elected Members, five to make a quorum. Three of the twelve elected members shall retire annually by ballot, but they shall be eligible for re-election.

4. The Annual Subscription to the Society shall be One Guinea. The publications of the Society shall not be delivered to any Member whose Subscription is in arrear, and no Member shall be permitted to receive more than one copy of the Society's publications.

5. The Society will undertake the issue of its own publications, *i.e.* without the intervention of a publisher or any other paid agent.

6. The Society will issue yearly two octavo volumes of about 320 pages each.

7. An Annual General Meeting of the Society shall be held on the last Tuesday in October.

8. Two stated Meetings of the Council shall be held each year, one on the last Tuesday of May, the other on the Tuesday preceding the day upon which the Annual General Meeting shall be held. The Secretary, on the request of three Members of the Council, shall call a special meeting of the Council.

9. Editors shall receive 20 copies of each volume they edit for the Society.

10. The owners of Manuscripts published by the Society will also be presented with a certain number of copies.

11. The Annual Balance Sheet, Rules, and List of Members shall be printed.

12. No alteration shall be made in these Rules except at a General Meeting of the Society. A fortnight's notice of any alteration to be proposed shall be given to the Members of the Council.

PUBLICATIONS.

GLAMIS PAPERS; including the 'BOOK OF RECORD,' written by PATRICK, FIRST EARL OF STRATHMORE (1647-95), the DIARY OF LADY HELEN MIDDLETON, his wife, and other documents, illustrating the social life of the seventeenth century. Edited from the original manuscripts at Glamis Castle by A. H. MILLAR.

JOHN MAJOR'S DE GESTIS SCOTORUM (1521). Translated by ARCHIBALD CONSTABLE, with a Memoir of the author by ÆNEAS J. G. MACKAY, Advocate.

THE DIARY OF ANDREW HAY OF STONE, NEAR BIGGAR, AFTERWARDS OF CRAIGNETHAN CASTLE, 1659-60. Edited by A. G. REID, F.S.A. Scot., from a manuscript in his possession.

THE RECORDS OF THE COMMISSION OF THE GENERAL ASSEMBLY, 1646-1662. Edited by the Rev. JAMES CHRISTIE, D.D., with an Introduction by the Rev. Professor MITCHELL, D.D.

'THE HISTORY OF MY LIFE, extracted from Journals I kept since I was twenty-six years of age, interspersed with short accounts of the most remarkable public affairs that happened in my time, especially such as I had some immediate concern in,' 1702-1754. By Sir JOHN CLERK OF PENICUIK, Baron of the Exchequer, Commissioner of the Union, etc. Edited from the original MS. in Penicuik House by J. M. GRAY.

In Contemplation.

SIR THOMAS CRAIG'S DE UNIONE REGNORUM BRITANNIÆ. Edited, with an English Translation, from the unpublished manuscript in the Advocates' Library.

THE DIARIES OR ACCOUNT BOOKS OF SIR JOHN FOULIS OF RAVELSTON, (1679-1707), and the ACCOUNT BOOK OF DAME HANNAH ERSKINE (1675-1699). Edited by the Rev. A. W. CORNELIUS HALLEN.

www.ingramcontent.com/pod-product-compliance
Lightning Source LLC
Chambersburg PA
CBHW020932030726
47496CB00005B/1156